THANK ___ ___ your
Light As Fire TO THE PLANET.
MAY THIS BOOK inspire you to BOTH
LIVE AND SHARE EVER MORE
EXTRAORDINARY STORIES
WITH THE WORLD.
I LOVE YOU
BROTHER.
WE ARE ONE!
Chip

Chip Richards

WRITING the STORY WITHIN

BECOMING THE WRITER
YOU CAME HERE TO BE!

BLUE ANGEL®
PUBLISHING

WRITING THE STORY WITHIN
A Dynamic Creative Journey - Becoming the Writer You Came Here to Be!

Copyright © 2012 Chip Richards

Published by Blue Angel Publishing®
80 Glen Tower Drive, Glen Waverley
Victoria, Australia 3150
Email: info@blueangelonline.com.au
Website: www.blueangelonline.com

Edited by Tanya Graham
Spiral story illustration by Jimmy Manton
Cover photos: Sunset by (5-year-old) Pearl, Sand Mandala by Chip Richards

Blue Angel is a registered trademark of Blue Angel Gallery Pty. Ltd.

ISBN: 978-0-9871651-4-5

To Joshy, for igniting the story Muse in me on a daily/nightly basis.

To Ash, for "answering the call" to share this magic life
and your beautiful spirit with me.

I love you both in heroic proportions.

Contents

Foreword

Today's shaman, just as they have been throughout recorded and even unrecorded history, is a storyteller. They weave light and shadow together, with more than a dash of imagination, to create something completely new – a story that has the power to change the world. The process begins somewhere deep within the soul, percolates up into the mind, then is finally released through the voice or pen of the magician. That's right, magician, because that's what a shaman storyteller really is. They make the impossible seem possible – they make us believe – and most of all, they remind us that we all have the power to create entire universes from wisps of thought.

Are you a shaman?

You wouldn't be reading this book if you didn't feel something inside that needed to be released or expressed. As far as I'm concerned, this is a natural, even essential part of the human condition – we all want to share the deepest part of ourselves, that well of inspiration with the power to enlighten and transform others. We long to describe the moments when we stood balanced at the edge of some real or imagined cliff, and the decision we made there that changed everything; or we invent – yes, the magical world of invention – a world where imagination overcomes the concrete, static realities we have been trained to obey, just so we can remind ourselves and others that there is a higher power that created and maintains us – the power of story!

Once again, that's why you're holding this in your hands right now. You were led here, and not by accident.

I can't tell you how excited I was to hear that Chip Richards had decided to write this book. My first thought was – Finally! I've known Chip for years, and was immediately impressed by his comprehensive understanding of the art of storytelling, as well as his deep knowledge of what I think of as 'story-scaffolding', the framework one builds before weaving their tale, or writing a single word. The true master is the one who sees past the curtain or even the stage itself, to the actual building blocks where the story is given life. It's like a great pianist who learns the theory of music before forcing it forever from their mind. If you don't have the knowledge of form – or the structure that makes a story great – then you'll miss the writer's greatest opportunity and gift – the freedom to fly, knowing that the wind will support your slow, looping descent back to the earth.

And then there's the ascent back into the sky! That's where a good story takes us, and it's where this book is about to take you. If you apply what you're about to learn, I promise you'll fly like the great storytellers of this and every period of history. You'll gain the tools to dive into your heart, into your mind, and even into your soul, and unearth the jewels that have been waiting for your vivid attention. Once you find them, they will set you free. The very act of breathing life into them breathes life into you – or at least ignites the life that's been sleeping inside you for a very long time. These tools are more than what they seem, just as anything of true value tends to be. They are simple and obvious, but they'll also sneak up on you, showing you the depth you didn't witness at first glance. All I can say is that when it appears – follow. You have chosen a great teacher, and now it's up to you to trust what he's about to reveal.

I could go on and on about the gift you're about to unwrap, but sometimes it's best to step back and let it be opened. My words aren't important here – yours are. Your story is about to jump forward in ways you cannot even imagine, but someday you'll look back and realize that it started when you began reading this book. So good luck, and trust your instinct. It's brought you to this moment – the only moment that's important and necessary.

James Twyman
Bestselling author of *The Moses Code* & *Emissary of Light*

Introduction:
The Power of Story

"The destiny of the world is determined less by the battles that are lost and won than by the stories it loves and believes in."
– Harold Goddard

I've been passionate about story for as long as I can remember. I used to love watching my grandfather, Pops, leap his wiry frame from the chair in our living room as he spun feverish yarns about vampire bats landing in his hair and riding elevators with Al Capone in the 1920's. Pops had stories about everything from ghosts to boxing and how to make pasta, and each tale had a way of transporting my brothers and me right into those places. We were those creatures, riding those elevators with those gangsters too. And while at some level we occasionally questioned the validity of Pops' stories, in truth we didn't care. It was in those moments perhaps that I began to realize that the truth is often found not in the moment itself, but in what we see and experience within it. It is our perspective that gives meaning to our experience, and with that meaning… we discover the seeds of story.

In our modern information age, we have been packed to the brim with new concepts and ideas. They seem to be tunneling in from every direction and dimension – books, TV, film and the web now find us in our homes, in our cars and on the touch screens of our mobile phones. We are virtually swimming in a giant spaghetti bowl of concepts, thoughts and opinions. On the bright side, we are certainly becoming much more aware of a lot of information. But perhaps because of the rapid pace of its arrival, a large majority of this information (no matter how revolutionary) is getting stuck up in our heads – or flying right past! Sure we can talk passionately about these concepts and ideas… we can write about them, and we may even find ourselves arguing on their behalf – or judging others for thinking otherwise. But the real truth is that many of the most powerful concepts we're learning – from ancient wisdom to quantum physics – aren't making it past the front door of our brain into our bodies and our beings. They aren't becoming cellular… they aren't being lived. Sure we 'get it'. But how many of us are actually, genuinely living it?

In my own quest to find ways to embody more of the truth I've been exposed to in this life, I have discovered one constant wellspring of indescribable power to both bring myself into deeper levels of genuine experience in life, and to simultaneously share that energy with others. That wellspring is the power of story.

*"There have been great societies that did not use the wheel,
but there have been no societies that did not tell stories."*
– Ursula K. LeGuin

It is well known that many of the greatest teachers and luminaries throughout time, as well as virtually every tribal culture on record, have passed on wisdom not through concepts and ideas but through stories and parables… But why? If they knew the truth, if they held the wisdom, why not just speak it plainly for all to hear?

For me, the answer to this question has come strong and clear in the past decade as I have set out to share truths from my own life journey with my now 11-year old son, Joshua. Josh and I share an amazing bond, but from early on, it seemed that whenever I tried to explain principles about life, he would often just sort of 'switch off'. It was like he had an anti-preach meter built in from a young age, and listening to life teaching was like eating steamed kale (which was also going on at that time). At first I got offended, but then one night at story time, I began spinning a tale about a couple of kids in the forest with a Druid and a glowing sword… it was quirky and funny with a touch of old Pops woven in, and Joshy loved it. As the story built to a climax, his eyes got a little wider, his mouth dropped open… and suddenly I realized, he wasn't just hearing the story, he was 'in it'. I could have shoved a fork full of kale into that little mouth right then and he would have eaten it. But instead I just dropped in a simple theme about the tangible power of thought, and the idea that 'thoughts are things'. After the story, Josh drifted off (to be honest, I probably fell asleep first), and then I forgot about the whole thing. About a week later we were running late for a movie and as we pulled around the corner looking for a place to park on the busy street, I blurted out, "We're never going to find a park in time!" Josh shot me a scornful glance. "Not if you think that way, Dad. Come on. 'Thoughts are things', remember?" As if on cue, a parking spot opened right in front of the theatre… touché.

The bottom line is that story is one of the greatest known bridges from our head to our heart. It is a genuine mode of energy transference, literally altering the chemistry of our body. When we listen to or read an authentic story, we are taken on a journey, and in that journey it is our own story that we hear within it. Great masters and indigenous elders have always known this to be true. When we share information we speak to the head, but when we tell a story, we speak to the experience of another. While facts are contained like a pool… stories run like a river. Their flowing rhythms allow those of all different walks to draw whatever they may need to take the next steps in their own journey.

Some cultures believe that the living pulse of a story actually seeks out specific people through which to be told or written (Australian Aborigines believe these stories even stalk their tellers!). For those cultures, the ones whose task is to receive and share new stories and songs are greatly revered, for it is known that in the sharing of story, we not only honor the wisdom of what has been, we weave new possibilities into the fabric of reality.

If you are holding this book right now, perhaps a story has been calling you – seeking (or stalking) you out – ready to be brought forth into the world. Like a seed sitting in a jar on the shelf… it waits for the right season when you will choose to hold it in your palm for a moment, then submerge it in the ground with a commitment to steward its journey to fruition.

If you are feeling this call but are not sure where to start, how to finish, or otherwise what to do with this rising inspiration… WELCOME. This book is designed as a bridge. It's a creative path to walk from that shelf in your mind, out into the garden of all possibilities, where you can fully plant that story seed into the soil of reality.

The truth is there has never been a better time to step on (or back on) the story path. In times of big change on the planet like this, we need new stories. Stories that reconnect us to the currents of life, so that our stride may be truer in the future. Stories that churn the soil of our existence so that we may begin to plant seeds for tomorrow's dreams and to grow a world of positive self-expression.

Some people say that if you want to be a writer, you need to read a lot and really saturate yourself with other writer's styles. While reading can certainly serve as a spark to light the kindling, in my experience, the best path to become the writer you really came here to be, is to put down your literature for a while and enter the book of your life. Take your shoes off, walk into the wild grass and genuinely engage with the Source of all story. Bring your genuine presence to even the smallest moment and there you will discover the currents of story being woven and shared all around you – in the sound of rain landing on a leaf, in the nasal breathing of a sleeping child, in the conversations and quiet dreaming of those all around you. In pain and pleasure, in yearning and fulfillment… and simply in being, there is story. Through our connection to the intimate we discover our doorway to the universal STORY of life.

Over the past two decades of travel and connection to people of many walks of life I have come to discover that we each have a wellspring of pure story energy within us. Stories of genuine inspiration, hilarity and discovery. Stories that are worth sharing. Stories that could actually be of great benefit to humanity at this time – because of the message they carry or the simple act of making us laugh, cry or consider our reality from a slightly different angle. But without a clearly defined pathway and knowledge of how to translate a story vision into a form, many of these great stories go untold.

Whether your story is fact or fiction, memoir, fantasy, comic book or an epic feature film trilogy, the purpose of this book is to help guide your path, by sharing a progression of key lessons in the art of writing/creative expression while helping you access the timeless story wisdom contained within your own life experiences. The book itself is a journey into an archetypal framework of story structure that has woven its way from ancient Greek mythology right through to modern 3-D cinema. While gaining an experiential understanding of story form, we will also open a path of genuine connection to your true creative voice so that you will clearly hear the pulse of the stories you feel most called to share… and the ones that feel most called to be shared through you.

Along the way, my intention is that we each gain a deeper sense of reverence for the hero's journey of our life, ultimately revealing that the true Muse we're seeking has been waiting right there within us all along.

So with great gratitude and humble excitement, I offer this quote by Thomas Drier to help us hoist our sails and head out into the living waters that writing holds for all who are ready to embrace its currents…

"As a writer, I only have one desire. To fill you with fire. To pour into you the distilled essence of the sun itself. I want every thought, every word, every act of mine to make you feel that you are receiving into your body, into your mind, into your soul, the sacred spirit that changes clay into men and men into gods."
– Thomas Drier

CHAPTER 1:

Prelude to the Journey

*"There are two mistakes one can make along the road to truth...
not going all the way, and not starting."*
– Buddha

How to Experience this Book

The *Writing the Story Within* journey is based on guiding principles that have emerged from my own baptism by fire on the page along with my passion for cross-pollinating common threads of various philosophies, schools of thought and theories in the story world. The aim of this book is to synthesize a wide variety of lessons, enquiry and exercises into a genuinely unified pathway, leaving you with the tools and confidence to answer the call of the stories that are ready to come through you... and to powerfully, joyfully bring them through onto the page – and beyond.

To do this, we will spend time exploring both the raw energy of creative flow and the disciplined form of story. We will swim in the waters of unbridled inspiration and we will also attune to the natural rhythms of archetypal story structure, aiming to weave these two polarities into a unified force. In so doing, we will ground the more ethereal inspiration of our stories into a form that feels true in its expression and speaks to the heart of our readers, viewers and listeners.

Because much of my own writing experience and story passion has been focused in the arena of film for much of my life (from childhood school assignments and free-time adventures through to years of professional focus), the structure of this book will follow somewhat of a cinematic theme. This does not mean the book is aimed specifically at aspiring film writers... I just find cinema to be a very dynamic and accessible arena to explore the framework and inner workings of story.

From time-to-time throughout this book I may make reference to specific film stories to exemplify certain story structure points. The nice thing about drawing on film in this way is that most readers have the ability to rent DVDs or download films quite quickly, so in a matter of hours you can seal your understanding of a lesson (as opposed to taking days or weeks to read the book). This is not in any way to discourage you from reading the written word, but for the purposes of grounding our understanding of the *structural* side of story, it will help us streamline the learning process, crystallize our understanding and keep the magic ball rolling (we gotta get these new stories out there!).

Whether your particular story vision is actually for a film or not, the principles explored apply equally. For those who do have a desire to write movies, the framework explored here is based upon the 3-Act story form that has been passed down from the ancients and now governs 99.9% of today's film stories. A basic understanding of this form will greatly infuse your structural decisions as a screenwriter, while bringing new depth and clarity to your moment-to-moment writing. For those who do not have a cinematic motive for your story, the structural guidance will help you drill into the heart of your story in a way that is both intimately connected and universally engaging.

In basic terms, the book is divided up into ten chapters, eight of which follow essential phases of story as I have come to experience them in various mediums. Each section dives into a different phase, so that as we journey through the book we not only gain an insight into the natural structural progression of story, we also get to see and experience how that progression mirrors our own journey and story of life.

Honoring a Master... and the Hero Within

In his profound work and study of the archetypal path of the hero, philosopher Joseph Campbell helped to define and articulate a form and rhythm for story that has woven its way through virtually every society and culture since the beginning of time. Campbell called this story form the "Hero's Journey" or "Monomyth", and demonstrated (among other amazing things) that all of the stories we dream and share contain a similar rhythmic pattern and progression, quite simply because they reflect the phases of our own path of growth and transformation in life. Campbell showed us that no matter what the story looks like on the outside, there is always an undercurrent of transformative change calling us/our hero into an inner journey of true discovery. The hero must choose to answer that "call to adventure" and cross over from his/her ordinary world into an extraordinary new world of possibilities, where lessons must be learned and fears conquered en route to claiming a new truth or "elixir" to be brought back and shared. Other pioneering authors (such as Christopher Vogler in the film world) have gone on to crystallize Campbell's teachings as they relate to modern story telling and the writing craft.

We experience the pulse of the Hero's Journey in different forms in virtually every story we watch, tell and hear – from ancient Greek mythology to modern 3-D cinema. The life stories of Prometheus, Moses, Buddha and Jesus all track closely to the rhythms of the Hero's Journey, as do stage and screen stories from Shakespeare through to *Toy Story*. As we experience these stories and others, we don't always know what's going to happen next, but there is a part of us that often knows what to expect energetically for our hero. The reason is that at a base level, the themes and rhythms of the Hero's Journey reflect the very fabric of our own transformative experiences in life. We are each drawn into the power of the Hero's Journey in different ways throughout our life, which is perhaps why we feel drawn to these reflections in literature, history and film. They inform the magic of our own steps on the path. By gaining an understanding of the patterns and rhythms of the archetypal Hero's Journey in story, we naturally open a doorway to recognize and embrace the journey of the hero we are becoming in our own life.

Writing the Story Within aims to open a bold new step on the story path by not only exploring the rhythms and principles of ancient story form as they relate to our own writing, but by guiding us into a genuine *experience* of these archetypal rhythms in our own life. In this way, the real invitation is not to read the pages here, but to embark upon a journey into yourself as a writer and a person – gaining a genuine, cellular connection to the Universal rhythms of the stories you both live and share.

My goal is for you each to have the opportunity to experience the lessons of this book on three levels:

1. To gain a deeper connection to the STORIES you are writing.
2. To gain a broader perspective of the LIFE STORY you are living.
3. To gain a powerful experience of the WRITING CRAFT itself.

How to transform raw inspiration into engaging story form is one of the greatest challenges I have discovered in emerging writers, so my aim is quite simply to help open that path for many more inspired stories to come through into the world.

I have always been a very experiential learner, so I have endeavored to make this book as interactive a journey as possible. Each of the primary chapters (Chapters 2-9) are named after a different key story phase, with the aim of experiencing the lessons of these story phases as we move through them. So overall, the book itself is designed as a living journey through story... Your story. Most of the chapters start out with a short personal story, along with a structural explanation of a specific key story phase. The rest of the sections within each chapter offer more open creative lessons and exercises to help expand your voice on the page and anchor the essence of that story beat in dynamic ways in your work. By the time we reach the end of the book, we will have literally journeyed right through each of these nine key phases of story – as writers, storytellers and people on the path of this great story of life.

We're not going to overdo it with this structural stuff, but within the overall mission of bringing creative visions into the real world where they can be shared, I will do my best to pass along key pieces about structure that to me have been the most liberating. For the most part, the guidelines provided here are not manmade rules. They are living patterns that reflect Universal Law and our own inner make-up. It's not so much about learning to follow these patterns as it is about learning to recognize them as they emerge, so we know how best to make the very most of the moment. I wrote my first screenplay before learning any of the structural concepts shared here. After studying screenplay structure I re-read my script and discovered that I had essentially managed to hit each of the vital structural components pretty much in their 'proper' place – without even knowing that they existed. The reason, I believe, is that archetypal story is engrained in our very DNA. It reflects who we are and how we become. I'm not teaching you these patterns to show you how you should structure things... I'm sharing them with you to give you a greater appreciation of the patterns that are probably already flowing through your life and your stories. The sharing of these concepts then becomes more about confirming, enriching and calling out what is already naturally there, ready to emerge.

Keeping it Real & Getting on the Page

Along with the key structural pieces that will come through each step along the way, we will share and explore dynamic exercises designed to help you anchor each chapter theme into your writing straight away. This whole book is an interactive writing experience, and I strongly encourage/invite/call you to engage with it as such. I will only be truly successful in my intention if you have written many new and inspired words throughout your *Writing the Story Within* experience, so please do your part by rolling up your sleeves, sharpening your pencil and diving onto the page whenever the moment calls.

I suggest that you buy yourself a nice, good-feeling journal for the Writing the Story Within journey. Not so nice that you are reluctant to use it, but nice enough to be a worthy container for your emerging brilliance. Nice enough that it feels good in your hands and makes you smile a little as you open the page. Nice enough that you feel inclined to bring it with you out into your world more often than not – to the park, to the café, into the movies (my wife and son would laugh at this because they have never seen me watch a film without my journal). I suggest you have that journal open as you read each chapter of this book, and as much as possible, take time to do the exercises as they come up. Resist the temptation to tell yourself you'll do them later. This is a dangerous trick of the mind and often leads to chronic delay.

There will certainly be lessons and exercises that you choose to come back to when you have more time or revisit later, but when the moment calls, do your best to jump in for at least an initial momentary blast. Dig in, have fun. Let whatever comes through, come through. No matter what the initial topic or creative call-to-action may be, if you bring your genuine presence to the page, you will almost always be positively surprised by what is waiting there just beneath the surface, just beyond the veil, ready to come through.

PACING AND 'BUILDING A PRACTICE' FOR YOUR WRITING FUTURE

This book has emerged from a series of 1-2 day workshops and an 8-week *Writing the Story Within* mentorship program I have been running for the past few years, and so it is fundamentally designed as a progressive experience, to be explored in a given amount of time. For the benefit of the stories that are waiting on your internal shelf of possibility, I invite you to embark upon the book in a similar fashion as you may enter a workshop or mentorship experience – with a commitment to complete the journey in a given time frame.

For those on a committed path with a bit of available time, one chapter per week (tackling a new sub-section every day or so) is a great way to experience the work, and will really help build a solid daily writing practice. If this is too much for your schedule, then find a different pace that works for you. Whether you stick right to the plan from start to finish or shift and evolve it as you go, my strongest suggestion of all is that, no matter what, you take time to WRITE EVERY DAY.

Making writing part of your daily practice in life is like running fresh water down a streambed each day... it feeds everything. The exercises and enquiry on the following pages will help spur this daily practice in many enriching ways, so pick a time (preferably first thing in the morning or at the end of the day) and honor this time as a sacred contract between yourself and the living stories that are ready to come through you. Don't make appointments or set meetings during this time. If someone asks you to see him or her during your writing time, tell them that you already have a meeting scheduled at that time. A very important meeting.

This may feel awkward at first – particularly if you're not yet sure what story you want to write – but as you begin to gain momentum in this daily ritual, you will foster a level of trust within your creative self that will open inner doorways you never knew existed. Soon you will have no problem protecting this time period from intrusion, for you will recognize it as one of the most vitally important aspects of your day.

SHOULD YOU WRITE YOUR STORY
WHILE YOU'RE WORKING THROUGH THE BOOK?

The answer to this question is different for everyone. You may wish to carry your story with you like a packed lunch on a mountain path, stopping to dig in and really chew on it at various parts of the journey. Or you may choose to follow the topics and exercises for their own sake with no immediate or specific story focus – taking notes for future reference along the way. You may have arrived here with no conscious awareness of what story to tell and then suddenly in Chapter 3 it lands like a special package in the mailbox of your mind. Or you may come into this experience with a very specific vision for a story you want to tell, only to find that your vision begins to change, transform or morph into something else as you move through the lessons. This too is part of the journey, and one of your great ongoing challenges/opportunities as a writer – to honor the initial vision of what brought you to the page while staying open to the energy and inspiration of what emerges once you are there. More on this later. For now, know that however you step onto the *Writing the Story Within* path, you will surely discover your own unique way to integrate and apply the lessons into your own writing journey and your life.

Part for Story... Part for Life...
Part for the Writer Within!

Lastly, as you move through the different phases of the *Writing the Story Within* experience, you will notice that some of the lessons are geared specifically toward the story you are writing and the heroes involved, while other lessons and enquiry are focused more directly toward you as the hero of your own life story. The reason for this is that the stories we tell are always – at some level – reflections of life. Even if the themes we choose to write about have no relevance to our specific life circumstance, the emotional undercurrents of these themes will always be enriched by our own unique connection to the river of our human experience. I may not have had the specific experience of leaping from a moving train onto the top of a moving car (as my hero may be propelled to do), but I have had experiences from my life that are charged with similar emotions. In this writing journey we will discover that if we can connect to the emotional truth of the scenes and stories we are writing, then we have the key to writing words that resonate clearly with that energy. And while we may not have had every experience that our characters will have, we have each experienced a full array of emotions.

As writers, this connection allows us to access our higher capacity to write from a place of genuine, heartfelt truth. As human beings, gaining an understanding of the universal patterns of story opens our lens to perceive and experience our reality in profoundly more empowered ways. When we can begin to recognize the archetypal story rhythms unfolding in the daily challenges and breakthroughs of our life, we gain access to a more heroic perspective and we begin to harness our capacity to transform simple life moments into vital steps of growth and realization. We begin to recognize when we are being 'called to adventure' or drawn into our own 'inner most cave'. We know when the hero of ourselves is being tested, and we can see our life like a writer sees a story – with one foot in it, and one foot above it – guiding, stewarding and learning each step of the way.

In this way, writing becomes like a tuning fork to help center ourselves – not only around the stories we wish to share with the world, but around the person we are being/doing/creating/becoming within it. As we travel together, I will share a glimpse into several of my own life and story experiences, as a way of demonstrating certain principles and story keys, while encouraging you to tap into your own life journey as the ultimate source of your truest story wisdom.

Wherever you currently find yourself on the story path and whatever has lead you here, I look forward to the great creative waves that will be initiated through your connection and commitment to the path ahead. You have 'answered the call' simply by being here, and you now stand poised to take your next steps into the rich arena of writing the stories within you... HERE WE GO!

CHAPTER 2:

Your Opening Image

"Australian Aborigines say that the big stories – the stories worth telling and retelling, the ones in which you may find the meaning of your life – are forever stalking the right teller, sniffing and tracking like predators hunting their prey in the bush."
– Robert Moss, Dreamgates

Why We Write

"The pages are still blank, but there is a miraculous feeling of the words being there, written in invisible ink and clamoring to become visible."
–Vladimir Nabakov

*

It's three hours before dawn... I fell asleep putting Josh to bed so now I'm up and grateful to be so. As is always the case when I rise early or have stayed up, there is a feeling in the air that makes me feel both peaceful and excited. I know that very few are awake at this time, and if you are one of us, you will agree that everything feels different. The air is different. There is a quietness of being that seems to illuminate everything. Maybe it's more of an absence of energy, an open space that's normally filled with movement and voices, mobile phones and vehicles. But it's palpable. Even the wind and the waters settle in this time. I used to wonder why the lake was so clear and calm and silky in the morning. Why the ocean showed up so smooth. But now I know. It's because of this pre-dawn time of quiet. A mandatory pause between the exhale of yesterday and the in-breath of tomorrow. Farmers, bakers, monks and young mothers. These are the only ones awake at this time. Quietly, mindfully tending to the task at hand. Tilling soil, needing dough, seeding prayers and feeding children. Creation time. New beginnings.

My family and I arrived to the USA from Australia just a few weeks ago with the intention of staying for a year, maybe more. Since landing back in my country of birth (and life until 17 years ago), the river has not stopped moving. Every day is full of movement, searching, seeking and feeling. Old friendships rekindled, old tracks re-discovered. New towns, schools and projects explored. Each day has become a quest, and each night a time to discuss, reflect and review. We came here with a vision to spread our wings for a time and explore the question of where on this great globe we are truly meant to BE. So far the path has been complex and in many ways the land has felt quite foreign. But here in the quiet of the night I am reminded of what my soul truly yearns for more than anything. Stillness. Quiet connection and inspired creation time. And so, amidst the movement of our new adventure, I will claim this time here in the wee hours as a sacred container to keep me connected to my truth, and to plant the seeds of new possibilities into the soil of reality. This is where I begin... to write myself home.

*

I won't lie. The writing path is not always easy. It is not all flow and grace with the magic dance of the Muse blessing each word, note and comma… At least it hasn't always been that way for me.

While I have certainly had my share of times when I feel as though the words are coming through me like a mountain spring cascading from a lofty peak, I have also had my share of moments when I feel like I'm turning on a stiff garden hose that's been sitting under the house all winter. You know the ones that make that distant, echoed coughing noise as the water crinkles and seeps its way through kinks and blockages, finally arriving in spattering bursts of rusty spit like a cat choking on a liquid hair ball... By the time those first words hit the page (if they ever arrive) my critical mind is already fidgeting, doubting and rewriting them – questioning the validity of the impulse that brought me to the page in the first place.

The truth is, writing can be awkward, painful, confusing and overwhelming… It can be boring, lonely and intimidating. Writing can bring up dormant feelings of self-doubt and criticism. It can unearth energies of angst, judgment, procrastination, resistance and guilt – to name a few. It might even make you vomit. Just kidding. But it might!

So why do we do it?

In my experience, we write for the same reason that surfers rise before dawn, that drummers play into the night, that mountaineers endure sub-zero winds on the ledge of a snowy peak (all of which I have also done in order to compare notes). We write to connect with and express a part of ourselves that we yearn for but don't always get to experience in everyday life. We write to feel the energy of the Universe being expressed uniquely through us. We write to come closer to God.

Call it what you will (Source, Energy, the Universe, our Higher Self) but at the base of all of life's peak moments, rich experiences and creative endeavors exists an opportunity to genuinely align with the connective energy of life itself. In truth, this opportunity stands poised within *all* experiences (from writing, to swimming with whales to brushing our teeth), but sometimes the extreme examples offer a more obvious doorway. It may initially be easier to recognize the miracle of life in the eyes of a sentient ocean being than in the bristles of your new Colgate electric (unless of course you're brushing your teeth while swimming with whales), but the opportunities to experience the inner pulse of life are available in both ends of the spectrum, and most spaces in between. We each have our own unique ways of accessing this space of connection that some call 'flow'. Whatever our particular flow doorways may be (and writing is certainly one of them), they call us to move through layers of unnecessary limits and to shed the trappings of our outer world, for the opportunity to claim and experience something greater… something deep and true.

Like a surfer who overcomes the temptation to stay in his warm, safe bed in order to drive down a cold, empty road, wedging himself into an already damp wetsuit, wading awkwardly across slippery sharp stones, paddling through froth, currents and crashing waves, in order to wait, breathe, watch and paddle some more... we must often journey through layers of challenge and resistance before reaching our own space of true expression on the page. But just as the surfer turns and strokes into alignment with a rising wall of water, gliding for a timeless moment within a curling tube that has literally traveled thousands and thousands of miles just to meet him at the shore... we too will reach that moment where nothing else matters or even exists outside of our creative connection with the wave of story that is moving through us, carrying with it the full power of the sea itself... reminding us what is possible and what is true.

In my experience, this is why we write. This is why I rose at 4:30 this morning and why I will likely do the same tomorrow, with my feet close to the heater; torso bundled in layers, hat and scarf. I can say that I'm working on a book, but in truth I'm using these words like the surfer uses waves, to guide me to that place of connection with the ocean of life... with the aim of bringing a bit of that magic through onto the page for others to share.

YOUR WRITING AS A DOORWAY TO YOU

As we find with any genuinely pursued endeavor, writing – especially when engaged on a daily basis – quite quickly becomes a doorway to personal discovery. In order to write something of truth we must at some level feel that truth in our being, so the process of clearing the path to do so often becomes a journey in itself. You could say that we get clear in order to write, or you could say that we write in order to become clear. Both are true.

Writing is, at its core, a 'practice'. Similar to meditation, yoga, martial arts, fine art, gardening, woodwork, sculpture, archery, surfing, drumming, dancing and, well, pretty much any other activity we bring our committed presence to, it has a way of peeling back the layers of our own perceptions and revealing an entire world within. It is exciting that from this journey into self we can produce a body of work that can be shared with others, and in my experience, the more we bring our focus to the 'practice' of writing for the pure purpose of expanding our connection and expression of self, the more that expression will naturally reach out and resonate for others. But first, we must be willing to show up.

To reach the mountain summit, to ride the wave or capture the rhythm, we must be fully present and committed to those endeavors. Sure we may be able to fluke a great ride now and then just through raw talent, but in order to flow with grace and power on a consistent basis, we're going to have to build a new type of fitness.

The nice thing about writing is that if you are reading this book right now, chances are very high that you already know how to write. If anything, you have probably been over-taught, over-critiqued and over-engineered – to the point that you may have come to believe there is a very specific right and wrong way to express yourself on the page – a thin path with many thorns, and you are not often on it. If you have not had such conditioning, then consider yourself one of the lucky ones. Your doorway to the expression of your truth may be easier to find and walk through, and we'll do our best to keep it wide open during the process of this book. And if you come to this space with some literary wounds and grammar school shell shock, then I look forward to rekindling the fire of your connection to your true creative voice. Believe me, it's in there, and if you've made it this far then my sneaking suspicion is that it is ready to come OUT.

Regardless of your background, the great news is, writing truthfully and engagingly actually takes a lot less energy than one might imagine. Much like the other activities mentioned so far, when we're in tune and expressing from our natural center, the act of writing actually gives us energy, fills us, infuses us, lights a torch inside that quite literally makes us feel more alive. It's like a magic walk (or sprint) down a dapple lit forest path. Every step and word reveals some new gift, perspective or aspect of ourselves waiting to be explored and experienced. When we trust our footsteps on this trail, the path will continue to rise, word for word, and meet us along the way. Each sentence leads to another, ultimately carrying us right where we need to go. And while there are certainly guidelines and structural 'laws of story' to be aware of, some of which we will explore in detail within this book, I have found the story path to be less about acquiring skills and techniques as it is about acquiring trust and confidence to simply listen and follow that quiet, creative voice that's been within us all along.

In my experience, the only part of writing that is actually painful is the process of clearing our internal pathway to enable this to happen. We must let go of judgment long enough to allow the energy of what is alive and closest to us to come on through.

Why We Don't Write
(A Glimpse at our Creative Antagonist)

"I wish I could show you,
When you are lonely or in darkness,
The astonishing light of your own being."
– Hafiz

*

4:47am. I've been up for 17 minutes. I've had a shower, cleared my desk, brewed a pot of Yerba Matte and lit a candle in the window. I've sat here quietly for a few minutes looking at the page and now I'm hoping that something will come along to help inform my fingers as they hover above the keys... please. Last night I felt inspired, so clear and in the flow, but this morning I feel confused and unsettled, questioning the validity of the creative impulse that brought me here. I feel overwhelmed. Fearful of locking up and losing momentum. Fearful of letting people down... letting myself down. Questioning whether I'm really the one to bring this story through, or whether there's anything of substance to bring through in the first place. What if this whole idea was just a random thought – nothing magic or special at all? Seriously, who is going to want to read this? It's a peaceful winter pre-dawn moment on the outside, but inside I'm churning with waves of doubt and resistance... memories of moments lost, of soccer goals I should have kicked and dreams I never acted on, rising inside with sharp voices that are building a solid case against me writing a single meaningful word. Conscious of the power of my thought to affect reality, I now find myself fearing the fear I'm feeling, lest it stacks up and makes the situation worse. If I took a step back and viewed myself from above I'd see that I have every reason to be inspired in this moment... the piece I am writing has been commissioned and it's set for print as soon as I send it in. In truth this is a moment I have longed and waited for, but for some reason here and now, I feel paralyzed. It seems easier to stand here full of potential, full of percolating ideas, than to roll up my sleeves and roll the dice out there and really see where they fall... So I dance around the edge for a while. Type a few sentences and circle back, picking them apart and starting over. Trying to see my way into the piece far enough to know my steps will be safe. I start feeling tired and the thought occurs that maybe I just need a little more sleep. It's a bit crazy being up this early anyway, right? My beautiful wife will surely welcome me back into bed with more warmth than the blank laptop screen before me. Perhaps a few more hours of sleep and I will be more clear... then it will be easier and I will know what I really have to say. Then I will have more courage and I will jump right onto the page and say it. Yes... just a bit more sleep and all will be clear...

*

*"Yours is the energy that makes your world.
There are no limitations to the self except those you believe in."*
– Jane Roberts

Because of the often cathartic nature and transformative power of writing, it is also one of those activities that can be the easiest to resist, postpone and procrastinate. It's amazing what crazy, damaging words and judgments can fly around inside of our heads, sucking our energy dry and diverting our attention from the call of our story. The above real life episode (to be continued!) is just a glimpse at some of the key players in my own personal team of resistance. You may be familiar with some of these voices in your own creative path and you may have other forces to contend with as well. Fortunately we'll have plenty of opportunity to see what's waiting just beyond this thin (but often LOUD) veil of resistance throughout the *Writing the Story Within* journey, and for now it's just good to open the vents and get a sense for where and who *they* are. Often the simple act of naming and expressing these forces allows them to move outside of our body into the light of day where they naturally begin to lose their power over us.

You may have bought this book a while ago and perhaps it's been sitting on a table or bookstand where you see it and feel a slight twinge each day as you pass it. There's a part of you that reaches out like a kitten swiping at your feet as you walk by, calling out for you to stop and play. There may be specific reasons why you've put off your writing in the past, and perhaps why you've questioned the endeavor of writing itself. Decisions and beliefs that throw into question why you are or are not worthy, qualified, acceptable to venture down this path. "Who would want to read my stories?" Maybe you've had a mixed bag of childhood writing experiences – some that gave you a taste for the elixir of writing from your heart, and some that slammed or closed you down for doing the same. So while you may have some positive reference points for what is possible in this creative space, there's also a part of you that feels like you're diving into the ocean on a moonless night or walking into the woods after dark. You hear the echoed reminder of when your brother told you that sharks (and mountain lions) feed at night. Bringing our pen to the page can be a scary thing for sure, but like the ocean and the woods, it is also a world of immense possibility and normally the scariest place is just before you begin. Right before you commit to dive in… You're squinting your eyes trying to see below the surface, but you see only the reflection of your tense face. You're trying to sense if the story you are entering will be there to catch you when you leap, but in truth, only the leap itself will reveal what this world has in store for you.

There is a yearning and a readiness, or else you surely would not be standing here at the water's edge. But this yearning may also bring with it a level of resistance and clinging to what you know, what is safe. The great gift of these antagonizing forces is that they will ultimately press us all to go beyond what we once thought possible. We will discover throughout this journey that the process of moving through these resistant forces (inside and out) is actually a vital part of the hero's journey to become all that we, and our heroes in story, came here to be.

WRITING EXERCISE: PURGING THE RESISTANCE

As we take our first few steps on the path of Writing the Story Within, *I invite you to take a few minutes to reflect and then write freely about whatever past obstacles, resistance and limiting beliefs may have held you back from committing to your creative path in the past. What past experiences have you had that may have caused you to hold back or suppress your creative voice? How have these experiences influenced your beliefs and creative expression since?*

Looking forward, what is your biggest fear or reluctance with regards to committing up until now? What has stopped you from committing in the past?

What if the OPPOSITE of your greatest fear were true, without you even realizing it? What does the opposite of your greatest fear look like?

When you consider the creative seeds you currently carry (and the ones that may not have even revealed themselves to you yet), how would you feel if these ideas were never acted upon? In what ways might your life be affected if you never gave full voice to your creative inspiration? What does that feel like to consider?

On the other hand, if you were to open the flood gates and fully go for it, fully commit, fully allow what is brewing inside of you to come through... what great possible benefits (to yourself, your family, your relationships, the planet!) may emerge from the full expression of your creative gifts. What good will come with your stories and what does that feel like as you imagine it?

Who would you be and what might you be doing right now creatively if you were totally free from all limiting beliefs, fears and experiences? If your creative voice were FREE and fully empowered in you right now... what would that look like?

In my experience, what waits just on the other side of true creative commitment is always far more expansive and fulfilling than we could have ever imagined. So the real question is are you willing to put your past limits in perception on hold for long enough to take a few bold steps into the wild open fields within, and see what is there waiting for you?

Why is NOW the perfect time for you to bring your stories through?

The great truth is that if you're sitting here, standing here, lying here reading these words, then you've already pushed past whatever initial dragons of resistance you may have encountered en route to this place. You may have stirred a few inner resistance pots to be here. You may feel a bit exposed, overwhelmed or unsure. But you're still here… and that is awesome. So let's get into it!

If need be, I suggest that you make an envelope for the voices of resistance that may emerge in the coming days. Give them a chance to express themselves as they rise up and then put them in a special place to live over there on the other side of the room for a while. You can revisit and hang out with those guys a little later if you'd like, but for now, we've got stories to write and Muses to follow, so let's clear some space in our mind and heart and step back on the path.

In the words of the master poet Rumi, *"The door is round and open, don't go back to sleep."*

Starting Where You Are

"Do not wait until the conditions are perfect to begin.
Beginning makes the conditions perfect."
– Alan Cohen

Several years ago I read the *The Artist's Way* by Julia Cameron (a magnificent book by the way), and in the very first chapter she gave a name to a simple daily writing exercise that I had been doing since I was a kid without realizing it. Cameron calls it 'Morning Pages' (I had always called it 'Writing freely in my journal before I do anything else'), and the simple task is to begin each day expressing openly on the page. The idea is to write without agenda, absolutely whatever comes into your mind. Stream of consciousness, with the only rule being that you have to keep your pen moving. If you can't think of anything to write, you simply write, "I can't think of anything to write…" until you do. In Cameron's practice she suggests to write 3 pages each day and never look back. I normally give myself a timeframe, like 10-20 minutes, and I often bookend my day with this activity (once in the morning and once at night). The fundamental aim of the exercise is to clear the slate of your mind, to give your dreams and subconscious a chance to vent and express in order to prepare your inner space for what really wants to come through. The very cool thing is that whether you are a writer, painter, housewife or advertising executive, it really, REALLY works.

Often times I find that during the process of free writing in this way, I begin with one voice, expressing simple thoughts and ideas, frustrations, desires, confusions, hopes, realizations, etc… and then somewhere in the middle the voice gradually begins to change and shift to one that is speaking *to* me instead of from me. Amidst that transition, I often discover answers or insights into whatever questions or thoughts I may have come into my writing with, and almost always finish the exercise in a very different state of being than when I started. This free writing exercise helps us move and align energy in ways that are difficult to describe but incredibly potent to experience. In a world of structures and schedules, this free flow writing is a chance to run wild on the page. It's like giving a young colt a chance to sprint around the paddock before entering a morning lesson in the ring. And while these words are initially for your eyes only, with no other aim but to clear the pipes and open your creative river, you may ultimately discover that some of your very best writing comes through during this time of simple free expression, particularly if you get in the habit of doing it every day.

WRITING EXERCISE:
ENTERING THE FREE FLOW

So today, in fact right now, and for the rest of your life perhaps, I invite you to give yourself 10-20 minutes to write freely in this way. To put your pen to the page without agenda and to write whatever comes. Don't edit, don't censor and don't even pause to read it... just write. Write and feel the simple, freeing feeling of energy running through you unimpeded onto the page. Ahhhhhhhhhhhhhhh.

A powerful thing occurs when we build a daily rhythm of free flow writing. At first we may move through layers of resistance and uncertainty... confusion, frustration and even anger (especially those who have been storing up creative fire for a long time!) but as we continue to "show up" each day we begin to put these feelings of struggle to rest, simultaneously drilling deeper and deeper into the substance of ourselves... and our art. It is this rhythm of consistency in the most ordinary actions that often illuminates the path to the extraordinary creative breakthroughs we all love and live to experience. So commit to clearing your vessel in this way each day (for the rest of this book at least) and prepare to witness and ride the waves of new possibility that emerge both on the page and in your life as a result.

NATURE AND THE PULSE OF ALL STORY
Once you have cleared your 'inner slate' with your free writing, you are usually much more ready to take a few deep breaths and genuinely turn your attention to the moment and story at hand. Even if you are pressed for time with looming deadlines, you will find that 10 minutes of free writing actually, literally lines you up to save hours (sometimes days!) of time trying to filter through all of your thoughts to identify what most wants to be expressed. With a clear space within, your senses come alive... and your inner eye naturally begins to see, discern and guide you into fresh new places on the page. I know this because I have experienced both sides of the spectrum in full, unbridled glory. I have spent days upon days locked in my studio working on a single scene with no success, only to stop and write freely out of pure frustration for a few minutes. I put down my pen and step outside onto the grass and suddenly the whole sequence unlocks in a single nanosecond.

The "step outside" part is not an excuse to put off your writing, but in many instances I often find it an important part of the equation. In the same way that free flow writing can work to clear our inner slate, often the act of stepping away from our desk and physically moving our bodies (particularly in nature) allows creative energy to shift and move in other ways. The process of putting on (or taking off) our shoes, unlocking the door, navigating the steps, greeting the dog, etc. serves to occupy our conscious mind in simple ways, creating space for our subconscious to bubble up from below and reveal hidden keys we may have been searching for. The other thing that happens when we step outside is that we have the opportunity to engage with the elements and energy of the natural world and in so doing we expose ourselves to the *story* of creation unfolding all around us. As we give ourselves the gift of connecting in a genuine way with the rhythms of nature, we find that our senses and our creative impulses begin to reflect a more natural, more truthful and universal cadence. We drop into a different space within ourselves, and as a result, everything we perceive and share begins to come from that space.

I went for a morning run the other day and then stopped to do some Qi Gong at the base of my favorite redwood tree. For a few minutes without realizing it, I was plowing through this sacred martial art with the same vigor I had carried into my run. My mind was partly present but at the same time was already leaping forward into my day. Dropping my eyes to the ground to begin a movement, my gaze happened to fall upon a banana slug inching his way across the pine needles at my feet. If you've never seen a banana slug, just imagine the love child of a banana and a large shell-less snail. Quite big, quite slimy, very yellow and very, very slow. Anyway, this little guy was moving along at his normal pace and the moment my eyes fell upon him, it felt like I entered his world. As I did, everything in my perception shifted. My breathing slowed and my body settled into the soil beneath my feet. My mind went quiet and my senses came alive in ways that I had not perceived in months! The whole world literally looked like a different place. A much richer and connected place than what I had been seeing through my busy-minded, to-do-list lens. A few more breaths with my banana friend and I realized that in truth the world not only looks different, it IS different depending on our pace and level of connection with it. Any time we give ourselves the chance to genuinely slow down and commune with the energy of nature – at whatever level – pretty much everything in our life becomes richer, more in tune and 'naturally' aligned.

So along with our ongoing morning free-writing assignment comes a strong suggestion for regular time spent breathing, moving, connecting, being away from our desk – ideally in the natural world.

As Paramahansa Yogananda tells us, *"When you increase your perception and feeling... you automatically absorb truth from the book of life."* Whispers 'out there' are very often doorways to the answers we're seeking 'in here'.

WRITING EXERCISE:
THE POWER OF SLOWING DOWN

Once you've cleared the slate with your free writing session, put your pen down and step outside. Step outside with the intention of connecting with something in the outside world that may have a message for you today... Into your garden or yard or someplace nearby (ideally with some element of nature), take a few breaths, shake your arms free and then allow yourself to become fully present. Slow down your stride and allow your steps to guide you to a spot to stand or sit for a moment. When you feel to stop, stop. Take another few breaths into your belly and allow your gaze to connect with something, anything, in your immediate environment. Could be a drop of dew on a blade of grass, could be an old sock that the dog's been chewing on... just take a moment to connect with something and get a sense for its details, its STORY, its message.

Connect with this something for just a few minutes, and when you are ready, step back inside (or grab your journal where you sit), and WRITE. Give yourself 10 minutes to write whatever comes. No pressure. Just the joy of giving voice to some little special piece of life, some simple story living out in your garden. It's been there all along, you're just setting it free... like blowing the seeds from a dandelion stem... Whooooosh.

CONGRATULATIONS! You are now officially on the page for the second time in this chapter!

I have found this simple warm-up exercise to be one of the most illuminating not only for bringing me into a great creative state of being, but for bringing fresh perspective to the stories that I am working on. Throughout this book we will explore many simple writing exercises – ranging from the natural to the bizarre, with two common threads of realization moving through them all:

1. **Since the essence of creativity exists *everywhere*, we can begin *anywhere*.**
Wherever we start, if we move on the page with a simple sense of trust, our inner voice will always find a way to lead us into the expression of what it wants to share. If we don't start, we will never know what we're missing. This idea may take some getting used to but once you realize that it's not what you write about but the energy beneath it that matters most, you may experience (as I have) an incredible sense of renewed freedom to realize you can begin ANYWHERE. And more specifically, you can write from exactly where you are – knowing that if you're writing from a place of genuine connection to the moment,

it will always lead you to a truthful expression. I could ask you to free-write about paper napkins (and I may!) and as you begin to write, the faculties of your inner creative voice will begin to draw upon reference points from your experience and perspective that will naturally permeate whatever you're writing. And at the end of the piece, everyone who reads what you've written will have a greater sense for who you really are and what you really have to say, even if you are writing about paper napkins. Different choices may lead to different destinations and expressions on the page, but all roads – when followed with trust and connection – have the potential to be alive with your energy and engaged by the reader.

Prior to realizing this, I used to spend hours, days, weeks trying to figure out the best entry or starting place into a scene or story. But through trial and discovery (and the drafting of many scenes!) I came to realize that if I am clear *energetically* with the scene, all roads will eventually lead to where the scene needs to go. Suddenly I was freed up to begin a scene or a moment wherever I felt most inspired to begin (even if it didn't make sense at the time), and then watch in wonder how the creative trail would wind its way around to a magically fulfilling result. Sure you may at times choose to write down the highway of an idea rather than wander down the country road, but it's quite liberating to realize that even those country road wanderings lead us to interesting places that are genuinely reflective of truth. Every real moment offers the opportunity for authentic creation. Every word could be the beginning of a poem. Start where you are and trust the path.

2. **Our greatest path to writing uniquely is to trust and allow our own voice to come through.**
We each have a unique perspective and creative lens. No two stories are the same. Even if the topics are identical and the writers are best friends. I could ask a thousand people to free-write a story about paper napkins and each would come up with something unique and different than the rest. I first realized this concept in a college filmmaking class where the professor gave each student the same raw reel of film and asked us each to edit our own piece from it. As I was working away, my choices seemed so obvious to me that I was sure that my final film would be strikingly similar to everyone else's. But when it came time for the viewing, it was literally mind-blowing to discover how different each student's perspective and edited piece was. So much so that unless you knew the assignment, most viewers would not even recognize that the same footage was used for each of the 20 films. I have explored this idea of unique voice in many ways since and am continually delighted to discover similar reflection in the writing world by giving entire groups the same exact words to work with, only to discover every piece to be totally different – and (more importantly) uniquely expressive of each individual.

In the world of writing, it is incredibly liberating to realize that our greatest creative power and most unique expression usually comes through our most naturally unique way of seeing and being in the world.

In many cases our most truthful and universally appealing words are often the ones that seem so obvious to us that we feel most tempted to edit or change them. Our greatest beauty often comes from a willingness to let go of how things look. Our greatest path to perfection is often to allow our flaws to flow freely. Our clearest path to genius is our willingness to appear a fool... And our greatest defense against procrastination is simply to begin. So here we go... let's begin. Again.

Starting at the End: Your Heart-based Intention

"What we call the beginning is often the end. And to make an end is to make a beginning.
The end is where we start from."
– T.S. Eliot

As we go from our connection to the wide open field of creative possibilities into a more focused, conscious intention around the specific stories that we want to share, it's a bit like sending sunlight through a magnifying glass. If we do it at the right angle, it heats right up and soon we have a fire on the page. This is what we want – to feel tapped into our limitless creative source, and yet focused and laser-like on the page.

Through our more non-directive free writing we open new pathways of creative flow. From there the question is, how can we allow the full expression of this raw energy, while also harvesting our words into a unified story form?

While there are certainly some key structural tools and guidelines to help us do this (many of which we will explore along the way), in my experience the first and most powerful step is to set what I would call a clear *heart-based intention* for our story.

This isn't an outline or a bullet point layout of the story itself. This is an imprint of emotional intent that will inform and align each of those structural story layout pieces to come. When we know energetically where we want our story to go (or where it may be calling us to take it!), when we know what lies at the heart center of our story, what *feeling* it will convey for our audience… and when we take time to impress that intention into our consciousness, it's literally like setting our internal compass for true north. We may be required to travel across vast, uncharted landscapes and waterways to get where we are going, but when our heart-based intention is clear, each step and creative decision on the path is guided by a quiet sense of inner knowing.

And while we may need to come back to this intention time and time again throughout the journey, and while the intention itself may shift and evolve over time, the inner pulse of our heart-based intention will become one of the most powerful and necessary gifts upon our story writing path. This intention will both reflect and honor our visions, and if we remain open to its promptings, will lead us well beyond what we initially thought was possible – in ways we may never have imagined.

In my experience of both life and story, the process of shifting an idea from our head into a genuine feeling or emotion in the body, is often the very first step to making it real in the world. What that means in terms of writing is that if we can start by connecting with the underlying feeling and emotional truth that our story wants to share, then as we write, the very words we choose will permeate with and be informed by that feeling. The end result will not be a story that is *about* a certain message or idea, but it will be a story that *is* the energy of that idea. And there is a difference between the two. A palpable difference. It's like the difference between talking about love and being in love. When our writing comes from a space of clear feeling, we don't need to question the words we choose because they emerge from a place of deep knowing. A wisdom well beyond our thinking mind. Our story brings a living pulse to the page and its message will stay alive in the hearts of our readers long after their experience of it.

The process of building a feeling-based intention for our story (or article, scene, song or poem) not only vastly enriches whatever we create, it also saves hours and hours of time. If you find yourself wandering on the page, flipping back and forth between ideas, questioning your decisions, impulses, and grammar, it's often because you have simply not taken the time (and it doesn't take very much time) to come to center and clarify your vision for what you are writing. I'm not suggesting that once we have a heart-based intention for our story that every word and scene is going to reflect our intention. But when we are connected to the underlying feeling of our intention as we write, every word and scene becomes infused by a knowing of where this path is leading. This knowledge gives us courage to take risks and follow paths that we may otherwise not have even considered because deep inside we know where we are going to end up.

The following exercise is an inside-out approach that I have developed in my own writing path as a way for me to center myself and cultivate a clear feeling-based vision when I am just beginning, or when I am lost in the trees of a story, article or scene. It's a way of providing a rudder for my journey so that I know if I'm on track, and if I'm not, I can quickly navigate myself back to where I need to be in order to most powerfully deliver the story I came to share. It's not a technical writing exercise, but if done well, it will inform every structural and technical decision along the way. It has a way of placing my whole writing path into a container that is aligned with my highest intention for the story to come.

WRITING EXERCISE:
FINDING FORM THROUGH THE FEELING

Close your eyes and take a few deep breaths into your lower abdomen and allow yourself to relax. Let your face soften and shoulders drop. Breathe out your day and all your to-dos. Breathe out what has been and all that may be waiting for you on the other side of this little session here. You've chosen this moment to expand your creative capacity, so breathe in that intention and let yourself just be here for a moment. Here on the page. A storyteller and a messenger, stepping boldly onto the path.

Imagine yourself holding the seed of your creative potential in your hand. Imagine imbuing it with all of the positive energy and nurturing support that it may require in the coming months as it grows, evolves and blossoms. Imagine your story seed growing to full fruition, fully realized, fully expressed through you and delivered in its highest form. Rippling out into the world creating waves of new possibilities, new perception and new experience for all who encounter it.

When you imagine yourself reaching the end of your Writing the Story Within experience, what would you love to have achieved (or taken great steps towards) in your creative work? How would it FEEL to know you have done this?

Looking out a bit further to the completion and release of your great creative work into the world in whatever its highest form may be (book, film or simply in your journal)… What is the underlying FEELING that you wish for your writing to carry and share with those who experience it?

When you consider the story (or type of story) that you feel most called to share or bring through at this time, what key question might this story pose to readers and viewers, based on your own experience and enquiry in life? What unique gift do you, the storyteller, bring to the telling of this tale?

Imagine a reader or viewer coming to the final moment or final image in your story. What will they see and experience? How will they FEEL when their journey through your story is complete?

While your story may bring with it many messages and gifts for readers and viewers, if you could only deliver ONE key gift, message or deeper meaning, what would that be?

What do you FEEL is the fundamental PURPOSE for writing and sharing your story at this time? In other words, why must your story be told? It need not be noble or grandiose... just real for what it is. Feel the energy of WHY now is the best time for this story (or these stories) to enter the world, and why YOU are the perfect vessel for them to come through... What question might your story pose based on your own experiences, and how might the telling of this tale explore the answers to that question?

Take a final moment to imagine YOURSELF at the end of this creative endeavor and to really saturate yourself with the positive energy of its full, triumphant completion. Bring yourself into this picture and allow yourself to feel how you will feel when the inspired call you have now answered has been fully delivered and realized through you. When the message and truth of your story is now weaving its way into the hearts and experiences of many... Take a moment just to breathe and move and smile how you may when you are on the other side of this creative journey. What is your heart-based intention, how do you wish to FEEL when this creative journey is complete?

Are you ready?

Starting at the Beginning: Your Opening Image

"Take the first step in faith. You don't have to see the whole staircase,
just take the first step."
*– **Martin Luther King Jr.***

The final exercise for our first chapter is quite simple, yet may have a lasting imprint on the entire story landscape you are here to explore.

Many great books and film stories have been sparked by a simple moment in time... a passing image or experience in the life of the writer that may have emerged spontaneously but has remained, germinating like a grain of sand in the tender heart of a clam... added to by layers and layers of impulses and ideas until it opens into a fully fledged story.

When we think back upon our lives, we each have these moments that have marked or hinted at the beginning of a new chapter or experience. Moments that may initially sneak in like the calm before the storm, but carry with them a whisper of what is to come. We may not always be fully aware of the impact of these moments when they occur, but in retrospect we will come to see them as symbolic doorways to a new opening in our world and all that has happened since.

*

I remember the very moment I first crossed the International Date Line, en route to Australia seventeen years ago. A subtle moment that came and went for most on board without so much as a shift in their open-mouthed, head-back, sleeping breath. But for me, as I watched the TV animation of the plane crossing that line on the map, something woke up inside of me. I was writing in my journal at the time. I had been writing my way through the pains of saying goodbye to my family and friends, indulging that deep and hollow sense of loss that comes with letting go, when the pilot's Date Line announcement quietly climbed inside and shifted my focus altogether. I suddenly found myself grappling with the whole idea that as this plane crossed over an imaginary line in the sea (depicted by a solid white vertical on the screen) somehow I was going to lose an entire day in my life. I had taken off from LAX on the evening of 25 May, and after 13 hours of plane food and movies I would be landing in Indonesia on the 27th? What happened to the 26th? My feelings of loss about leaving my home were suddenly amplified by the realization that I was not only giving up the life I knew and the people I loved for a mostly unknown adventure for an undetermined amount of time, I was also giving up an actual day in my life. Just vanished as though it never existed.

Perhaps it was part of the entry fee for my quest, the toll-way for my heart to cross from one world into another. Up until that time I had always enjoyed traveling west because you normally gain time when you head that way. In fact I had written poems as a youth about the possibility of remaining in a constant state of sunrise if we could run fast enough to match the pace of the rising sun. It was a perfect theory so it seemed, to always have the sun at your back... But here I was facing a human-imposed limit, a virtual wall of time constructed in the middle of the ocean, not only blocking the fulfillment of my eternal sunrise aspiration, but actually punishing all of us who tried, by taking a whole day out of our lives. Do we give it back when we fly east back across this line?

After trying to work the math out in my head for quite some time, I decided that the only way to counter this 24 hour thievery – at least until I found a way to balance the equation – was quite simply to claim back the _essence_ of the day that I had lost by living more fully in the days that I still had. While this day had been physically removed from my life, other days could be lost just as easily through simply not being fully present or immersed in what I was doing. In fact, I had just lost a few minutes in the day that I _did_ have, by worrying about what I had lost!

I knew that in the coming days of riding my bike through the jungles of Bali, of coaching skiing in the mountains of Australia, and wherever else the path may lead, each day I would come to new thresholds and crossroads where I would have the option to choose the well trodden path, to go with what was comfortable, cling to what I knew... or to step across my own imaginary line into bold new discovery. To chase the sunrise not from the seat of an airplane but in the very way that I lived. I decided then and there that the only way to claim back any time loss from the past was quite simply to be fully present and engaged in the present. "Squeeze the towel dry." Those were the words my brother Scott had always used to describe such commitment to the moment.

So as I crossed the date line for the very first time, I found myself stretching myself to write a wide-open vision for the time ahead. I challenged myself to look beyond self-doubt and uncertainty, to write the most glorious view I could imagine. In my journal it came through more as a prayer. I prayed for calm connectedness and clear action and synchronicity. I prayed for the path to rise and meet me, to guide me into the fullest experience and expression of my true self. I was alone. I had just left everyone I knew and loved in the world and this date line was my tipping point into a new day. As far as I could see, the only way to truly master the time aspect of this equation was not to race or conquer the date line guardians, but to continually bring myself purely and completely to the tiniest time element that I knew of... this very moment.

*

Looking back, this simple, mostly internal moment of crossing the International Date Line is what I might call the "Opening Image" of what was (and continues to be) one of the greatest journeys of my life. I had not even landed or begun my official adventure, but there in the quiet hours of Air Garuda's trans-Pacific flight to Bali, I received a momentary glimpse into the essence of the path ahead. A spark of new awareness lit from within, shining toward a world not bound by place and time, but by genuine connectedness to the simple pulse of the moment. I had begun.

In the visual landscape of cinema, many of our film stories take advantage of this opening moment to plant a symbolic seed of the path ahead for our heroes. To create an imprint of the beginning of our story that will ultimately come full circle, leading us back to where we began – having grown, evolved, changed and expanded in more ways than we ever could have imagined. The Opening and Closing Images of our story often work as bookend moments, standing at opposite ends of the main story content, reflecting each other and creating a container to hold all the elements of the story in place. As with an effective bookend on a shelf, they are often subtle and may even go unnoticed on first view... but in retrospect we will come to value their presence and recognize the poetic role they play. A well-crafted Opening Image will often offer a simple but profound reflection into the whole story. It will say everything in a single moment, without saying anything at all.

The film *Forest Gump* does this in a beautifully poetic way with its opening image and beginning sequence, which follows the whimsical path of a feather being swept into different places and experiences – sometimes noticed, sometimes not – throughout the city and the country until it lands at the feet of Forest. When we first see this feather drifting along, we know it only as a feather. But once we've experienced Forest's story and arrive back here at the end, we realize that the feather and Forest are one. Watching the opening again, we discover that the opening minute of the film actually gives us an energetic glimpse of the entire journey we are about to take.

In the movie *Avatar*, we begin inside the flying dream of paraplegic Marine, Jake Sully, as he travels through space toward his mission on the planet of Pandora. Soaring over a pristine jungle landscape, flying is the furthest thing from his current reality (as a disabled veteran) and at the time neither he nor we know what this dream means. But by the time we reach the end of our story, we will discover that this opening moment carries a symbolic imprint of the path ahead, and all that Jake is destined to become.

We have all had simple moments like these in our dreams and experience that leave us with an impression or an image... and visual seed or expression of some future idea. Within that vision is a pulse... an energy of something more. Perhaps at the time, we do not know what it means, but something inside, something deep inside, rings true. There is a familiarity to this moment and we will one day look back to recognize it as a message from our future self, giving us a glimpse of the path ahead.

In writing, I sometimes find it is actually easier to write my Opening Image once I know what my Closing Image will be. Once I have traveled to the end of my story and I know where my hero is going to end up, it can be much easier to pull back to the beginning like a sling shot and craft just the right Opening Image. On the other hand, sometimes there is great wisdom in simply trusting an impulse we may have about how our story wants to start (even if we don't yet know where it's going to lead us). The act of following the raw impulses of an Opening Image often reveals creative rivers we never even knew existed. So while we may wish to circle back to this lesson later on and revisit our Opening Image once we have our ending, let's start right now by simply trusting what visions emerge when we open ourselves to the opening of our story.

WRITING EXERCISE:
YOUR OPENING IMAGE

Having considered the overall intention of your story (in the previous section), now is a great time to sit quietly with this intention... breathe yourself into a calm, receptive state, and ask your inner voice to reveal to you an IMAGE. An Opening Image, feeling or moment that may serve as the beginning few moments/minutes of your story.

Ask to be shown and then simply, quietly wait and listen...

Depending on how you normally connect creatively, you may see an image, hear sounds or simply get a feeling. Be aware of how this opening image or moment comes, and simply write down what you see/hear/feel. Even if it does not initially make any sense. Even if it is different than how you had previously envisioned your story starting. Even if you don't yet know what story you want to write. Just ask yourself to show you an Opening Image worth exploring... and when it comes, allow yourself to follow it on the page.

There's no need to force it to make sense or fit in with anything else as you write it. Don't put a lot of pressure on this. Just trust and enjoy the act of writing what comes. What you write may change, evolve or lead to something else all together – and all of that is fine. For now, just connect, ask, listen, receive and write.

An image or a moment to begin with is all that we are seeking. Write for 5-20 minutes – or as long as you feel compelled to express. Then give yourself mighty THANKS for giving you a glimpse at the story currents within. May the river run free.

Creative endeavor is one of the most powerfully transformative pathways available to humanity. It's like stepping into the center of a volcano. Sure it can be hot and uncomfortable… but this is the energy that literally creates and moves mountains in our world. The simple act of opening the creative space, of beginning a new song or story, of listening to and following the pulse of an Opening Image, is indeed a sacred act... an act of genuine creation.

Congratulations on completing Chapter 2! We have set the stage for an epic story journey. Keep that pen moving and I look forward to our next bold steps on the path!

"From small beginnings come great things."
*– **Proverb***

CHAPTER 3:

Hearing Your Call
to Adventure

"A hero ventures forth from the world of common day into a region of supernatural wonder: fabulous forces are there encountered and a decisive victory is won: the hero comes back from this mysterious adventure with the power to bestow boons on his fellow man."
– Joseph Campbell, The Hero with a Thousand Faces

The Mythic Story of You

"All of life can change in a moment.
But that moment rarely comes how or when we imagine it."

*

Standing at the top of the in-run, I hear the announcer call my name. Friends and teammates bark cheers from the side as the course official waves his flag from the knoll. I take a breath of mountain air, focusing down the snowy runway to the top of a large jump waiting for me there. Fourteen feet high at its peak, 60 feet back from the <u>beginning</u> of the landing hill. In a matter of moments I will arrive at the top of this jump traveling at full speed and I will launch up to the tree line – well above the judge's stand, sound system and crowd. I will perform a series of coordinated maneuvers in the air and a few seconds later, I will land. It's been a long winter and my body is tired, but this is my moment. This jump is the only thing standing between me and the top national ranking I have been working toward, so in truth, this is the moment I have been waiting for. It will all be over in less than a minute, then I can rest for a time and ready myself for the wide-open path ahead. I force a deep exhale, tap my ski poles together in quiet ritual and push off down the track.

I'm not sure what lured me into the sport of Freestyle Snow Skiing as a kid, but I know what kept me there for over a decade growing up – rising before the sun on the coldest days, packing our family van to drive into the mountains, pushing through days of sweat and fear, pain and exhilaration. It was that moment just after lift-off from the top of the jump when you go from warp speed along the snowy earth to weightless and timeless, way above it all. Quite literally flying. Only the sound of clean wind through thrilled lungs, as the world opens to an eagle's view in human form. I've always believed there's more to our reality than what we see from the ground and the aerials event confirmed this to my core. So Freestyle Skiing became one of my first doorways to explore the greater possibilities of life. But on this particular day, on my final jump of a major national event – just weeks before the World Cup qualifications and the next magic step in my own Olympic dream – I was about to meet one of the less forgiving elements of our 3-D world… gravity. I had landed similar jumps from similar heights hundreds of times with no problem, but for some reason, on this clear afternoon in Telluride, Colorado, in that split second when my 19-year-old body arrived back to earth from 40+ feet above, the two forces did not agree. A lightening bolt of pain shot up through my right leg, stopping briefly at my knee before rippling through to the rest of my body… and the moment fades to black.

I remember the regretful blink in my doctor's eye as he cradled my knee joint in his hands... I remember the disbelief in my coach's eyes, and the tears in my dad's as he met me on the street. I remember the chemical taste in my mouth just after surgery and the iodine stains on my withered leg in the early days of rehab. In one fraction-of-a-second moment I had somehow gone from the rising peak of a lifelong dream to a pit of pain and uncertainty. As I lay there in the hospital bed, trying somehow to go back and choose differently, to undo or bend what was now confronting me as reality, I could not imagine what good could come from this place.

How could I possibly foresee that in one year's time, as a direct result of this injury, I would be lead to discover the extraordinary world of coaching? A natural gift that would open in accelerated form, leading me to Australia, where I would meet and marry my soul mate, fulfill my Olympic dream as the coach of the Australian team, buy a farm, co-create a beautiful son, learn to surf, write movies and create a whole LIFE here on this side of the world? Hard to believe that a moment of such painful surprise could give birth to so much good... that such momentary loss and confusion could lead to such positive, lasting discovery. Such is often the way of the Hero's Call to Adventure.

*

Amidst the rapid pace of our modern world – now full to the brim with technology, to-do lists and earth change – it is easy to be lulled into reactive, unconscious patterns of living, where every day is a race to simply stay on the treadmill and satisfy expectations from the world around us. But as we paddle hard to keep up with these surface waves of life, there is a powerful undercurrent steadily drawing us into deeper waters... into the experience of our true Self in full heroic form. Occasionally, as we race from point A to point B, something happens to rock us from our boat and open us to the wider currents. It may come in the form of a quiet whisper, great blessing, challenge, crisis or even apparent tragedy. However this moment appears, one day we will recognize it for what it really was – an inner call for us to journey into a greater experience of ourselves and harvest some deeper, latent capacity to create and express in the world. In retrospect, these are the moments that call us into becoming the hero of our own life story.

As discussed in Chapter 1, the Hero's Journey – or Monomyth, as referred to by scholar Joseph Campbell – is an energetic template and pattern for story that spans from ancient Greek mythology to modern 3-D cinema. In the Hero's Journey, the hero begins in his/her ordinary world, where s/he receives a 'Call' to enter an unknown arena of strange powers and possibility. This call may be initially refused, but ultimately the hero will answer, crossing the threshold from the ordinary world into the extraordinary new arena, where he or she will face tasks and trials, meet allies and opposition en route to reaching their 'innermost cave' of personal challenge and discovery. There the hero will acquire a great gift, 'boon' or 'elixir', which he or she must carry back into the ordinary world, ultimately transforming their ordinary world into an extraordinary place.

The following is a basic story map that I have used throughout my screenwriting work as a way to visualize the overall structural flow of the story I am writing with nine of the key 'story moments' or turning points found in most cinematic hero's journey story forms (the Hero's Journey story form has 17 phases in total, but for the purposes of this experience we've honed it into nine).

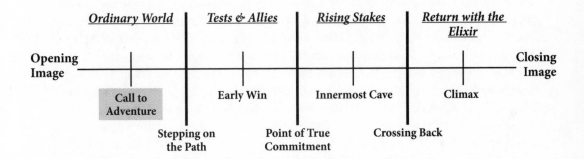

In a sense, this whole journey is like climbing a mountain, and each of the vertical lines on the story map represent key shifts and turning points on the path. Challenges that must be overcome. Breakthroughs and realizations of self along the way. If you imagine a mountain climber… waking up, feeling called, thinking about it, debating it, deciding to go, so he begins… It's colder than he thinks, more difficult than he thought it would be, but slowly he adapts, he finds a way within himself to keep going, to notice the beauty, to gain momentum… until he reaches a moment of true commitment, where he knows he cannot go backward, but must continue on to the top. There's great physical challenge, his food runs short, he gets frostbite and a terrible mountain storm drives him into a cave. He loses his map and much of his supplies, but deep in the depths of this mountain cave, something inside of him wakes up. He realizes that in truth it doesn't matter if he makes it to the top of this mountain or not… this journey is about him being on the mountain, becoming the mountain… enjoying the adventure. With that, he sort of let's go and surrenders to the greater power of this mountain. The light shifts and he steps from the cave to see that the storm has broken. There's a break in the clouds and he spots the mountain summit in the distance… It's closer than he thought! So he musters all the courage that he has and goes for it… Step for step, breath for breath he moves along the snowy mountain path, guided by that deep inner light, until he reaches the peak. In one sense his journey is complete… in another it has just begun, for now he must find his way back down from this lofty peak to his family, to his home, to his people. So that he may share all that he has gathered on the journey.

In the ten minutes it took me to conjure that sequence, I essentially touched on each of the key moments and story phases of the story map above. We will continue to move through and reflect upon these key phases as we travel along the mountain path of *Writing the Story Within*. And whether your vision is actually to write a feature film or simply a poem, song or children's book, you will find that the guiding principles shared here will apply and enliven your focus on the page. For now it's just good to realize that the first big kick-starting moment in story is our 'Call to Adventure'.

In cinema, we know that some time in the first 10-15 minutes, our main character's world will be penetrated by a force that will in some way act as a spark of story ignition. That moment when Frodo is first given 'the ring' by Bilbo in *Lord of the Rings*; when Ray first hears the whispered voice, "If you build it, they will come" in the cornfield of *Field of Dreams*; or when Jake Sully first meets his big blue self in the movie *Avatar*. As an audience we wait for this moment like the lighting of a firecracker fuse, because we know that no matter what our heroes were doing when we met them, the real journey is about to begin. And whatever this catalyst moment looks like on the outside, we recognize it for what it really is… a bold beginning to a journey that must be taken. We revel in the opportunity to fasten our seatbelts and prepare to cross a threshold with our hero into a new world of tests, allies, lessons and messages – knowing that we will all return somehow transformed. As an audience, we willingly say, "Yes" and leap into the story, trusting that the journey will ultimately lead to some point of discovery, where – with our hero – we will vicariously claim some new gift to bring back into our own world. Even though this Call may bring us discomfort (even watching!), ultimately this is why we came.

We certainly don't all see ourselves as heroes (at least not all the time!), but the gift of the Hero's Journey story form reveals a natural, archetypal rhythm in the way that we all experience change and transformation in life. No matter where we begin, we each receive our own unique "calls to adventure" at various stages of life – beckoning, urging, and thrusting us out of what is comfortable, into more of what is possible.

Looking back on the moment of my ski injury, as I was jolted from the peak of my athletic career into injury, surgery, recovery and new discovery, I was in essence, experiencing the pain of being 'called' (or rather ripped) from my 'ordinary world' of elite sport into the extraordinary world of life beyond. And while in time I would begin to sense a profound undercurrent of new possibility opening before and within me, at the moment of impact I had no idea what I was being 'called' into.

The truth is that we are always being called to adventure in some way or another. Every day situations rise up in our life to challenge our current perceptions and experience. At first we may push back or try to resist… but if we look openly, we will often recognize a deeper wisdom to these moments. In retrospect, we will usually find that whatever form the Call comes in, it is just what is needed to catalyze a vital change. Sometimes the Call starts out as a whisper, but if we ignore the quiet voice, ultimately it will rise in volume and in consequence until it is heard. In my own case, I like to think that I would have found my way to coaching and the rest of my life experience without damaging my body to do it… but the truth is that without my physical body putting the breaks on, I would have likely just kept on plowing forward as an athlete, and could have walked (or skied) my way right past the entire life I have discovered since.

WRITING EXERCISE:
WHAT'S YOUR CALL TO ADVENTURE?

Take a moment to consider a few moments of big change or challenge in your life. A time when your life flow was suddenly interrupted and you were shaken from your tree. When you felt in some way called to make a shift, embark upon a journey, break from the old or commit to something new. Looking back on a few of these moments, can you recognize the Call within them and how that Call may have been nudging, drawing, perhaps throwing you into a new phase of your existence?

The Call heralds critical, life-changing moments, and can also be seen on a much smaller scale in the way unexpected developments enter the rhythms of our day-to-day life. Do you notice a pattern of how or when these moments arrive in your life? How do you normally respond? Do you embrace the lightning bolts of change on your path or do you run the other way? Do you move with the shifting currents of the river or do you find yourself resisting and trying to push against the flow?

Take a few minutes now to describe in detail a specific moment from your past when you were 'Called to Adventure'. When the path you were walking was directly interrupted, causing a shift in direction that has since rippled through your whole world. What moments lead up to this Call and how did you respond when it came? Write about the feeling of that single piercing moment when lightning struck your path.

As we open our perception to the inner promptings of our day-to-day existence, we begin to realize that the Call is everywhere – in our relationships, in our creative pursuits, within our finances, our body, our quest for home and beyond – because in truth, we are always being beckoned by our true Self to open up to being more of who we came here to be.

In what ways – large or small – are you currently feeling 'called'?

Perhaps now is the perfect time to answer.

The Nature of Desire

"Don't ask yourself what the world needs - ask yourself what makes you come alive, and then go do it. Because what the world needs is people who have come alive."
– Harold Thurman Whitman, Philosopher and Theologian

As a coach and creative guide, I know of no other question that so powerfully stops people in their tracks, than simply to ask, "What do you really want?" In the modern world we are so hemmed in by expectations and roles that we rarely give ourselves the chance to ponder such a question, and if we do, we tend to limit our view of the possible by focusing in the direction of what we *don't* want instead. In life and in story, the courage to genuinely ask and honestly answer this question is quite often the key to opening a whole new path of possibilities.

The Latin word for 'desire' can be translated into the words 'of the father', suggesting that when we have a true and deep desire – one that transcends our surface world of simple wants and whims and resonates at a Soul level – we are tapping into the energy of God/ Life itself, yearning to be experienced and expressed through us. While some philosophies perceive our higher spiritual path as a 'letting go' or an absence of desire, others believe that desire, in its purest form, is an energetic force that allows us to pierce through the veils of our preconceived limits and actually reach the heights of true connection with the Divine. On the hero's path we will discover that the truth lies somewhere in the middle... and that our highest dreams call for both bold yearning, to reach beyond the possible, and quiet surrender to the greater guiding currents.

Sometimes, like children, we know exactly what we want and we call for it with zero inhibition. Yet sometimes, through lifetimes of societal training, we censor our desires to be 'appropriate', 'realistic' or to be somehow less than what our soul truly yearns for. Sometimes still, what we *think* we want is just a doorway to a bigger world of what we may truly *need* just beyond. A good story may explore any or all of these levels of desire en route to leading us to a fulfilling resolution, but in one way or another all of our stories will be driven in some sense by the desires (denied, fulfilled, pursued, embraced, etc.) of our characters.

In the beginning of a story, desire is one of the fundamental driving forces that propels almost every plot and character into action. What our characters want sits at the core of their behavior and is one of the very first things we are aware of as an audience. Even the noblest of stories often begins with a simple, primal and even selfish desire. And while our heroes may not always get what they *want* on the surface, their pursuit will almost always lead them to discover and fulfill what they really *need*. Our characters' desire is also one of the primary ways that we, as an audience (and author), connect with our characters along the way. The more we resonate with our hero's base desire, the more we will connect with them and cheer for them as they move along on the path toward reaching it. We all know what it's like to want something and we also know what it's like to have that desire held back from us in one way or another. In story, this energy of yearning transfers from the writer's experience to the character's expression, to the reader's engagement in reading it.

As a general guidepost, the stronger and clearer the desire (even if it is initially suppressed or hidden from view) the more likely we are to follow our heroes emotionally when the call comes to initiate their journey. This desire must feel natural and real, not superimposed. If our characters don't have a clear aim or desire, it can be very hard for us to want something for them. In my experience as a sporting coach, if ever I wanted something more than my athletes did, the road was always a struggle. But if their path was lit from the spark of desire within, it was immeasurably easier to coach and navigate them to victory. If the call to adventure is like a stick of dynamite, our character's desire is like the fuse – it gives them (and us) access to the pure power of the call. Sometimes it's a bit explosive, sometimes it makes a mess when it first expresses itself, and that too is the nature of desire.

THE POWER OF CONTRAST

One of the clearest ways to introduce our character's desire and to prepare them for their journey is by commencing their story in a reality that is in stark contrast to their desire. If we know what they ultimately want and what they will ultimately gain, it can be quite powerful to let the hero's story start as far away from that truth as possible. In *Kung Fu Panda*, the main character 'Po' reveals his great desire to be a Kung Fu hero in his opening dream within the story. But then he wakes to the reality of his life as an out of shape, overfed panda bear, waiting tables for his dad's noodle bar. Straight away we feel the contrast and the inner pull between what our hero wants and what he is currently experiencing. In Po's case, his desire to be a great Kung Fu master and his life as an overweight noodle bar waiter come to a palpable head when he sees a poster announcing the great 'Dragon Warrior' Kung Fu tournament about to commence at the Jade Palace. This is Po's call (initially a desire to go watch), which he cannot help but answer, and thus our story begins…

> *"When I used to teach creative writing, I would tell the students to make their characters want something right away even if it's only a glass of water. Characters paralyzed by the meaninglessness of modern life still have to drink water from time to time."*
> **– Kurt Vonnegut**

WRITING EXERCISE:
EXPLORING OUR RELATIONSHIP WITH DESIRE

Can you think of a time when you knew exactly what you wanted and your focused intent catalyzed powerful action toward receiving it? Or perhaps a time when you weren't sure exactly what you wanted until something happened that really made things clear for you? Maybe there have also been times when you knew what you really wanted but didn't act for one reason or another? How did you feel afterward, letting that doorway pass? Take some time to write about your relationship with DESIRE, how it registers in your body and how it has propelled, infused or even stifled your steps.

Wants vs. Needs
Can you think of a time when you wanted something enough to pursue it passionately, only to fall short or 'fail' in some way... but your pursuit of what you 'wanted' ultimately brought you into connection with something greater, deeper and more appropriate for you at the time – what you really 'needed'. Perhaps you started with an initial desire that opened to a much wider path than you could ever have imagined (i.e. my journey from athlete to coach to living a full life in Australia). Take some time to explore the power of your surface wants and how your steps on the path have exposed you to your deeper needs and truest desires.

What About Now?
Consider an area of your life that you are not currently fulfilled in or experiencing at the level that you would like. This could be a relationship, a job, project, aspect of your own well-being, etc. If you quiet your mind and let go of the voices that may wish to censor or judge your truest soul desires, what would emerge in your heart of hearts? What do you really want? How would you feel if this ultimate inner yearning were fulfilled? What would the fulfillment of this desire give you? And what would that give you?

Keep asking this question until you arrive at a core FEELING... a single emotional essence that sits beneath the worldly masks of all our desires... A feeling which – if we are willing to follow it – will lead us beyond the surface "want" to the real soul desire within.

What About Your Characters?
If you are currently writing a story, consider the same for your main character (and all of your characters for that matter). What do they want, what do they really need underneath and how do these two energies interface with their reality? How is their desire aligned or contrasted with their reality as they come into the story?

The Call to Adventure may wake our heroes up, but the energy of their DESIRE is what will propel them into action. The energy of desire will allow them to pierce through the bubble of their perceived reality into the wide-open field of their story.

Allow yourself to connect with the energy of DESIRE today, in yourself and in your writing. See what feelings, thoughts, words and actions spring from this fire into the stories of your life and the lives of those you now scribe upon the page...

"God picks up the reed-flute world and blows.
Each note is a need coming through one of us, a passion, a longing pain.
Remember the lips where the wind-breath originated, and let your note be clear.
Don't try to end it.
BE Your Note.
I'll show you how it's enough.
Go up on the roof at night in the city of the Soul.
Let everyone climb on their roofs and sing their notes!
Sing loud!"
– Rumi

Nature of Resistance (Refusal of the Call)

"Nothing will ever be attempted if all possible objections must be first overcome."
– Samuel Johnson

If our characters enter their story knowing what they want, and if their path is met with a clear and compelling Call to Adventure, it's hard to believe that they would hesitate or delay from stepping on the path. But within many truthful and epic stories (including our own) we often find the immediate time period after the Call to be one of internal question, doubt and resistance. In the Hero's Journey story form this story phase (between The Call and Stepping on the Path) is often referred to as the 'debate' or 'refusal', because it marks the time where our hero must reconcile the contrast of his/her current reality with the invitation that life is now offering.

Why would we resist the very thing we want most in life?
Why would an author resist committing to writing a story he knows wants to come through? Why would an artist resist painting what she sees in her heart? Sometimes we resist the call because there is a part of us that is afraid to go beyond our current bubble of comfort. Afraid to step out and experience the limitless potential of who we really are, and certainly afraid to share that with the world. This part of us – some would call it the personality self, some might call it the ego – wants to keep things the way they are because, more than anything, it wants to keep us safe. This is one reason why we might resist or refuse the Call to Adventure… and even stay within the discomfort of our ordinary world. Simply because it is what we know.

Another reason we may resist the catalyst moments in our life (and our stories) is because they are often masked as something else or come in a way that we don't expect. In fact, the greatest Calls often come in such disguise that we may initially see them as opposing forces to our wants and needs. When I first injured myself skiing, it was simply perceived as a test to be overcome. There was no 'Call' in the incident, except simply to rehabilitate and strengthen my resolve. But when I recovered from my first knee re-construction and regained my number one ranking, only to shatter my other knee the following year, I began to sense a deeper message in the moment. The Call had become stronger, and in the forced pause on my path, it began to penetrate through my focused resistance to a place of higher truth.

This veil of resistance that we may find ourselves facing at the beginning of a new creative endeavor or chapter of life is quite parallel to the energy of resistance that often rises in the lives and minds of our heroes as they enter their journey in a story. Story in its very essence is about change, growth and transformation. It's about going from one level of experience to another. Whenever we embark upon such a journey, we must first, in some sense, break free and depart from what we know. As we learn about the power and purpose of our Call to Adventure, it's equally important to learn to recognize the surge of resistance that may rise as a veil between the Call and our bold answer to it.

As creatures of habit, we resist change, even when it's for the better, simply because it calls us to step (or leap) from the safety of our comfort zone into the unknown realms of the hero we truly are.

Whether the moment of our call comes in the form of something pleasant or challenging, positive or critical, these times where the path suddenly shifts beneath our feet, almost always come in ways that we could not have imagined, and with timing we would not have consciously picked. The reason for this (in life and story) is that the fundamental role of the Call is to break our current patterns in such a way that we have no choice but to see and choose a higher path. Like an infant at the time of birth, the Call pulls us from the womb of our normal world, and it does so with great reason – to lead us into a whole new dimension of experience.

If we can hear the call in a quiet whisper, so be it. If we need a lightening bolt to shake our tree, well that can be supplied too. **In most cases, the magnitude of our 'Call' is in direct proportion to our level of resistance to listening and our attachment to what we *think* is supposed to happen.** More simply put, the more we resist the Call, the louder it gets. Following my own story as an athlete, based on my level of passion and commitment to my external goals as a competitive skier, I can see now that nothing short of a major physical interruption (a.k.a. knee explosion) would have pulled me from my path as an athlete. In the end it took two major surgeries plus a minor one before my perception opened enough to see where my soul was being called.

The same is often true for our characters in story. When we meet them in their ordinary world, they are quite often blinded by the confines of their circumstance, deaf to the quiet whispers of their own hero's call. And so it takes a lightening bolt of some description to penetrate their path and wake them up to a new way of experiencing life.

While it can be nearly impossible to see the bigger picture in moments of great change, in retrospect the synchronistic precision of these experiences with the greater flow of life is almost always apparent. And while these moments may come in disguise, there is something about them – at a cellular level – that also feels quite familiar. The reason for this is that at a deeper level, we know. We know that we are being nudged by a force greater than us to step out into a new level of experience. Here in the debate, we get a chance to hear all the voices that ever would have stopped us from pursuing our desire in the past. It is these voices we must move through or leap past in order to genuinely answer the Call and cross over into the extraordinary world of our story.

WRITING EXERCISE:
EXPLORING THE POWER OF RESISTANCE

Think of a time in your past when you initially resisted a change that ultimately proved to be for the better. A time when your comfort zone may have been stretched or you may have gotten just what you asked for, but the timing or form of delivery caused you to initially resist against it. How and why have you refused the Call in the past? What have you discovered on the other side?

Think of something that you really want now... A new relationship, better job, improved finances, triumphantly completed creative project? In what ways are you inviting this experience into your world? In what ways are you perhaps putting up barriers or resisting the flow?

Is there an area of your life that you sense is calling for change, where the whispered Call has already come, but you may be currently be refusing to hear it for fear of what's on the other side? What would happen if you answered?

Take some time to consider the energy of resistance in your life, in your writing and in the lives of your story heroes. What stops you from answering the Call? What will it take for you to move beyond your resistance into the open space of your journey? And what would the ultimate consequences be if you don't?

"How many pages have I produced? I don't care. Are they any good?
I don't even think about it. All that matters is I've put in my time
and hit it with all I've got. All that counts is that, for this day, for this session,
I have overcome Resistance."
– Steven Pressfield

The Nature of Conflict

"As long as a man stands in his own way, everything seems to be in his way."
– Ralph Waldo Emerson

Following our exploration of Desire and the internal resistance that often comes with it, today we're going to dive into another essential story component: Conflict. In story, once we get a sense for what a character really WANTS or NEEDS, usually the next thing we are exposed to is 'what is stopping them from getting it.' This contrast between what is wanted and what is currently being experienced by our hero is a powerful doorway of discovery. As our heroes seek to bridge the gap between where they are and where they want to be they're going to have to deal with what's in the way. As they dig deep and stretch themselves to face challenges, both inside and out, we begin to peel back the layers of their ordinary self to discover who they really are inside. This is fundamentally the purpose of almost every journey worth taking – it causes us grow into more of who we came here to be. In story, conflict is a great ally in disguise because it gives our heroes no choice but to step up.

If you and I were talking about an area of your life you wish to improve and I asked you what you really want, in the process of giving me an honest answer you would be become instantly aware of two things – both what you want and what you currently have. In our modern world they are like two sides of the same coin. As soon as you think of one, you have a constant reference point to the other. That edge between the two faces of the coin is the rich landscape where story evolves. I'm in Melbourne and I want more than anything to get to Byron Bay. The story exists in between. The story isn't in Melbourne or Byron Bay, it's in the why and the how I get from one to the other, and what obstacles I might have to overcome to do it. It is this gap between what is and what we yearn for that makes our journey both possible and necessary. And while in our lives (and our character's lives) we often may wish this space between would evaporate so we could just get on with having/being/doing what we really want, in truth what we *really* want – what our soul wants at its deepest level – is to experience ourselves *in* the journey of reaching for, moving toward and becoming our ultimate outcome.

As sweet as the apple tastes when it is harvested ripe from the tree, we know it would be nothing without the seasons and storms, the waiting and growing, the reaching and sprouting... the long days of becoming that lead to full fruition. And so in story, it is through the tension, conflict and challenge of moving toward what is desired – despite what comes up or blocks the way – that we truly get to know who our characters are, and who they are becoming.

As writers, one of our temptations is to want to protect and shield our heroes from difficult conflict and challenge. We love these guys, they are like our children, and so we have this quiet subconscious desire to deliver them to the promised land without major cuts or bruises. Without flaws, failures or genuine setbacks along the way. As a peaceful guy to the core, this was certainly the case for me when I first started writing film stories. But it wasn't long before I began to realize something that seasoned parents get early on with their kids... that challenge, in the right dosage, is a great gift. That every obstacle overcome, every fear faced and every conflict defused makes our heroes stronger, and more importantly, shows us who they are – their shadow sides, flaws and vulnerability. Places within them that need growth and transformation.

In film writing circles it is often said that "character is revealed under tension." The Hollywood arena has certainly milked this notion into sensory overload, particularly in big budget action-adventure stories, but there is a subtle truth to the concept that is worth keeping in mind as we continue on the story path.

In a basic sense, conflict comes to us and our heroes in three primary ways:

EXTERNAL CONFLICT – People, places, elements and circumstances that challenge our characters from the outside (i.e. Storms, broken bridges, 'bad guys', bullies, etc.).

INTIMATE CONFLICT – People and circumstances that oppose our characters from within their intimate circle of life (i.e. Parents, siblings, lovers, friends, pets, etc.).

INTERNAL CONFLICT – Energy, emotions and internal blocks that oppose or challenge our characters from within (i.e. Fears, memories, stress, self-doubt, etc.).

In a well-told story, aspects of all three of these types of conflicts will weave their way into our character's journey, and in most cases feed and bounce off each other. Often, there may be a tremendous amount of challenge and conflict imposed upon our hero from the external and intimate worlds around them, but the ultimate key to resolving these challenges will come from a more subtle shift within. It is almost always this breakthrough on the INSIDE / INTERNAL level, that enables the character to resolve conflict in both INTIMATE and EXTERNAL realms.

In this sense we can begin to see the whole external 'reality' of our characters as a symbol or reflection of what is really going on within. They may win great battles and gather new skills but only when they really 'get it' on the inside, will things really shift and change with certainty on the outside. And in this way, we can actually begin to see the great gift that conflict brings to our heroes – the opportunity to ignite inner change that will ripple into their outer world. That's what it's all about. That is when the warrior becomes the chief. And isn't that true of life itself?!

We will continue to explore the notion of conflict throughout our journey, with an aim of awakening a new paradigm approach to story that is less reliant on the old 'good vs. evil', 'right vs. wrong', 'good guy – bad guy' perspective, and more openly connected to an authentic experience of human transformation and discovery. It's not about making conflict wrong, but about choosing how we use this potent tool to draw the very best from our heroes in story and in life. For now, let's just take some time to get comfortable with this notion of conflict as an ally on the story path. See it like the tension on the guitar strings that allows the music to come through… and let it come on through!

WRITING EXERCISE:
3 LEVELS OF CONFLICT

EXTERNAL CONFLICT

Think of a time when your steps toward a certain aim or goal were blocked or opposed by an outward or EXTERNAL conflict. Stormy weather on a mountain challenging your attempts to reach the summit. Traffic blocking your path to reach an important meeting. An opponent on a sporting field, challenging your skills and efforts toward victory. Conjure the feeling of EXTERNAL conflict in these experiences and connect with your own response/reaction. How did this external energy effect, humble, off-put and perhaps enhance your efforts or outcome? Describe this moment and see what comes up for you.

INTIMATE CONFLICT

Now consider a time when your steps were challenged INTIMATELY... by someone who was/is close to you? A life partner, a parent, close friend or a child. Someone who knows which buttons to press and how to reach beneath the surface. Think of a time when you were genuinely conflicted or challenged because of your intimate connection to another? An offer to move to a new city conflicted with your love relationship where you currently live. A desire to give your children a healthy upbringing challenged by their relentless desire for ice cream. A desire to be on time for work, challenged by your dog who is pleading, begging, asking you to go for a walk. Our INTIMATE conflicts are often the most challenging to face because they involve those we love. How do these moments feel for you and how are they different than more purely external challenges in your life? Looking back on a specific moment of deep intimate challenge, what was beneath this conflict and how did it resolve? If there was a gift to be discovered in resolving it, were you available to see it at the time? What about now? Describe a moment of INTIMATE conflict and see what comes up for you.

INTERNAL CHALLENGE

Now think of a time when your steps were challenged by INTERNAL conflict. Perhaps an area of your life that is blocked in your life right now... A desire to put your work out into the world conflicted by fear of rejection. A desire to follow a dream or live your purpose, challenged by the voices inside reminding you of the practicalities of life. An overseas job offer, challenged by a quiet voice calling you to build rhythms of home in a single place for a time. A yearning for a loving life partner conflicted with memories of relationships that ended in pain. Scan your life and your current endeavors to see where you feel some sense of resistance or inner conflict. In one sense, our INTERNAL conflict is the least visible in our life, but in another sense, all we need to do is scratch beneath the surface of our EXTERNAL and INTIMATE challenges and we will usually reach a core that is fueled by something waiting to shift within. How does the energy of INTERNAL conflict feel compared to the other two levels of conflict in your life? When you are out of alignment INTERNALLY, how does this affect your relationships and your ability to take action and navigate your EXTERNAL world? How might a genuine shift on the inside ripple out into the world around you? Describe a moment of INTERNAL conflict (past or present) and see what comes up for you.

BRINGING IT ALL TOGETHER

Once you've had a bit of fun with the above, the last challenge for today is to pick a moment in your (or your hero's) life where these three elements of conflict (EXTERNAL, INTIMATE and INTERNAL) all came into play in different ways to challenge a desired outcome... Allow yourself to build up and reveal the fullness of the conflict and when you're ready, show how, through a breakthrough in one level, you/your hero were able to resolve this challenge on all levels – fulfilling your desire and/or discovering what you really needed!

By diving into our own experience of conflict, we gain a genuine insight into how these various levels of challenge reveal, influence and ultimately ignite the paths of our heroes. As we seek to understand and portray the true nature of conflict and the treasures that it carries for our heroes in story, we take a step toward expanding the human view and approach to conflict on the wider stage of life.

> *"There has been opposition to every innovation in the history of man,*
> *with the possible exception of the sword."*
> **– Benjamin Dana**

Finding Your Unique Voice
(The 5-Word Experiment)

"You are unrepeatable. There is a magic about you that is all your own."
– D.M. Dellinger

One of the most consistent quandaries – and factors of resistance – among artists and writers is how to find their unique voice or approach. How to stand out and do something different than what everyone else is doing, and different than what others expect... but to do it in a way that also resonates with all of those reading, watching or experiencing our work. If pursued externally, this quest to be unique can become somewhat maddening, pushing us into fear and reaction each time we see someone's work that we like, but don't want to imitate. The fear of appearing like everyone else can be paralyzing. The fear of appearing like no one in particular can be even worse. So how do we find our unique voice amidst 7 billion, and express it in a way that not only feels good, but serves the whole?

After working with many very gifted writers and artists across a vast array of mediums, and after leading hundreds of emerging storytellers through similar creative exercises, I have come to a very clear conclusion that while much of our formal school training and instruction tends to angle our creations toward similarity and to fit within accepted norms, at our very core, our most natural expression is totally unique.

No one sees or experiences the world exactly as we do. Therefore no one will ever express creatively what we do. Even if we stand together, telling the exact same story, we will each have a different take, a different view, a different way of bringing it through. We each truly have a unique note or verse to sing and it is my growing realization that this unique note is required in order for the great song and story of creation to be complete. The main mission is not to impose or assert our voice, but to open ourselves to genuinely let it come on through.

As we stand on the threshold of our own creative potential, this information can be a catalyst for both inspired action and petrified procrastination. How can we know what creative truth wants to come through us? What makes my idea or creative seed special or important to share? Maybe you know that you have an amazing idea swimming in your being, pulling at your soul to be shared, but you find yourself staring at the blank page, wondering where to begin. I would imagine that for every great story told, there are a thousand more that never reach the light of day beyond the doubtful doorway of their steward's mind.

One of the very first moments of genuine connection that I shared with my wife Asheyana – one late, late night in the mountains of Victoria – was staring together at a blank canvas, sharing the simultaneous conflict of invitation and intimidation that often comes in the early moments of creative endeavor. As a result, early in our relationship we began creating paintings together by simply taking turns making seemingly random marks on the page until a picture began to form, which we would then follow to colorful completion.

In the past ten years I've spent much of my creative time in the writing space and have come up against many of those early phase moments in storytelling or screenwriting when the pressure of a project seems to weigh extra-heavily on those first few words. This is the writer's opportunity to move through the 'refusal of the call' and catch a glimpse of what's really on the other side. Amidst this journey, what I have learned is that often the more we want to write or create something of importance, the more pressure we put on ourselves, which in turn restricts our creative flow to the point that what emerges feels stifled and forced. Simultaneously, I have also realized that when our agenda is simply to explore raw creative energy on the page (as we might in our journal), often truly profound expressions come through.

So the question is, how can we have both? How can we effectively channel our creative voice in the direction of meaningful expression, but do so in a natural and free flowing way, so that it feels effortless and genuinely expressive of our true essence?

Today, as we consider how best we can respond to the great creative 'call' within us, I will offer a simple exercise that has been a fun and potent doorway for many emerging writers and creative beings to do just that.

This exercise is one that I often share early in workshops as a way of helping different people with varying creative intentions move onto the page with a real sense of connection. It is a very simple exercise, and like many of life's truest gifts, it never ceases to amaze me how powerfully revealing it is of two things:

1. We each have a truly unique perspective and way of expressing our creative voice.

2. Even a very simple exercise can become a powerful doorway for our higher self to come through.

It's called the "**5-Word Experiment**" and here's how it works. I will give you five random words and 5-10 minutes to write a simple story, poem or descriptive moment that incorporates all five words. We can sit for hours (or years), wondering how best to start a story, but if we give our conscious mind a simple task like the 5-Word Experiment, it opens the door for our subconscious to naturally rise up and show us where it wants to go.

WRITING EXERCISE:
THE 5-WORD EXPERIMENT

Are you ready? OK. The five words for today are: **breath, imagine, free, belong, fly.**

Take a few moments to reflect on these words, and then begin to write whatever comes. Give yourself 5-10 minutes max, to write whatever you see or feel, incorporating each of the words in whatever order or tense you choose. If you get stuck, just take a breath and ask what next? Then follow what comes. There's no right or wrong, just you opening the path for your creative voice to come through and express. Enjoy.

In the workshop setting, it always, always, always blows my mind to see how unique each person's expression is, and how even the most resistant writers spring forth with prose and verse that send chills of truth through the spines of all in the group. So, as we stand on the threshold of our leap into the extraordinary world of story, I invite you to take five minutes to explore this exercise.

Again, the words are **breath, imagine, free, belong, fly.**

I did this exercise (with these same words) recently with a group. As always I was inspired beyond description by what emerged from the different individuals. Below is what came out for me, which was also a surprise at the time (Please wait to read until after you have written your own!):

"Is this truly what I must do to be free?" thought the young brave, staring out from the cliff top to the grassy knoll way beneath. It seemed a very long way to drop. He had seen this done before many times. He had imagined this moment himself many times. But to be here standing on the edge, wings of the bird tribe fastened to his arms, the elders chanting behind him... his family and grandfather waiting around the fire below. Is this really where he belonged? Maybe he could just turn back... What was he seeking anyway, in making this big leap? As if reading his mind, the Chief stepped up, with kind black eyes and said, "It's not what you are seeking that is calling you. It is who you already are, that is waiting to greet you as you fly." With that, the young brave took a breath and stepped out into the sky."

Enjoy where the 5-Word Experiment leads you (and really let it lead you!), and I'll meet you back here for Chapter 4 as we cross over the threshold into the next phase of story and our journey toward expressing our unique tale in the great creation story of life.

"We are each gifted in a unique and important way.
It is our privilege and our adventure to discover our own special light."
– Mary Dunbar

CHAPTER 4:

Stepping on the Path

"We must be willing to get rid of the life we've planned,
so as to have the life that is waiting for us."
- Joseph Campbell

From the Ordinary to Extraordinary

"The distance is nothing; it's only the first step that is difficult."
– Marquise du Deffand

*

Athens, Greece – August, 1992. It's 6:30 pm and I'm sitting against the whitewashed stonewall of the Athens airport arrivals section. I've been traveling for over 24 hours since saying goodbye to my folks and friends in Denver, but in truth my adventure has not yet even begun. I walked through graduation in June with my class at Dartmouth College, but because I took most of my winters off to train and compete in skiing, I have a few extra credits to pick up before they send me my diploma. Having just recovered from my third knee surgery in as many years, I'm feeling ready to shift that broken record to a new song, and primed for a dose of soul questing. My last college term begins in Meinz, Germany in just over a month, so I have answered an inner call to spend five weeks of solo adventure in Greece. I've never been to Europe and I've never traveled alone, but for some reason Greece sent an invitation to me, so here I am answering.

My plan is simple. Step off the plane, find a bus to the ferry port and take the very first boat I find out into the deep wide blue of the Aegean Sea. Something about that water is calling to me. I don't know why. I just know it is. And while I'm sure that Athens literally has worlds of magic to explore, advice from those who've been here at peak season is to bypass the crowded summer smog and hit this ancient city on the way back. This is fine by me. My sights are set firmly on the blue.

This is my plan, and in the spirit of adventure I have chosen not to crowd this vision with any other details or logistics… trusting that the 'how' part of this plan will reveal itself as clearly as the water I am aiming to sail on, just as soon as I land in Athens. What I somehow failed to anticipate was that I'd be landing 1) At night, after the last of the ferries has left the port, and 2) During a citywide transportation strike, with no way of getting to the port anyway! I'm a pretty adaptable and spontaneous sort of fellow, and it's been said that my optimism (and stubbornness) sometimes leads me to ignore, or at least postpone my acceptance of the facts. What are the facts anyway, but someone else's perspective on reality? Aren't we here to create our own? Even so, if there's a fine line between positive thinking and flat out denial, after four trips to the airport information desk and several failed payphone calls, I begin to realize that I'm walking it. I also begin to realize that I may not be going to the islands that night after all… and in fact, unless I want to walk the 30 kilometers into the city, I may not be going anywhere at all.

I share my story with the program leader of a group of American students I met on the plane hoping she might smile and say, "Come join us for the night and we'll drop you off at the ferry in the morning!" She does smile, but says instead that she was sure I'd work it out.

The airport starts to empty and I can feel my mind reaching for options and slowly spiraling in on itself. I'm standing on the threshold of what should be a great life-changing adventure, but here, just one step in, a simple kink in my 'plan' has left me paralyzed. In one breath, I've gone from being a solo traveler on my first bold adventure to a lonely unprepared tourist, and the rapidly emptying airport just magnifies my feeling of being alone. What am I doing here? I'm a stone in a giant slingshot ready to be released, but something has blocked the gate... and now I'm about to drop.

The American group gathers in a huddle for instructions, and then starts flooding out the doors to their vans. Disappearing like leaves on the river. I'm sure they've got some extra seats in those vans, but no invitation comes. I'm just sitting here like a log in the current. Slowly starting to decay. Immoveable. I'll probably still be here when they return in a month to head home. I will have made some friends by then... a few stray cats and security guards. This could be home for a month. I'm sure I could find a comfortable plastic chair to sleep in... How bad could it be?

The last few students are sucked out the exit, followed by the group leader. She offers a departing smile and the glass doors close behind her. Scouring my 'Let's Go Europe' for a message from the Greek gods, I glance up to see the doors re-open and the leader comes back in. In fact she's walking across the concourse right towards me. I thank Zeus, thinking that she must have found an empty seat and decided to welcome me into the group for the night. Instead, she stops short about six feet away and leans in a little to simply say, "You won't find your answers in here. You've got to go out there to get them."

She offers the kind of curt smile teachers give when they are satisfied with what they've said, and before I can respond, she's gone. I look down at the stagnant scattering of papers and tourist material I've gathered since my arrival. I know she's right. There's nothing for me here. Unless I'm in a Die Hard *movie, this adventure is not going to happen in the airport. So I saddle up my bag, chuck the papers and phone scribbles into the bin and step toward the sliding glass doors. As I approach, a thin band of energy starts tightening around my stomach. It seems to be saying, "What the heck are you doing?" But I keep walking. Approaching the doors, the band gets tighter, the voice gets louder... The doors close behind the last person and I pause right there on the edge. Another step and they opened wide again, and I burst through like a breaching whale, filling my lungs with mid-summer Athens smog. Strangely, it tastes great. I join a short line of folks waiting for private taxis and within moments I've struck up a conversation with a young couple in a similar situation to me. We agree to share a cab, which takes us into the tiny-street centre of La Plaka (the oldest and perhaps most enchanted part of the city). Together, we find a rooftop room to rent for the night, spend the evening strolling the sites of ancient Greece and within twelve hours we're making our way to the islands.*

From this moment forward for the rest of my journey (and well beyond), I will practice crossing the threshold from the known to the unknown every chance I get. I will introduce myself to those I feel called to meet. And as I step off trains, boats, planes or horses, I will take a breath, feel in my heart which way to go, and simply start walking. Past hotel hawkers and restaurateurs, past tour groups and map holders, onto whatever road or path is shining brightest. I will walk with a sense of purpose until I find myself walking and talking with someone positively important to my path, and I will trust that I will find myself arriving right where I need to be... at just the perfect time.

*

> *"All great deeds and all great thoughts have a ridiculous beginning."*
> **– Albert Camus**

Just as the butterfly builds all of its essential flying muscles during its struggle to escape from the cocoon, we each expand our life strength every time we cross over into the unknown of a new experience. Crossing that simple threshold at the Athens airport was just one small moment in the big picture of my next few months of travel (and well beyond), but it has stayed with me as a turning point and poignant reminder during moments of new life experience since. The awkward tightness still surfaces from time to time as I step beyond what's comfortable, but now I recognize this tension as a positive sign, that I am on the cusp of crossing another border into a field of new possibility. I am leaving my ordinary world yet again and entering into the extraordinary world of the hero's path.

When I stepped from the Athens airport I didn't know what experiences awaited me on the other side and I had no concept of the deeper lessons I was learning about life. I was just responding to the awkward demand of the moment – I had no place to sleep and the airport was closing. But in doing so, I crossed over into a whole new world of experience. In our stories, whether this crossing requires our hero to plow up the cornfields, climb into a space ship or step through the sliding glass doors of an airport, it is a critical moment in the journey. A 'first action' moment for our characters in story. Later decisions will be far more informed and conscious, but for now the hero must move, must leap, must step across the line with only a glimpse of what is to come. A sense of blind faith is required here; a trusting that something or someone will be there to catch their fall.

STRANGERS IN A STRANGE LAND (A.K.A. TESTS AND ALLIES)

In the film story world, after the 'Call' and a brief period of 'debate', our hero usually 'Steps on the Path' about 25-30 minutes into the story. This is often called 'crossing the threshold' and is often signified by a literal change in physical and geographical experience. In this moment we depart from the domain of the hero's ordinary world, and we cross into the extraordinary world of the story. When Frodo Baggins first leaves the safety of the shire in *Lord of the Rings*, when Jake Sully first lands in the jungle of Pandora in *Avatar*, when Po is first carried into the Jade Palace in *Kung Fu Panda*... these are all moments of 'crossing the threshold' as our heroes enter the world of their story.

No matter how much of a master or an expert our character may be in his/her ordinary world, the moment s/he crosses over into the extraordinary world, everything is different. Instantly we have a feeling of being a fish out of water, a stranger in a strange land. The people, animals, culture, the language of LIFE itself often feels new, different and overwhelming. Often against their will, our hero is forced to enter into a state of 'beginner's mind' where s/he literally must begin again, and learn to live in a whole new way. In *Avatar*, when Jake Sully (in the form of his blue Avatar body) lands in the jungle of Pandora for his first mission, he has almost no reference point for the drastic difference in the plants and animals. He's quickly thrown into life-threatening tests, which soon-thereafter lead him to meet his first real ally in the extraordinary world, the beautiful Neytiri (who saves his life from a pack of scary hyena beasts). When Neytiri turns scornfully to Jake and says, "You're like a baby!" she is announcing to all of us that Jake has now officially crossed into the extraordinary world and the 'Initiation' phase of his journey. This phase is also called 'Tests and Allies' as it will lead him through stages of awkward learning and new discovery, ultimately to a place of true commitment (see Chapter 5) and onward into his Inner Most Cave (see Chapter 6) and the ultimate realization of the deeper purpose of his journey. But right in this moment, he is clumsy, out of his depth and quite literally "like a baby."

The purpose of the *Tests and Allies* phase of our journey is to break apart the limiting patterns that have held us captive in our ordinary world and to literally awaken the dormant capacities of a true and higher self. We may have entered this new world with no real conscious desire to be there, but in time it is here in this new world that our true nature is ultimately realized and revealed.

THE EARLY WIN

Having crossed the threshold into the extraordinary world, having experienced an onslaught of new tests, conflict and challenge, and having been mostly (often severely) humbled each step of the way, there comes a moment early on where something happens to give us and our hero a minor glimpse of positive possibility. Up until this moment, the hero has likely spent most of his time getting tossed around in the washing machine of the new, but here we receive a glimmer of positive hope. It's a moment I like to refer to as an 'Early Win', because it gives our hero a dose of synchronistic good fortune that's often just enough to keep him/her alive and moving on the path.

Avatar gives us a very clear example of this Early Win during Jake Sully's first night stranded in the jungle. After almost dying a few times and proving himself to be moronic in the eyes of warrioress Neytiri, Jake follows her through the jungle, trying to engage and connect. This just makes her angrier and she's about to shove him off the tree when out of nowhere, a 'seed of the sacred tree' floats down, landing on Jake's arm. He tries to swat it away, but within moments there are hundreds of them all settling on his body. Neytiri looks at him in wonder, and she knows... this is a sign. With that, Jake is taken to 'Home Tree' where he meets the tribal elders and commences his journey of discovery with the tribe.

In life, this 'Early Win' moment often comes to us when we first step out into something new, as a sort of North Star to help keep our ship moving in the right direction. During my athlete days when I was learning a new skill or technique I would often watch the coach perform the maneuver then somehow follow suit, performing the task nearly perfectly on the first try. This little miracle would give me a momentary boost of ego, but then it would usually take me the following two weeks to figure out how to get it right again! I would have to break it down and dissect it into separate components, then put it all back together again before I could express this skill on a consistent basis. I would have to learn what, at some level, my body already knew how to do.

During that time I started to recognize this process as one of the fundamental ways that we acquire mastery in many areas of life. If we are open to the possible, we often get a glimpse of our own perfected form early on – way before we have actually trained ourselves to consistently embody that perfection. This sense of 'beginner luck' may be a blind glimpse as we don't really know how or why we did it right in the first place (Jake Sully had no idea why those little white flying seeds were landing on him), but it's usually enough to spur us on, so that as we move through the various stages of actually learning and integrating this new skill, there is a sense of knowing somewhere inside that it is actually possible!

The transition time between our Early Win and future mastery is often dictated not only by our commitment to the path but by our willingness to let go of what we *thought* we knew in order to allow a truly new experience. Are we willing to drop what we think we know in order to discover something greater within?

Within the Initiation phase, each challenge or test that comes our way is almost always coupled by an ally or gift. And while the challenges may push us to exhaustible limits, each new obstacle overcome reveals another layer of unrealized potential. In our *Avatar* example there is a whole sequence of scenes that depict this growth for Jake Sully while we watch the Marine in him die away as he learns to hunt, run, eat, ride, fly and sleep in new ways. We gradually watch him transition from utter awkwardness through stages of growth, into a true warrior amidst the Navi people.

Looking back on my Greek Island adventure, as I journeyed through early days of feeling very much like a tourist, into a more seasoned traveler and explorer of life in a new land, each experience peeled back another layer of who I thought I was, honing me into a centre point in the middle. My movements became more natural, pure and aligned, my perspective became expansive and inclusive. I felt at once independent and somehow part of a greater whole. It was a gradual process but by the time my journey in the islands was over I had acquired a host of new skills, perceptions and friends… and more importantly I felt genuinely connected to their culture. I could carry on a simple Greek conversation, I knew how to bargain for what I needed, how to find a safe spot to sleep on the beach, and how to move in time with the rhythm of Greek life as I journeyed around from place to place. I had made lasting friendships with people from many nations that I would visit in the months to come and overall I felt like a greatly expanded version of myself. All of this made possible from a simple willingness to cross the threshold, step on the path and say YES to the journey that was calling me from inside the airport that day.

WRITING EXERCISE:
STEPPING ON THE PATH

Take a moment to consider when the circumstance of your life brought you to a point of necessary departure from your ordinary world. Whether you chose this new experience or whether you felt thrown into it, remember as clearly as possible what it felt like to step to the threshold of that new experience and cross over into the new arena. The first day at a new school, a new job, a new marriage, a new litter of puppies... How did your call to adventure lead you to this moment and what was on the other side waiting for you? What new tests, challenges, gifts and allies met you on the path?

Take some time to connect with this turning point moment at various times of your life, when you had the opportunity to step into the unknown and you took it. What does it feel like in your body and your senses when you make this sort of leap? Pick one of these moments and take the next ten minutes to write the details of that Turning Point moment.

When you're ready, do the same for the hero/character of your story.

STORY CHALLENGE:
Watch a film (or two!) this week and see if you can track the phases of story we have discussed so far. Keep your stopwatch handy and check the timing of these key story beats. Do they match the story map we have created? Do these key moments work well in the story? Knowing what you now know, how might you improve or enhance them if it was your story?

"Two roads diverged in a wood, and I,
I took the one less traveled by,
And that has made all the difference."
– **Robert Frost, The Road Not Taken**

Looking for Dolphins,
Discovering Your Muse

"If a dolphin comes to you in a dream, it was not a dream.
The dolphin has really come."
– A Maori saying

*

"Oh my God! What happened to you?!" Ash said with frightened alarm, staring at the stream of blood running from my forehead, across my ocean-wet face. All I could do was smile. "I just had the most incredible experience of my life!"

A few years ago, my wife, Ash, son, Josh and I lived near a special beach in Byron Bay, Australia, where our daily rhythms were woven into the lives of a local pod of dolphins. It started with an intimate encounter one day while I was out surfing with a friend (the above described head wound came just after, while riding into shore in a state of ecstatic joy, my board caught an edge in about 6-inches of water sending me headlong into the sand!) and developed into a genuine friendship, or rather mentorship – they being the teachers. During our first month after arriving to the area, we had so many encounters with whales and dolphins in the wild that it felt like we were being stalked. While at first it appeared like they were simply everywhere, on further reflection, we started to see a pattern in their appearances – one that coincided with our own willingness to follow moment-to-moment impulses and sparks of intuition. It seemed that whenever we made ourselves available to hear and openly answer the spontaneous call of the moment, so would they. That quiet voice that calls us up from the computer mid-sentence to run down to the beach, despite the pressure of impending deadlines... that shift in breeze that makes us turn left on our beach walk, when we normally turn right... that whisper that says to stay and surf just one more wave before going in... These quiet streams of inner promptings, which are so often drowned out by the rivers of our busy minds and daily to-do lists, seem to be the realms in which the dolphins exist and communicate. And the more we allowed ourselves to follow and move with the quiet voice of flow within, the more we found ourselves in the same place at the same time, doing the same thing as the dolphins.

Anyone who has ever spent time with dolphins and/or whales knows that they have a way of being that seems to almost perfectly align with the elements of what we call synchronicity. I don't know how they do it, but they seem to arrive, breach, surface, breathe and then disappear in perfect response to moments of our own thought, spoken word and action. Recently, on a road trip down the California coastline with my family, I was telling a story to my son Josh as we drove. We'd been driving inland for about 3 hours with no sign of the water, when the road began winding back toward the coast. It was near sunset and the story I was spinning was reaching a climax where I was about to introduce a new character, a giant whale. Without planning it, this whale character came into the story just as we rounded the bend on Highway 1 and caught our very first glimpse of the ocean. And with the kind of cosmic timing that the greatest film director couldn't dream of, just exactly at the moment I uttered the word 'whale' for the first time, a migrating Humpback surfaced on the sunset horizon and breached right in our line of sight! We all gasped and I nearly drove right through the guardrail. I don't know how many (or if any) other people saw the great breath of that whale on the water or what it may have meant to them, but to us, in that moment, it was a stroke of magic that came in direct response to our creative musings. And that's just the way they do it.

If I go to the beach specifically looking for dolphins, they are often nowhere to be seen. I could (and have) spend hours seeking, searching, watching, hoping with no result. But if I let go of the search for a few minutes and allow myself just to settle into my surfing, enjoy my swim or my walk – to be present with the white morning light, the diamonds on the water, the precisely whimsical flight of pelicans along the wave face – and let go of the need to see anyone, suddenly "Pffwooosh", there they are, right behind me or surfacing in the wave beneath my feet. It is as if they have been there all along under the surface, just waiting for me to stop looking and start being. Waiting for me to raise my sense of presence and connectedness to the moment enough for them to meet me there, because quite simply, that's where they exist.

*

Our relationship with the Muse is the same. When we go looking for our creative spark often it seems to elude us. We can dance around the edges of commitment to a story or a song for days, weeks or lifetimes, just waiting for the right magic impulse to show up and guide the way. What we do not often realize is that the Muse is like a mirror. As we wait, so does the Muse. Like the dolphins, she waits for us to enter the space and connect with the elements of creative energy that are already present. And as we find our flow and connection with what *is*, the Muse meets us there in response, shining light on the path, bringing meaning to the moment. Often she seems to sort of sneak in beside us as though she has been there all along waiting… and in truth she has!

Our willingness to show up to the moment and to get our energy moving – to find a sense of flow by bringing our pen to the page or our fingers to the keys even in the simplest ways – is often just the energetic movement required to bring ourselves up to speed with the moving, growing, dynamically flowing energy and inspiration of our Muse. You can't catch a wave while you're sitting still. You have to paddle yourself up to speed in order for it to carry you.

HOW DO WE MEET OUR MUSE IN TIMES OF CREATIVE UNCERTAINTY?

If I'm preparing to write a scene or a story section that I am unsure about... if I have called for the Muse to help but have not yet felt the answer, and if a looming deadline means I can no longer wait, I will often give myself the gift of starting my writing session somewhere I know the energy *is*.

It may mean starting my writing with a scene or segment I *do* have a sense of clarity about, or maybe it comes from writing a goofy, no-agenda email to one of my brothers. Maybe it's a five-minute poetry session with the magnetic words on our refrigerator... Or maybe I simply need to go leap into a heatless swimming pool and come back to the page, dripping wet. If I'm looking for my Muse and she hasn't shown up... the first step to making the connection is usually NOT to tense up and push harder. Like with the dolphins, finding our Muse is not a matter of searching and hunting her out. But rather to do whatever we need to do to feel like we love to feel when we're in a state of positive creative flow. It's not an excuse to walk away, abandon the mission or procrastinate. It's an invitation to do what's necessary to raise our own creative state of being to a different place, to feel alive in what we are doing, no matter what it looks like. To stop racing forward with pressure and agenda, and for just a moment to stop and really be present with what magic potential is all around us. In this space, our communion with the Muse becomes second nature.

When we are stuck and unsure, we tend to question every word and comma. It's like we're walking through a thorny path and there's pain with every step. When we are in flow, we seem to glide right through that same field in a quiet blur. Somehow above it. What the words look like at that point, we do not even care... Are there spelling mistakes? Have I left out a comma? So what? In this moment it doesn't matter because suddenly the words are alive. They have a pulse as they come through us, and so the very act of feeling and writing them down becomes the elixir we are looking for. Both the seed and the harvest. Our prayer and the answer all bundled into one, building and growing inside of us as we move along the page. If the words are pleasing to someone else as they read them, all the better. But regardless of where these words end up, no one can deny the experience we have had in writing them. Even if we emerge with our face dripping with blood, we will stand smiling with the deep knowledge that we have been swimming with the Muse.

In the quiet moments of my soul I know that this is the first and most important gift of the creative path. As I write these words, I suddenly realize they give a whole new meaning to the title of this book... As we take time to genuinely connect with the higher creative energy within us, as we journey through the process of writing the story within, bringing to the page the inspired currents of our connection to the Muse, we are not only making this energy available for others to share… we are writing the essence of our inspiration into the fiber of our being. We are actually writing the story *within* ourselves.

WRITING EXERCISE:
MUSE LIST

Make a list of all the activities that you do – or could do – to enhance, ignite and illuminate your own sense of creative flow. These are often activities that take little effort but deliver simple and great pleasure. Things that make us smile, open our hearts and connect the synapses of our mind in different ways. Simple endeavors that work like tuning forks in our body and our being. Activities that give us a sense of time stretching or standing still. Activities that leave us feeling energized and empowered. Calm and connected. Quietly grateful. By doing our part to elevate our own state of being on a regular basis, we open the channel of communion with our higher creative voice and we leave a space for the Muse to move in. Inspiration follows inspiration. And whales breach on the horizon at just the perfect time.

PART 2 - TAKE IT TO THE PAGE
Describe a moment of pure connection and flow with something or someone in your life. Watching a sunset, riding a wave, dancing the salsa, playing the drums… Whatever this moment is for you, pick an experience from your life where you felt truly connected to something 'more', something beyond your normal self. Where your perceptions and your actions felt propelled, guided, lifted by a higher force within you. Describe the moments leading up to this experience and what happened when you truly 'dropped in' to that place of higher flow. Can you recognize any similarities to other moments in your life when this feeling has emerged? What allowed this moment to happen? What made it possible for you to be right there in the flow with the Muse of YOU?

The Balance of Character and Plot

*"Sow an act, and you reap a habit; sow a habit, and you reap a character;
sow a character, and you reap a destiny."*
– George Dana Boardman

Which came first, the character or the plot? Along with lifelong debates of chickens, eggs, cavemen and amoeba, depending on who you ask you might get a different answer. The truth of the matter is that it is quite difficult to have one without the other, and in many cases they somehow happen simultaneously. Story plots (what the story is about) come to life through the actions and heartbeats of the characters within them. Characters come to life through the stories that they live and express. You could have a great character who sits on the couch doing nothing, but unless he says or does something to impact the direction of the story, we will probably not gain much from him or care much for him. You can also have a great story that's full of impactful action, but unless we feel genuine connection to the characters expressing that action, the same will be true. The task of the storyteller is to weave the elements of character and plot into a meaningful fabric where one leads to, feeds and completes the other, ultimately making something altogether more. Story.

The writing of a story is in some ways like the writing of a song. You could say the music is the plot and the lyrics are the characters. In the end, if the songwriter is successful, most listeners may not even be aware of the two elements as different... Sure they may appreciate the way the melody starts here, the way the rhythm kicks in there, the way that lyric brings home the message and gives them the chills – but in the end what they will be left with mostly is an overall experience of the song, which is invariably the blend of the music and the lyrics. I've talked to a lot of songwriters about their process for writing and composing. Some say they always start with the music, some say they always begin with the lyrics. Most have a 'usual' way it happens, but everyone also has extraordinary exceptions where it happened opposite to how it normally does. Often times the conversation ends up a bit confused and then they get sort of quiet and say something like, "Yeah... um... I don't know really. The spark could really come from anywhere."

The same is certainly true for character and plot. Some writers tend to start with story 'concepts' where they imagine a specific scenario, and then in the process of developing up that scenario they create the most compelling characters they can think of to populate and live out that scenario. Traditionally a lot of big Hollywood films are pitched and sold initially on their plot 'concept' – a sentence or two that captures the overall essence of story itself. In this light, the plot concept for *Avatar* might be pitched something like, "A futuristic environmental adventure where humans are attempting to mine the natural resources of a distant planet against the wishes of an indigenous alien culture." That's the plot of the story, without much specific focus on the characters.

On the other hand, some writers begin with the energy of a specific character or human experience and then allow the story plot to grow organically from that space. While the tides are certainly shifting, traditionally we find that a lot of European and independent films are more character-based stories. But even a giant like *Avatar* could be described from a character point of view by imagining *"a futuristic Pocahontas tale, where a young paraplegic Marine discovers his path of true leadership through an unlikely romance with a female warrior of an indigenous tribe during a military mining mission on a distant planet."* A bit of a mouthful but you get the picture. Instantly our focus is less on the major story plot and more on the arc of the characters who are living it. In the end, I have found the process to be a bit like tightening the spokes on a bike wheel. If you tighten one side down more than the other, the wheel will not run true, but if you crank each spoke a little bit at a time, balancing one with the other, the wheel will simultaneously strengthen and balance.

In my own writing process, there are times when it has really helped to separate out the elements of plot and character and work on them in isolation to each other – for a time. For example, I often start with an overall concept of the story plot, so while I might quickly map out an overall plot outline, I then find it especially helpful to shift gears and drill right into the characters, breathing their heartbeats into the scenes and plot points. If I remain open to the wisdom of my heroes (rather than thinking I have all the answers), they will often bring new elements to the story plot that I would never have thought of in the 'concept' development phase of the plot alone. To this end, I might do a whole pass through a screenplay where I simply focus on the arc and development of one of the main characters. I will start at the beginning – or before the beginning – and spend time fortifying my overall connection to who they are and the essence of their journey. If I have really taken time to get to know my character, I can bring them back through the plot and I will have a whole new level of appreciation for how they would respond and react to different situations. It might sound complicated but it's actually a really natural progression. It happens in layers and each time you shift from character to plot or from plot back to character, you will be astounded by how much each of these elements informs and ignites new insight into the other. Imagine if you and your wife/husband/partner were going to go to a party together and at the last minute s/he asked if you would go ahead and just give them a call when you get there to tell them if they would like it. If you agreed to this, you'd go to the party and you would instantly start imagining if the other person was there. You would picture them in different scenarios with the people there and you would quite quickly get a sense for how they would react and whether they would enjoy themselves. You make the call… and hope you are right, because now they are on their way! With our heroes we need to know them well enough (their character traits, quirks, strengths, fears and preferences) to be able to place them into any scene and really know how they would respond. It's not a matter of getting them to do what we want them to do. It's a matter of placing them into the scene and being willing to openly watch how they respond – even if it means changing your outline of what's supposed to happen next!

As you flow between character and plot, between music and lyrics, between this spoke and that, the veil between the two becomes thinner and thinner until you are working with one multilayered, cohesive experience. Story.

WRITING EXERCISE:
INFUSING PLOT WITH THE ESSENCE OF CHARACTER

To give you a brief example of how the worlds of plot and character, character and plot can work together and infuse/inform/inspire each other, I have laid out a simple process below which starts with a simple character-based enquiry and leads into the spontaneous telling of a tale. The object of this exercise is not to labor or dwell on any single question too long, but to move through quite intuitively, responding in the moment. This exercise can be very powerful to do with the actual characters of your stories (see the extra Story Challenge below), but the first and easiest place to begin is to do this with you as the hero. Take 5-10 minutes to respond to the following enquiry. No more. Just your stream of consciousness response. Breathe deeply, try not to censor. This is just for you, so just write what comes up first. Ready? Here we go...

My earliest strong memory is...
At that moment a part of me decided...
When I was a child, what I truly loved was...
What I wanted more than anything to be/do/create was...
When I was a child, my greatest fear was...
When most people meet me, they think that I am...
They think this because of the way that I...
What most people don't know about me is...
One of my secret passions in life is...
In the past I have felt held back by _____, limited by _____, challenged by _____ .
Right now, my greatest fear is...
I demonstrate, overcome or try to hide that fear in my life by...
Deep down what I know is...
And what I truly want more than anything right now is...
The reason I want this so much is...
Once I have it I will feel...
I love the sky when it's _____ because...
I love the season of _____ because...
My favorite element is _____ because...
My favorite animal is _____ because...
My favorite thing to do with others is...

My favorite thing to do when I'm alone is...
My favorite moment so far today was _____ because...
If the child I once was could see me now, s/he would probably say...
I believe that life is...
The world is...
People are...
If you could sum up the theme of my life right now in one word, it would be...

OK, now that you have built a simple internal framework of connection to some of the key elements of your character (in this case, you), take 5-10 more minutes and fill in the blanks of the sentences below, expanding your answers to create a simple story in the moment. Again, no agenda here. Don't try to bend the tale in any particular direction. Just use the energy of the previous exercise to naturally infuse your responses, and see what comes.

Today, the strangest thing happened. I was sitting there at _____, when all of a sudden...
At first I did not know what to do, so I...
But then once I realized what was really going on, I...
As soon as I did, suddenly...
Now, I know more than ever that...

STORY CHALLENGE
If you enjoyed the above exercise and are ready to bring your whole story journey to the next level, I invite you to bring one of the characters from your story (or from a story you'd like to write) through the same exercise. Answer all the questions again, but this time as though you are the mind and heart of that character. Let their qualities, desires, fears and connections infuse you. Then, when you are full of good character mojo, bring that energy into the fill-in-the-blank scene above, and allow your new awareness of the character to enliven your response.

As I mentioned, for me it is often quite natural to first map out a story idea, then drill into the characters as doorways to that story. Once I really know my characters, then I will bring them back through my story and usually the story will dramatically change as a result, leading me back into exploration of who these people are that I am *really* writing about. Flip, flop and back again. Before you know it there is a melody rising on the page and the actions and words of your hero are like the lyrics of a magical song.

"Everyone is necessarily the hero of his own life story." – **John Barth**

Starting with a Plan... and Trusting the River (A.k.a. The Art of Focused Surrender)

*

"What the hell is 'river boarding'?" This was my first response when one of my brothers suggested this as a "guys' day" in New Zealand several years ago. They had come to visit from the US and I wanted to give them a good adventure, so we went to Queenstown to explore the planet's epicenter of adrenaline. During our last day there we talked each other into going 'river boarding', which basically consisted of suiting up in the thickest wetsuits known to man (picture the skin of a rhino), and being dropped into a freezing, frothing, raging, rapid-filled river with nothing but a boogie board and a pair of flippers. Sound fun? We sort of thought so, so my brothers, dad and I signed up and took the leap. We started with a quietly nervous group of 20 in a glassy calm section of the river with a seemingly simple plan: float downstream to where the vans would meet us three or four kilometers away. But by about three minutes into the journey, as we entered a series of intense rapids and falls – fingers and faces already numb and feet beginning to cramp – we each began our own gasping version of a flailing hero's journey. With jagged stones, sharp cliff faces and deep spiraling holes to dodge at every bend, I found myself in pure feverish focus, desperately kicking myself this way and that to avoid danger and try to stay afloat. The problem was that despite my love of water and my passion for rivers, my efforts to navigate this flowing, writhing beast were revealing themselves to be futile. In fact, the harder I kicked, the further behind I seemed to drift, until I looked out through my cockeyed helmet to discover the whole group was actually way ahead of me!

By this time, one of the Kiwi guides had actually circled back to check on me. "You alright, mate?" he said as he dipped into my world for a moment. I sputtered a half-smiling nod, then watched him slip away through some secret current, instantly rejoining the others. That guy must have a motor on his fins... What was I doing wrong? By the time we'd been in the water for 20 minutes, my legs felt like a pair of fossilized oaks dragging through the eddies and my face was frozen into a permanent grimace. I had completely exhausted myself and could no longer fight the flow, but I knew of no other safe way through...

As I drifted toward the next set of rapids, I could barely make out the other helmets bobbing in the waves ahead, but at this stage I was too tired to care. So I decided to use what energy I had left to simply hold on to my boogie board and let the river take me where it wanted. Clinging to my foam biscuit like an otter with a clam, I rolled onto my back as I was sucked into the next rollercoaster section. I remember gazing up along the granite cliffs to the sky and thinking, "Well... if this is the way I *die, at least I'm surrounded by beauty. Raging, frothing, frigid beauty... but beauty nonetheless." And with that, I gave it over... and within a few moments, the strangest thing happened. Somehow, without kicking my feet or even so much as looking where I was going, I found myself drawn naturally into the very center of the current, where I was pulled along quite seamlessly through the entire section of river. No major collisions and still I was breathing. Remarkably, within a few minutes I found myself bobbing along right past many of the other participants. By the time we reached the next stretch of calm, I had actually passed up the entire group and was now out in the very front by about 50 meters. All without kicking once! Simply holding on and trusting the flow of the river.*

By the time we reached our exit point in the river an hour later, I was still numb but my heart was aflame with the embodied realization of a golden truth in the realms of flow. We can start with a plan and this is good. But as soon as we enter the river – of story and of life – in truth we enter a dance. We bring our presence, energy and intention to the space... and the river brings its own. And while the ultimate goal may be to navigate gracefully through, sometimes the river takes unexpected turns. In those moments we can exhaust ourselves trying to fight the flow, or we can trust enough to let go of how we thought it would look, and to realize we are not alone. We are part of a much greater current that is always flowing in, through and around us. We need only look to the sky within... and hold onto our board!

*

In life and creative endeavor, we often find ourselves moving with great focus toward what we think we want, only to discover (if we are open to seeing it) some greater treasure waiting for us just beyond our conscious aim. We may push with great passion and effort until we cannot take another step, only to be greeted by our goal in full form the moment we let go and in some sense 'give up' what we thought we came for.

This reminds me of an experiment I once read about the founders of the Esalen Institute in California in the early days of exploring human potential. In efforts to increase their ability to focus intention, they developed a device that measured energy and translated it electromagnetically from sensors on their body to a little needle on a scale. As they held their focus in a certain way, the needle would move along the scale. While the primary aim of the experiment was to expand their ability to focus energy (moving the needle further and further), what they discovered was something quite extraordinary... They found that while their conscious focus could indeed move the needle slightly along the scale for a time, the greatest movement (by far) came in the moment *immediately following* intense periods of focus, when they simply could not concentrate anymore and were forced to give up. In these precise moments of "Ahhh" release, the needle – which had been hovering just barely above the start line – would spring across the scale, maxing out the measurement. From this experiment emerged a whole meditative practice they named 'Focused Surrender', reflecting the ebb and flow, push and release of energy we often experience on the path of growing, becoming, pursuing our dreams and nurturing our creations in life.

The basic conclusion of the study was that in order to achieve the highest result in a given endeavor, both total focus and total release were required. Without the inertia of clearly focused intention, the needle would have no impetus to move, but without the equal willingness to surrender, the higher possibilities of the energy would never be fully realized. When I first read about this study, I felt like a clock tower bell rang through my body, as it helped me rationalize a bizarre phenomenon I had discovered during an intense drafting period of my first screenplay.

I had entered the film project knowing that we were racing against a rapidly ticking clock, but at the time of commitment, my Aries blood embraced the challenge. Several months and a few drafts later, I was sleeping very little, writing very fast and trying desperately to keep my heart in the center of the story current. To stick with our outlined 'plan' for the story, while also leaving room for the Muse to guide us to higher ground.

During this time I discovered a pattern in my creative flow that rings very true to the theme of Focused Surrender. I found that I could spend hours (sometimes days) in pure focus on a given scene or section of the story. I would drill in deep. I would write and re-write my way to the magic center. I would skip meals, sleep and sunrises to stay on course. Eventually, I would reach a place where whatever I was working on was *close*, but it wasn't fully dropping into place. Something was missing but fierce determination was not enough to find it. I would stay with it as long as I could until finally, through utter frustration, exhaustion, or both, I would close my laptop and burst out of my office. I would grab my keys and my surfboard, jump in the car and start driving toward the coast. I had done what I could for the moment and now I just needed to clear my head. Weaving along the narrow hinterland roads through rays of morning light, my conscious mind would begin to let go of the story, and like clockwork, all of a sudden, WHAM! It would hit me like a lightening bolt. The entire scene I had just spent 8+ hours working on would arrive in completed sparkling form right in the center of my mind. Issues resolved, dialogue resonating, missing pieces found. When this first started happening I would usually swerve off the road, dig for a pen and scribble whatever came through onto the back of a grocery receipt. After a few occurrences, I began carrying my journal and dictaphone in the car, so I could gather these pearls when they dropped from the sky.

The scenes that emerged in these windy mountain morning drives became some of the best scenes in the film. And they came through with such grace and ease that it made me wonder what the heck I was doing the rest of the time. While these breakthroughs did seem to advocate more frequent breaks and trips to coast (which suited my surfing passion just fine), I was quick to realize that the breakthroughs were the product of the exchange between my own energetic focus and my willingness to hand it all over. This was a dance and both partners were required. And while the time pressure of the project didn't allow for me to tinker with the formula (i.e. what would happen if I spent all day 'surrendered' at the beach?), what it did was force me to quickly refine my creative rhythms so that I spent less time in force and struggle, and more time in flow with the higher source of my creativity. And while I certainly embraced several opportunities to connect with this source on my way to go surfing, I also learned quickly that I could gain a similar burst of positive 'surrender clarity' simply by going for a short walk in the grass or playing baseball catch with then 3-year-old Josh.

I have found that this principle of 'focused surrender' applies not only to the ebb and flow of the writing process, but also to the actual unfolding of story itself. There are certainly times for us to bring our clear intention and focused plan to the page, following closely to the outline or treatment we have created. But once we are fully engaged and immersed in a scene or moment on the page, there is an equal responsibility to remain open to the greater currents flowing through. If we are open we will often discover that the initial impulse that got us onto the page is just a doorway to a much more expansive energy that has been lying just beneath the surface. Following the first impulse opens that doorway to let the second one rise up and reveal itself to us. So watch for this.

We can try to kick our way downstream, thinking we know how best to navigate the waters, but if we are open and honest in our writing, there will inevitably come a moment when the river will begin to flow in unexpected ways… Where a little tributary will whisper a new possibility into the current – some new creative impulse that may have been impossible to see from the outside of the experience. Do we trust and follow it or do we kick a bit harder and endeavor to stick to the 'plan'? Plans are static, rivers are flowing. Our hands grow numb and our face begins to grimace. Without the plan we may not have begun, but without letting go of it, we may never finish! **In time we realize that the real purpose of the plan is not to hem us in or put boundaries on a living outcome, but to give us the courage to enter the river in the first place. To trust enough to begin.** Sometimes fresh impulses can be seen as distractions from the focus, sometimes they are gifts from the Muse and just what the scene really needs… only you will know the difference, and you may only know by trusting enough to follow and see where the river takes you.

All rivers lead to the ocean. When we are willing to stay with the process, all creative journeys bear fruit, or lead to others that do. This rhythm of starting with a plan *and* trusting the river can in most cases be experienced quite gracefully. But sometimes, the currents run fast and full and it's all we can do to simply hold on! Had I known the level of physical punishment and exertion I would put myself through before I allowed myself to enter the genuine flow of that New Zealand river, I'm not sure if I would have begun (numb and near drowning was definitely not part of my plan). But had I not entered the river that day, I might not be writing this piece, living the truth of 'focused surrender' and sharing this story today.

WRITING EXERCISE:
THE BALANCE OF FOCUS AND SURRENDER

Consider your own creative process and the principles of Focused Surrender. If you imagine these two polarities on opposite sides of a scale, where do you find yourself spending most of your time and energy?

FOCUS ———————————————————————— SURRENDER

Do you tend to hold fast and cling to your initial vision of a project, trying to control the outcome even when the energy may be calling for something new? Or are you so quick to follow impulses that you find yourself distracted and scattered like a ship without a rudder? What is the balance of focus and surrender in your creative process and what is this moment on the path calling for? Is it time to strengthen your resolve and bring new levels of focused intent to your work? Or are you ready to let go and allow the greater river inside of you to carry you and your creations around the next bend?

Take a few minutes to write about your own balance between focus and surrender in life and on the page. How might you bring yourself into the flow of your great creative river today?

Finding Your Unique View

"Far better to live your own path imperfectly than to live another's perfectly."
– Bhagavad Gita

Many great books and film stories have been sparked by a simple moment in time… An image in the mind or experience of the author that germinates like a grain of sand in the tender heart of an oyster… an insatiable itch that grows silently, layer upon layer, until it opens into a fully realized story gem.

We have all had simple moments like these in our dreams and lives that leave us with an image – a simple visual seed or the expression of an idea. Some of our greatest inventions, philosophical theories and mathematical equations have emerged in such moments. And so has the life force of many sweet stories, songs and poems been born. Within that vision is a pulse, the hint or possibility of 'something more'. Perhaps not yet realized, not yet fully formed. Still floating out there in the ethers, waiting to be pulled down. And if, in this moment we pull just slightly, or open ourselves to see it more fully, we may just discover this image begins to unravel into 'that something more'… and well beyond!

As we take these early steps on the path of *Writing the Story Within*, and as we guide our characters through their first steps in the extraordinary world of their story, we and they have the gift of discovering the unique VOICE, VISION and PERSPECTIVE that we each carry… A view of the world that is quite literally 1 in 7 billion. Even if we each set out to write the exact same story with all the same characters, we would find that each story would turn out completely different from the others. And that's just the way it's meant to be.

At the end of last chapter we did a simple **5-Word Experiment** to give us a glimpse into our natural uniqueness and the different ways that we each process and create, even when given the same information. Today, we'll take another step of this exploration, into our unique way of seeing in the world.

This following exercise is poignant not only for where we are on the path of story, but also where our heroes find themselves in this phase of their journey. It is here in this time of the threshold crossing into the extraordinary world of the hero's journey, the Tests and Allies phase, that our hero will truly begin to question who they are and how they see the world. New sights and sounds, new currents and eddies, new dangers and gifts at every step. This phase of our story is about waking up. Their past world view may in fact collapse before their very eyes as they open their perspective to see and experience all of life and who they are with new eyes.

WRITING EXERCISE:
FINDING YOUR UNIQUE VIEW

Please take a few minutes to study the following image... and then bring your pen to paper and write for 15-20 minutes whatever comes naturally to you. Don't censor or edit what you write, just let it come through... What is the story that is unfolding HERE? Enjoy movement of your pen on the page (or fingers on the keys) and whatever may begin to rise as you simply bring your unique perspective to the energy of an image... see what rises in you from that image... and follow it onto the page.

I have done this exercise several times with this same picture and every time something totally new comes through for me, which is interesting considering I was also the person who took the picture and I know the 'reality' of what was actually happening when the picture was taken. Needless to say, my writing often reveals different 'realities' all together. Here's what came through in my most recent *Writing the Story Within* mentorship program *(Please wait to read this until after you have done yours!)*.

"In the whispers of red light dusk, comes sometimes a message. I was only six when Papa sent me down first to see what the Tree spirit spoke. Thought it funny to go to sand and water to hear Tree man message. I didn't know yet that Tree man speaks with smoke. Didn't yet know that deep tree secrets live deep inside his belly. Didn't yet know that sometimes you gotta listen real close. Sometimes you gotta sing it out. Call that tree to speak too. Maybe dance sometimes too. Stomp my feet into the sand. "Wake up sleeping spirit!" Twisted and drifting, lying there so long. Riding waves and wind from over there. Tree Spirit, where you been hiding at?

Wave wash my feet. Fire fills my hair. Tree man, I know why you been sleeping. I know those people cut you down. Maybe you think your message no matters no more. Tree man, you matter to me.

Come. Come wake up in the fire and tell me some stories. Tell me your story. I am ready now. I am ready now to hear. To listen. To run with the fire of your wise dreams."

Discovering our own unique perspective gives us the strength to commit to the journey, knowing that we each have our own view and voice to share… and that all are needed by the whole.

> *"Because there is a natural storytelling urge and ability in all human beings,*
> *even just a little nurturing of this impulse can bring about*
> *astonishing and delightful results."*
> **– Nancy Mellon, The Art of Storytelling**

CHAPTER 5:

Your Point of True Commitment

*"Until one is committed, there is hesitancy, the chance to draw back-
Concerning all acts of initiative (and creation), there is one elementary truth
that ignorance of which kills countless ideas and splendid plans: that the
moment one definitely commits oneself, then Providence moves too. All sorts
of things occur to help one that would never otherwise have occurred. A whole
stream of events issues from the decision, raising in one's favor all manner of
unforeseen incidents and meetings and material assistance, which no man could
have dreamed would have come his way. I learned a deep respect for one of
Goethe's couplets: Whatever you can do, or dream you can do, begin it. Boldness
has genius, power, and magic in it. Begin it now."*
– W.H. Murray

The Power of YES

Wheresoever you go, go with all your heart.
– Confucius

*

I remember sneaking up to the back of that seedy Denver, Colorado café with a friend who had come there for an oracle reading. I didn't even know what 'a reading' was, but there was a 'specials' sign that said I could pay $5 and ask one question, so I thought that might be fun. I forked out my $5 and said simply, "I'm getting ready to go on a trip... so, yeah, um... what about this trip?" I remember the strange eyes of the oracle man staring for a long moment before turning a single card and speaking the words, "Yes. This will indeed be a very big trip."

I remember thinking he was stating the obvious, shrugging my shoulders and not really giving it much thought after that. I remember the opening lyrics on the mix tape my brother Steve gave me the day before I left. "Hey... hey... I ain't never coming home." I remember thinking the lead singer was stating the absurd, but strangely tears were flowing down my cheeks as I listened. Flash forward five months and I'm sitting in the passenger seat of a borrowed car, riding through the suburbs of Melbourne, Australia. Spring flowers blur across the headlights mixing with the soft scent of the beautiful being next to me, and a single thought is about to land in my heart that would amplify those two prophetic quotes, and shift the direction of my path forever.

A month after my 24th birthday, I had left my Colorado home with the fundamental vision of following the whispered pulse of the Universe. I had graduated from college, coached skiing for a couple years to save money and now I was ready to venture out for 1-2 years and fully cure this travel bug before returning to start my 'real life' back home. I spent two months clinging to the handlebars of my bicycle on the single lane jungle roads of Indonesia (flinching at the courtesy horn blast of each and every car, truck and scooter that passed me along the way), and I had just spent the past three months coaching skiers in the mountains of Victoria, Australia. And now... well, now I was in love.

Asheyana and I met shortly after I arrived to Mt. Buller to coach for the Australian winter. I had never been to Australia and Ash had never seen the snow, so in a strange way, we were both equally out of our elements, housed in different floors of the same staff hotel, far away from most of life's ordinary reference points.

One of the things I have always loved about travel is that when we step away from our normal life in a genuine sense – away from friends, family and others who know us a certain way, away from roles and responsibilities and normal patterns of thought and behavior – we quickly find layers of who we thought we were starting to drop away, revealing a sweetly stripped back and quietly centered version of our true self. It can be a bit confronting letting go of parts of our identity that may have served to keep our tick-tock life in motion, letting go of comforts that may simply not be available in this new land, but if we are willing to go with this stripping back, our entire perception of life begins to change. On one hand, things begin to slow down. Without our normal roles and expectations occupying our mind, we find ourselves naturally aligning with the pulse of life in a more calmly connected way – following spontaneous impulses like a bee follows the scent of nectar through the field. And as this slowing down occurs, tuning us into the subtle rhythms of life, our ability to navigate to the very center of relationships and experiences has a tendency to speed up! Because our heart is open and our vision is uncluttered, our actions become ignited by a sense of direct clarity and boldness that accelerates us along the path with great synchronistic efficiency.

Such was the case with Ash and I. Amidst our different schedules on the mountain it took us a week or so to meet – and a few more days after that to fully 'recognize' each other. But once we genuinely connected, a spark was lit that quickly became a brightly burning, rapidly spreading, spontaneous-smile-evoking, sleep-depriving fire. She was unlike anyone I had ever met and yet somehow she was the most familiar thing I had ever encountered. Our backgrounds were totally different and we knew close to nothing of each other's lives, but this just seemed to leave more room for our souls to align. Looking back upon our meeting in this tiny mountain village so far from our respective lives, it now appears like a fragile and tenuous event, but in the moment, it felt like we were being carried by a giant wave... And who were we to hold back the tides?

After learning how to survive on about 1 hour of sleep (I worked all day and Asheyana worked at night so the only quality time we had to be together was between 3am when the bar closed and 7am when I started work again) while somehow leading the ski team to a record-breaking year, I now had a decision to make... where to next? There was a job offer on the table to spend the next 6 months coaching the Australian National Ski Team at the World Championships in Europe... I had a plane ticket set to depart for Thailand to continue my bicycle journey around the world... And while I would have eagerly jumped at either of those two options just a few months prior, strangely both seemed a distraction from the simple act of being right here, way over my head in love.

As the clock was ticking and the pressure was building with people waiting for answers, I searched for something to cut through the clutter and help me make a stand. Some way of unifying these seemingly opposing forces of career, travel and love... As a last ditch effort one afternoon, I called my oldest brother Scott. Having journeyed, lived and loved, he knew well each of these worlds and could surely offer some advice. I called from a city payphone but he wasn't there. So I emptied several dollars of change into the payphone and left him a 15-minute message venting spirals of my mind into the receiver.

When I finished, I had no new answers, but I felt just a little bit lighter. I walked back to Asheyana's Melbourne apartment, took a shower, and about an hour later, as we drove through the streets of Melbourne on our way to dinner, it hit me. Like a giant drop of rain landing on the center of my forehead, a single thought entered my mind, leveling virtually every other thought in my being. It was quite a simple thought really, but it quickly grew into a realization that would change my life forever.

I realized quite simply that I was going to love Asheyana more each day for the rest of my life. My love for her already stretched beyond what I had ever imagined possible, and in my deepest heart of hearts I could not see that horizon ever stopping to expand. This was quite an exciting realization, which quite quickly lead to another: If I really was going to keep loving Ash more each day forever, then it would be quite great if we were together during that time... And if we were going to be together for forever, then well, we should probably be married!

To be honest, I had never even really thought of the words 'marry' and 'me' in the same sentence, but here they were leaping around like a green tree frog in my belly, as we pulled into the Sandringham bottle-shop to buy some drinks for dinner. I must have looked a bit bewildered because Ash asked if I was OK. I nervously cleared my throat and leaned in to share my revelation, when suddenly there was a loud KNOCKING on the car window, revealing a second discovery for the evening – that Australia has 'drive-through' liquor stores. What the heck?

The lanky bottle-shop guy took our order and I regained my composure, thinking this whole marriage thing must've been a momentary whim. But once we started driving again, it resurfaced like a beach ball shoved under water. Blub blub, and there it was floating around my chest. Wow. Really? I sat and stared at it for a moment and it just stared back with a smile. So I took a breath and simply said, "Hey, I just had a crazy notion I feel like I need to share with you... Um...(pause, pause)... I would absolutely love to marry you."

Instantly the voice of fear rose up inside, convinced that I would scare her away, barking at me to add some sort of safety disclaimer like, "So... hey, maybe we will one day." But the deeper truth inside of me just held me there in silence. A silence that was matched by Asheyana for what seemed like about six days (in truth about a minute), before she calmly stopped the car, looked me square in the soul with her magic angel eyes and said, "Well... I would absolutely love to marry you too."

"OK," I said with a giant smile. "Let's do it." We both started laughing and crying at the same time, cracked open the drinks we'd just bought and toasted in giddy gratitude to our union.

We had no idea of the incredible acceleration of life events and ripple effects that this moment would initiate... But in this moment we were infused by the power of YES, and that was all that mattered.

On one hand you could say we were totally un-prepared, unmeasured and unqualified to make such a life changing commitment. But on the other hand, there was a purity there, a power in the soulful spontaneity of our "Yes" that seemed to dissolve all surface conflicts. A centerline of truth to gauge and balance all other decisions upon. Looking back now 17 years later on the incredible journey that has evolved since, I can plainly see that the pure power of that initial "Yes" carried Ash and I through the first several years of our life together allowing us to navigate the logistics of trans-continental love while getting to know the person whose soul we had fallen in love with.

In one sense the lyrics on my brother's mix tape were right... In truth, I would never return back to where I had come from in the same way as when I had left. It was as though a future part of me had planted a seed months before that was now sprouting up through the soil on the path before me. But in saying yes to the river of love unfolding before and within me, I was committing to a path that would lead me home in the truest sense forever.

*

In story, when our heroes first step on the path and cross the initial threshold from the ordinary world into the extraordinary world of their story journey, this leap is usually made with a sense of blind faith and 'hope' that everything will work out OK. At this stage of their journey, their actions are often reactive and unconscious, meaning they really have no idea what's in store for them. From here, they are thrown into the deep end of this new world with no choice but to learn how to swim. This might mean a new school, a new job, a new universe opening in the back of an old closet... in all cases our characters will face challenges, meet allies and be forced to gather new skills necessary to begin functioning effectively in this new world. Eventually (usually right around the Midpoint of the story) they come to a place where they have acquired a certain level of fluency and capability in this new world, and now suddenly a stronger, more pro-active and *consciously* committed step is required. This moment is like the tipping point of a seesaw and marks a real shift in pace and focus for our characters. Until this moment, it would have been easier for them to go back to the ordinary world from which they came – and indeed there may have been many moments when they have actually wished to do so (think Frodo Baggins longing to return to the 'Shire' in *Lord of the Rings*). But as our heroes cross the midway line of their journey, they must do so with the knowledge that there is no going back from here.

We call this place the 'Point of No Return'. Not because the hero will never return to where they came from, but because from this point forward they can no longer go backwards to do so. Up until this moment there was usually an 'out' if they needed one, and often at the Midpoint of the story our characters are given one last clear opportunity to 'get out while they still can.' But once they pass this doorway, the bridges to their past are burned and the only way home is straight through to the positive completion of their journey. In one sense the hero now has a much better grip on what s/he is saying "Yes" to, but in another, they are about to enter a whole new phase of unknown.

In the film *Avatar* – which we have been tracking along with so far – this moment is very clear to see. Jake Sully has been training to be a warrior with the tribal people of Pandora as part of his 'intelligence mission' for the Marines. In the process, he has been gathering skills, igniting a whole new awareness of the interconnectedness of life… and falling in love. He has passed the warrior test of bonding with his own 'Banshee' flying dragon and now he stands at a threshold of initiation into the Navi tribe as 'one of the People'. On the eve of his warrior ceremony, the Marine Colonel calls Jake back to the base and tells him that his mission is complete. He's been scheduled on a flight to go home (back to earth) and have the surgery needed to 'get his real legs back'. Three months ago, as a paraplegic, this would have been the greatest news Jake could ever imagine hearing. Yet here he is, midway through his journey, having integrated the lessons of his experiences to the point that many of his core values have now been altered. Jake asks to stay one more night to complete his manhood initiation ceremony – gaining authority to speak with the People and negotiate a truce for the military. But on the night of his initiation, Jakes consecrates his love with Neytiri under the white-light limbs of a sacred tree – an act that fully brings him 'across the line' from being a Marine on a secret mission, to one of the Navi People, committed by love to the tribe. As he drifts off to sleep in the jungle we see him awake in his 'link-up pod', and in the quiet of the chamber of his soul, he says to himself, "What are you doing?" He says this not with regret, but with the simple realization that he has just crossed the line. He knows not the ramifications of his actions, but on a deep level he knows that he has just past the point of true commitment – and no return. There will be no going 'back' from here.

Perhaps the biggest difference between our hero's initial decision to 'cross the threshold' into the extraordinary world and this midpoint moment of true commitment is that the first turning point usually comes as a moment of reaction – catalyzed by something that happens *externally to our hero* (Jake is stranded in the jungle of Pandora in *Avatar*, Frodo is sent from the Shire by Gandolf in *Lord of the Rings*, Po is carried into the Jade Palace by a procession of pigs in *Kung Fu Panda*, etc.), whereas what we're talking about there with our midpoint commitment is a more pro-active decision stemming from a genuine emotional shift that has occurred *inside our hero*.

What is most important about this point of true commitment is not the exact placement of the beat or what it may look like in your particular story, but to simply start to recognize the rising scale of commitment that matches our characters each step of their journey. Each time our characters grow, there is a greater need for that growth to be expressed in committed form in their actions. This commitment progression will continue to escalate right up to our story climax, but here in the Midpoint we see the first outward expression of a genuine shift in our hero's energy, from their connection to their past world toward the new future that is yet to be created.

THE POINT OF TRUE COMMITMENT FOR YOU

In the same way that our characters and stories reach these points of true commitment and no return, we will also arrive at these tipping points in our own journey as writers. Moments where we know we must strengthen our resolve and commitment to our own creative path. Like the heroes of many stories, we may have started our creative journey on a whim of inspired connection to an idea – a simple call to creative adventure. We may have crossed the threshold into beginning our story, our book, our film, without really knowing where it would lead us… what it would ask of us… what it would call forth in us. We may have moved through various layers of resistance and tests as we have traveled through early phases of drafting and now (or sometime in the future) we find ourselves at that point of deeper required commitment. That moment when we realize that the story we signed up for is perhaps bigger than we thought it was, and we know that in order to reach the end and truly bring this seed to fruition, a deeper level of devotion is required.

Sometimes these moments occur to us first as sticking points or creative blocks where we may find ourselves overwhelmed or questioning the validity of our work. It can be tempting to turn away, to put our manuscript back in the drawer and work on something more 'realistic' for a time… But in most cases, our story is simply calling us to stretch and meet it on a new level – to recognize this apparent sticking point as a doorway to a higher level of commitment and experience on the writing path. If we continue out into the deep from here, we may lose sight of land, but what great treasures may wait within us on the journey to the other side?

In story, in writing and in life, these moments of leaping off and genuinely committing ourselves define us. Our greatest fear is that commitment will lock us in and limit our options… But what we may ultimately realize is that true commitment is a doorway to the highest path of freedom.

WRITING EXERCISE:
THE POWER OF COMMITMENT

As you consider the Midpoint phase of your Writing the Story Within experience, take a few minutes to consider the role and the power of commitment in your life, your stories and your path as writer.

Describe in detail the following:

A MOMENT OF TRUE COMMITMENT FROM YOUR LIFE

Consider a crossroads moment where you really felt that choosing one direction meant burning the bridge to another. Where you had perhaps been traveling along a certain path and suddenly became aware of the need for a new level of commitment. What came up for you at that point of decision? How did you decide and what happened once you did? What steps did you take to seal your commitment into action in the world – and how were those steps reflected in the path that opened before you?

Is there an area of your life that you have been exploring on a certain level that is now calling for a sense of true commitment? What has stopped you from committing in the past? What would happen if you truly committed and crossed the line? What might happen if you don't?

A MOMENT OF TRUE COMMITMENT FOR YOUR HERO

If you have a story that you are currently working on, take a few minutes to imagine what happens at the Midpoint of that story. Where has your hero been so far, and what lies ahead? How might she consecrate her commitment to the path in such a way that we all know she has crossed the Point of No Return?

Have some fun with this, and if your story has not yet reached its Midpoint when you read this, feel free to conjure a simple tale, poem or moment.

Here, I'll help you out… take the next five minutes to fill in the blanks of the following sentences. Add, change and expand as much as you feel drawn to. No need to stay in the lines… use it as a doorway to write this hero across the Midpoint of her journey.

As the last rays of sun reached over the horizon, she stepped quietly to the fork in the…
She looked to the left and saw…
She looked to the right and saw…
Glancing back over her shoulder she squinted to see the path she had walked so far. It made her feel…

Smelling _____ in the breeze, she lifted her eyes to the sky, focusing in on_____ and in that moment, she knew just what she had to do. So she took a deep breath and...

A MOMENT OF TRUE COMMITMENT FOR YOUR PATH AS A WRITER

Consider where you now stand on your writing path. Look at the stories you feel drawn to share, the lessons and gifts you have acquired on your journey so far. What would it mean to truly commit to your creative path? To step across that safe line of untapped potential into the arena of committed realization. If you knew that your level of commitment was directly related to your level of true success/fulfillment in whatever creative endeavor you may envision... If you knew that your commitment is the key to unlock the true potential of any path, what steps would you take today to make that commitment real?

More than anything, this moment of midpoint commitment is a statement to the Universe that says, "In answering the call to this adventure I have tapped into a greater power within me that is ready for more expression in the world. I have seen new possibilities and glimpsed a new reality. I may still be reaching and grappling for it, but now I know I cannot go back to where and who I was before this journey. The way forward is full of unknowns but I now choose to release my hold on what was, and step completely into this adventure. I don't know exactly where this path will lead, but I know that in this moment, it is calling me to take another step. To fully commit in order to see what's on the other side. Here I go."

What are you *really* committed to?

> *"A people are as healthy and confident as the stories they tell themselves.*
> *Sick storytellers can make nations sick. Without stories we would go mad.*
> *Life would lose its moorings or orientation...*
> *Stories can conquer fear, you know. They can make the heart larger."*
> **– Ben Okri**

> *"All things splendid have been achieved by those who dared believe*
> *that something inside them was superior to circumstance."*
> **– Bruce Barton**

The Power of WHY
(A.k.a. Rising Stakes!)

A protagonist and his/her story is only as emotionally compelling
as the forces of antagonism make them.
– Robert McKee

By tapping into the nature of DESIRE (Chapter 3), we connect with the inner wants and needs of our characters. As our characters begin to take steps toward that desire we come into contact with the nature of CONFLICT (Chapter 4) and the elements (internal, external and intimate) that may rise to push 'against' or stop our heroes from reaching their desire. This convergence between the energy of what is wanted (DESIRE) and the energy of what must be overcome in order to achieve it (CONFLICT) is like the friction between two sticks that start the flame of a story. Once we know what our heroes want and what is stopping them from getting it, there is a third element that we must add to the mix that will act like oxygen (or lighter fluid!) to that flame. This third element is the fundamental ingredient that will not only require our hero to truly commit, it will ultimately allow him to transcend whatever challenge and conflict may come his/her way. What I'm referring to here is the element of STAKES.

While our desires tell us what we want and our conflict tells us what's stopping us, the stakes of our story essentially answer the question, "Why *must* we do it anyway?" Why must this happen? What is so important about this mission that we and our heroes must stay on the path despite the challenges that come our way until this journey is complete? And what will happen if we don't? Quite literally, what is at stake?

While not every story is loaded with life-or-death / save-the-castle / beat-the-dragon-or-the-whole-world-ends stakes, every compelling journey must have a deeply compelling reason WHY... some inner purpose or driving need that motivates the hero's action beyond the levels of resistance and opposition that may have stopped them from answering the call in the past.

In life, we can want something to change for months and years (maybe lifetimes!), but it is only when we have a genuine compelling reason, when we truly know WHY IT MUST HAPPEN that we are able to transcend all levels of conflict in order to stay on the path and claim it. When we see someone achieve something incredible in life, our first question is often, "How did they do it?" But what we should really be asking is "Why?" Without a compelling reason why, skill and technique is of little use. If, on the other hand, we are anchored deeply in our "Why", we become way less dependent upon skill and technique alone, because our actions are driven from a deeper place of truth within.

When I first met Ash, she smoked cigarettes. At first it didn't bother me (the smoke always seemed to quite magically evaporate away from her body as soon as it left her mouth), but as we became closer I began to feel a rising urge to help her quit. I loved her too much to see her do anything that could be damaging to her life. She wanted to stop too, but had never been able to move past the addiction. We tried several techniques and approaches including patches and hypnosis, but the internal conflict of the addiction was just too strong and this back and forth struggle endured for the first five years of our marriage. Then one day a simple thing happened that changed everything. One simple shift in our circumstance gave her the power to go from smoking a pack a day to quitting cold turkey on the spot. It wasn't a new technique or approach, it was a simple addition of a new level of 'Stakes' to her desire. She got pregnant. She had wanted to quit for herself and for me before, but neither of these were strong enough 'whys' at the time. But with the quiet pulse of our child growing inside of her, she instantly had an entirely new level of motivation beneath her actions. No special techniques were needed. Just the clarity of why it MUST happen.

Stakes are what enable us to rise above our current circumstance and go beyond our pre-conceived abilities – to drive through the night in order to reach a friend, to sleep very little for months on end in order to keep a newborn fed, to learn a new concept in order to pass a test, to run through a fire in order to save a dog. It may not be comfortable, it may not be easy, but when we truly know the reason why, and when we move with the power of that 'why' within us, the boundaries of the possible part ways.

THREE KEYS TO BUILDING EFFECTIVE STAKES

When we're considering how best to weave and raise the stakes in our story, there are a few keys that will help keep them real and powerful for our heroes and our readers each step of the way.

The first key is making them PRIMAL.

In film stories and fairytales alike, beneath the surface action and complexity of the story, what's at stake for our heroes is almost always something quite basic and instinctual. In most cases, if we boiled it right down to why our heroes are doing what they are doing, we will usually find one of the following desires/needs at play:

- **Survival** (doing what is necessary to satisfy basic human needs, stay alive)
- **Love / Procreation** (winning, saving, protecting or avenging a loved one)
- **Avoiding Death / Loss** (physical or energetic death/rejection/loss – of a job, a relationship, an idea, a kingdom, etc.)

Author Blake Snyder does a great job of hammering home the importance of keeping it primal throughout his screenwriting book *Save the Cat*. When it comes to layering our stakes in such a way that our audience/readers fully resonate at the most basic level, Blake sums it up with a very simple question: "Would a caveman understand?"

Snyder goes on to site a handful of blockbuster movies and their primal drivers. I'll do the same here with a few of the films we've mentioned so far (and a few others just for safe measure):

- *Avatar* (desire to protect their world)
- *Field of Dreams* (desire not to lose their farm)
- *Lord of the Rings* (desire to survive and protect Middle Earth)
- *Whale Rider* (desire to belong / be accepted and to save a species)
- *Motorcycle Diaries* (desire to survive and 'make it through')
- *Amélie* (desire to find/win a mate)
- *Up!* (desire to fulfill a promise to a loved one)

Even if the stakes of your story are not as extreme as life and death survival, there must be a basic instinctual drive around whatever the goal may be. It doesn't need to be life and death, but for our character, it needs to feel more important, more urgent and more of a *must* than their current life patterns... otherwise they would likely not embark or not complete the journey!

A child's desire to 'fit in' with friends, a mother's desire to protect her own, an artist's desire to stay true to her Muse, an entrepreneur's desire to keep the shirt on his back, may all qualify as primal stakes if they are driven by a deep seeded reason WHY.

We know this to be true even in the writing journey that we are now on together. We may toss a story idea around in our mind for years and not fully commit to it... until the stakes of our own lives or inner drives rise enough to get us going on the page. I myself have found that I often work much better to a deadline/submission date, simply because it activates a primal sense of urgency within me that forces me to show up and push through my own levels of resistance in order to bring the creative vision into form. Looking back, it's astounding to see how hard I have pushed myself at times, how many sleepless nights and practically meal-less days I have endured to complete a project simply because a meaningful deadline has been placed upon it. And while we may not consciously choose the high-pressured path, in retrospect it often reveals that with a bit of a sense of urgency, we are capable of far more than we give ourselves credit for. It's crazy that even our life's passion could require an extra primal push to get the job done, but for some reason (with me at least) it often really helps. Sometimes the heat just has to raise a little to draw that hero out.

When we consider how best to establish the stakes of our story, we begin here at the basic human needs for life, love, safety and survival. These needs may slide up the energy scale to include more expansive vistas for our heroes, but we start here with stakes that are real and visceral. We start by making them PRIMAL.

The second key to creating compelling stakes is to make them PROGRESSIVE.
In story, our characters often embark upon their mission with only a superficial or 'first step' understanding of what is at stake. They may have a sense that their mission is important, but early on they rarely see the bigger picture. Their initial stakes often revolve around personal preservation or reaction to some immediate challenge or threat to their own well-being, but as we move further into the story with our heroes, they will begin to sense that maybe this journey isn't just about them. In fact, there's a lot more at stake – both personally and way beyond – than they ever could have imagined.

In *Lord of the Rings* when Frodo first leaves the shire with the ring he does so as a simple short-term favor for Gandolf. He knows there is a sense of urgency and importance, but he does not really know why. He and the other Hobbits are instantly faced with challenges that are beyond what they have ever had to deal with before (in the form of creepy black horsemen) but what they deal with here is tiny compared to what they must ultimately endure to achieve the final aim of returning the ring to the fires of Mordor.

If someone had told Frodo everything that he would eventually have to do in order to complete his mission prior to leaving, there is no way in the world that he would have accepted the task. But because the stakes were progressive – increasing steadily as he went – he was able to rise to the occasion (just!) each step of the way. This is one of the main reasons why our stakes must be progressive… too much too soon and we risk losing both our hero and our audience before they even get started.

Each step the hero takes upon the story path is mirrored by a sense of stakes that is often just beyond their comfort zone. As soon as they start to get comfortable with one level, the goal posts shift again and they are once again thrown into the deep end. The key as storytellers is to draw our characters and our audience steadily out from the shallows into the very deepest waters, and to do so in a compelling, believable and progressive way.

While much of the first half of our story is often externally driven and somewhat self-centered for our main characters, the second half of our story is where the external and the internal worlds begin to converge. It is here where the hero's actions will really begin to matter, to count, and to play an important role in the world around them. It is here where they will begin to elevate from trying to save their own skin to contributing a vital piece to the greater puzzle of life around them. Why? Because they MUST… and because that MUST is growing!

As the plot boils beyond our midpoint commitment, the elements of conflict and stakes begin to accelerate, making it progressively more difficult AND more vitally important for our hero to fully complete the mission. The harder it gets, the higher the stakes must rise to keep our hero motivated to go beyond what he may have deemed possible yesterday. Necessity becomes the mother of invention.

Even if our story is a simple tale with no bad guys or epic world-saving consequences, understanding the power of stakes enables us to magnetically charge the beats of our story so that they build progressively throughout the tale, challenging and motivating our heroes' actions in steadily increasing amounts around whatever is vitally important to them and their world.

As writers, we are like chefs in a fancy restaurant and our ultimate goal is to have our customers reach absolute culinary euphoria by the time they finish their meal. We know that we'll be serving up a killer dessert when the time comes, but we're not going to give it to them at the beginning of the meal, are we? And we're certainly not going to serve all the food at once. We're going to draw it out. As experienced chefs we know we need to build each course upon the next. Our aim is to keep our customers totally satiated and at the same time yearning for more.

By building up our stories progressively – the desires, the lessons, the conflict and the stakes – we gradually lead our heroes into fuller expressions of themselves than they (and we) would have ever thought possible. When we finally arrive at the end we will all look back in utter amazement at the journey we have traveled. We will enjoy the dessert of this great feast because it has come with perfect, progressive timing.

The third key of effective stake building is the power of POLARITY (A.k.a. The Carrot and the Stick).
In a very basic sense, it can be said that almost everything we do in life is done in order to either gain pleasure or avoid pain… or both. We may want the Olympic gold, the soul mate partner, the recording contract or the business deal, but underneath those external desires is a basic yearning to FEEL how we think we are going to feel when we have achieved our goal, or to avoid feeling how we think we would feel if we failed. Beneath whatever things we're pursuing are always the feelings we associate with gaining or losing them. In this way, we can consider this polarity of pleasure and pain like the carrot and the stick of a racehorse. The carrot lures the horse toward what she wants, the stick drives her away from what she wants to avoid. While some research shows that people tend to be motivated more powerfully by the desire to avoid pain than by their hopes of gaining pleasure, in most compelling stories, these two elements weave intrinsically together adding depth and meaning to the stakes.

The polarity of stakes essentially forces us and our heroes to finish the sentence: "I must do this in order to _____, or else _____." The first blank in that sentence stands for the 'carrot', or the positive outcome our hero is seeking – the desired reward for the journey ("If I do this thing I will save the world, win the girl, acquire a fortune, win a medal…"). The second blank in the sentence stands for the 'stick', or the negative ramifications of falling short of the goal. What/who will be disappointed, what will be lost, what pain will come to the world if the hero falls short?

The athlete wants to win the Olympic gold to fulfill her inspired dream (the carrot). At times that desire may be eclipsed by the fear of failure and the pressure to perform, to fulfill their coach's and sponsors' demands. She may be driven in bursts by the fear of losing her spot on the team, her sense of purpose, etc… and while these pain-based pressures may be great motivators on those rainy days when the last thing she wants to do is get out of bed to train, they will be nothing without the deep seeded vision and glimmer of true positive possibility living in her heart. The pain of moving away from something uncomfortable is compelling, but in my experience the power of moving toward what is truly desired is the power that moves mountains. When we read of someone running through flames or lifting up a car to save a loved one, they are clearly trying to avoid pain and loss, but in the interviews and stories I've read, it is quite clearly the power of their LOVE for that person/animal/thing that empowers them beyond all other things to achieve their goal.

While life and story is not always this black and white, there is almost always an element of polarity in our pursuits. One leading us onward from the front, one driving us from behind. And while the avoidance of pain may at times be the louder voice and most compelling short term driver, in my experience it is that deeper, quiet voice of inspired vision that ultimately stands the test of time.

As we move along the story path it is great for us to get a sense for polarity balance within our own life and that of our heroes in story. Are we driven more by our fears or by our love? How does our fundamental driving force influence what we actually receive and create in our world? Or in other words, what is the end result if we focus more on avoiding pain vs. reaching the positive pleasure of our vision? What is the right combination that will truly inspire us to rise above all challenge and truly fulfill our calling?

The truth is that we are ALL capable of way more than we give ourselves credit for. We have capacities and dormant abilities as human beings that we have not yet even dreamed of. Many of the great spiritual teachers have pointed to this innate mastery within each of us and have called for it to be fully realized, not in some lifetime in the distant future, but here and now, just as we are. In my experience, the greatest challenge in life isn't in achieving that which we set out to achieve, the greatest challenge is actually to continue to expand our view of the possible and to reach beyond our preconceived notions to fully experience it. There is an immense joy in co-creating or achieving something beyond what we previously thought was possible. Each time we do, we catch another glimpse of the truly infinite field of potential within us. What greater aim in life could there be? For this I give thanks to the STAKES that often propel our thoughts and actions beyond our preconceived limits to get there!

Knowing the answer to "WHY MUST THIS HAPPEN?" plays a huge part in making the hero's journey possible... and worthwhile in the end. Making those stakes Primal, Progressive and Polar adds richness to the tapestry, which gives both our heroes and their journey more dimension.

No matter what the subject matter, a compelling story has a way of building and 'raising' the stakes throughout the journey, so that as the characters' steps strengthen toward their goal, so do both the opposing forces AND the underlying stakes (reason why) of the quest – all building toward the ultimate story climax where the only way forward is through a thin doorway of transformation.

WRITING EXERCISE:
STAKES AND THE POWER OF THREE

*Using what you now know about the nature of **DESIRE** (what our character wants/ needs), **CONFLICT** (what's stopping him/her) and **STAKES** (why it MUST happen), take a few minutes to write a fun and simple story:*

Imagine a young boy/girl who has been given a mission of going up to the local shop to buy something for his/her mom. Set him/her out on the path with a clear DESIRE (what does s/he want on the surface and underneath?) and a plan. Then start to weave into this path whatever CONFLICT and STAKES you can think of that could possibly get in his/her way. Start stacking up the challenges and see if you can build the conflict on all three levels (externally, intimately and internally – what/who is trying to stop him? What fears does he have? What's waiting at the other end?), and then see if you can raise the STAKES (with Primal, Progressive and Polarity!) from simple, self-centered motivation to some 'greater mission' and motivation at hand. Lead this journey wherever you feel drawn (as 'out there' as you can imagine) and then see if you can bring him/her back home, just in time, with just what s/he needs. Why MUST s/he do this? Why now?? What happens if s/he doesn't make it back in time? Who/what is waiting at the other end? Perhaps Mom is there to say, "Thanks," with no idea what her child truly had to endure to complete this quest.

Take 10-20 minutes and have fun with this. Open your imagination and let whatever you can dream up flow into the story. No boundaries on this one, except to build as much multi-layered conflict and progressive stakes into the scene as you can.

OK. Go for it, and we'll see you back here for the next step on the story path!

*"I'm not intimidated by lead roles. I'm better in them.
I don't feel pressure. I feel released at times like that.
That's what I'm born to do."*
– Morgan Freeman

The Power of Detail
Igniting Our Message with Our Senses

"Nothing can cure the soul but the senses,
just as nothing can cure the senses but the soul."
– *Oscar Wilde*

When we approach our writing with a sense of a desire to capture and send out a certain message, one of the temptations we may encounter is to jump right into the message itself. We have discovered this idea or ideal and we can feel the power of it, we know how much it's going to help and inspire people, so we just want to pour it out onto the page. However, jumping right to the message is often a bit like starting a joke with the punch line. It doesn't really work. Particularly with the savvy minds of modern audiences and readers, we need to find dynamic ways to build to our message so that when it comes, we, our heroes and our audiences can really soak it in. No one wants to be spoon-fed the story, they want be able to piece it together for themselves, connecting the dots, using their hearts and minds to stretch between moments and discover hidden gems on their own. As writers our goal is to deliver our story and our message in such a way that each person experiencing it has an opportunity to own it themselves as though it were their story and discovery. This, I imagine, is why Zen masters shared their lessons in koans and why Jesus taught in parables. By telling a story we create a container of connection and within that container each participant has the opportunity to enter and drawn from it just what they need. Rather than feeding our readers with a spoon, we can lead them to the river and let them dive in and fully quench their thirst.

Interestingly, one of the most potent writing tools that enables a story to elevate to its highest ideals and greatest message is our ability to ground it first in the finest of physical detail. I'm not talking about factual details that you can get from doing a Google search, I'm talking about subtleties of detail that are known only by those who have truly experienced that which is being discussed. It is these details that make a story truly come to life. Details and grounded specifics are what elevate a story from 'the facts' into the realms of truly engaging narrative. Details lift us out of a more expected and/or cliché perception of an event, into the genuine energy of the experience itself.

If I told you that my cat was curled up on my desk, purring, that's mildly interesting and perhaps a bit expected of a writer. But if I told you that Princess, our psycho kitten farm panther just leapt onto my desk with a strange dove-like yodel (one that my wife taught her as a kitten and which she now believes is cat language – much to the confusion of every other cat she meets), and she bolted across my keyboard typing "D)9jxxxxz~" in efforts to swat a moth… well then you're starting to get a more real-to-life and interesting sense of what's going on. Details. Real details from our real experience lift even mundane moments and objects into the arena of positive engagement.

Similarly, if I were to tell you that I am sitting here writing on my computer, that is a fact which may or may not interest you. However, if I were to elaborate just a little, you may find that your relationship to what I'm telling you begins to change… If, for example, I were to tell you "it's the middle of the night, and I'm sitting in the tiled bathroom of an 80's style beach hotel, with the sink as my desk and the toilet as my seat…" That suddenly gives you a whole different picture. If I were to go on to say, "The out-dated ceiling fan is buzzing above me like a bee hive, and that my bare feet are pressing into the shining white floor, sending an occasional shiver up my legs as they pick up grains of sand floating on the tiles from my son's last trip to the beach…" you're starting to get and even clearer picture. If I were to go on to say that "the faint scent of coconut sun cream is blending with the sub-tropic winter air, leaving my fingers and face relaxed but just cold enough to stay awake…" and that "I'm typing quietly, trying not to speak out loud as I often do (sounding out the words as they emerge on the screen) – so as not to wake up my wife Ash and Josh who are sleeping soundly in the other room…" and that I'm "racing to finish writing these words before the sunrise comes, because I promised my publisher he'd have them by dawn…" suddenly you're climbing into this space with me, ready to travel wherever the moment may lead. Add the kitten into the picture and the whole scene starts to come alive. Josh wakes up and needs to use the bathroom (my office)… now what?

Specifics and details ground us into the real world and provide a springboard from which we can lead and carry our readers to the greatest depths, highest heights and most interesting nooks in between. It is in the details of what we share from our world that we begin to reveal our own unique perspective, and in a way, we become the energy of our message, often eliminating the need to state it directly at all. It is in the details that we bring our message into material form so that it simply permeates the page. So that by the end of the section, we could ask the reader what they got from the passage and they will tell us straight away (in their own words!) even if we never once extended the spoon to their mouth.

WRITING EXERCISE:
THE POWER OF DETAIL

Part 1 – Here and Now
*Take a few minutes to observe your immediate surroundings right here and now...
then describe them in as much detail as you can. Draw upon all of your physical
senses (what you see, hear, smell, feel, and taste in the air) as a doorway to what
other more subtle and energetic conclusions you may observe in your situation. Try
picking the most mundane and ordinary object (a light switch, piece of paper, bit of
Kleenex, strand of hair, smudge on the wall, etc...) and see what story it has to tell,
what doorway it may provide when you dive right into the details.*

PART 2 - Revisiting the Corner Store Adventure
*Now that you're getting a sense for the power of details in your surroundings, let's take
this same sensory view and go back to the simple story you wrote in the previous section
(The Nature of Stakes) about the boy/girl on the corner store mission. Take the next
few minutes to glide through the story and notice areas where added visceral detail
may enhance or deepen our connection to the moment. What smells are in the air,
what are his/her eyes attracted to, what's the temperature outside and in the store, is
there music or other sounds in the background. Comb back through your story with
a fresh eye for detail and add whatever you see, hear, smell or taste along the way!*

And in our next section we'll take this little corner store quest to a whole new level through
the Power of Point of View!

*"We can tell people abstract rules of thumb, which we have derived from prior
experiences, but it is very difficult for other people to learn from these...
we can more easily remember a good story. Stories give life to past experience.
Stories make the events in memory memorable to others and to ourselves.
This is one of the reasons why people like to tell stories."*
– Roger C. Shank, from **Tell Me A Story**

The Power of Point of View

"It takes a thousand voices to tell a single story."
– Native American saying

*

Not so long ago we spent an autumn season in Melbourne. I was in between major projects and needing to do something more dynamic with my energy than sitting at the computer all day waiting for emails to come through. My income had been primarily project-based over the previous few years and it had been a while since I had had a simple regular wage coming in, so I decided to combine my desire for steady flow with a growing passion for the Earth and sustainability... and I went to work for a local biodynamic farm, harvesting apples. The notion was quite romantic initially. I'd spend my days wandering the orchard rows connecting with the Muse, and my evenings writing to my heart's content. As an Aries, I'm always up for new discovery so the first few days were pretty exciting – driving tractors, climbing through trees in the autumn sunshine, embracing the daily challenge of filling 2-3 big apple crates with about 2,000 apples each before sunset. But by about day four, I was starting to feel pretty restless... and exhausted. With bruised grooves in each shoulder from my apple pouch and carpel tunnel rising in both wrists from twisting and pulling Fuji's all day, I hadn't had the energy to open my laptop once, much less to write anything of value. I was starting to wonder if I was wasting my time – 'valuable time' I was telling myself, that I could be channeling into any number of potentially exciting activities or projects. Here I was, slaving away for a fraction of my normal fee for writing or coaching, the days were beating me up and the foreman had this way of applying subtle pressure to the pace of my picking that made me feel, well, quite inept. I'd be out there working my way up the rows, soaking wet with morning dew, and he'd stop by on his motorcycle, look into the bins and just kind of shake his head. He wouldn't say much, but what his eyes were speaking was, "Really? You've been out here all this time and this is all you got?!" By week two I was getting faster, but my restlessness was growing. I was still finding myself too exhausted to be creatively useful in the evenings (shower-food-sleep was the pattern, waking just in time to throw on my overalls and get back out there the next morning) and on top of that, I was having a heck of a time trying to field business calls while climbing ladders with a pouch packed full of Granny Smiths. I had been late for a couple of important afternoon meetings, I had missed a few key calls and this 40-acre property of fertile soil and prolific fruit growth had gone from poetically beautiful to overbearing, overwhelming and almost oppressive. So many apples... How would we ever get through them all? By the end of week three I was starting to seriously consider pulling the escape hatch... That's when George arrived.

George was a tall, thin Chinese man. I don't know how old he was but I would guess mid-fifties. He had run a successful importing business for many years but recently let it go because of conflicting interests with his suppliers. He'd come to Melbourne to live with and look after his parents for a while and wanted to learn a new trade. Somehow he found the orchard and had decided to drive 90-minutes each way across city traffic to be there picking each day. I was having a hard time dragging myself out of bed to make the ten-minute drive in time, so I wondered how long George would last. He was a quiet man and we didn't talk much for the first few days, but one thing I noticed straight away – which admittedly, did give me some comfort at the time – was that he was a much slower picker than me. I was about half as fast as the foreman, and George… well George was about half as fast as me. Within a few days, some of the harsh words I had thought I was hearing through the silent eyes of the foreman, I started catching out loud, muttered quietly in George's direction.

But the days were getting shorter and they needed the help, so as a couple of slow, misfit pickers, we were partnered up to work the same section of the orchard each day, sharing the harvest. Knowing that I would now have to pick even faster in order to make up for George if we were going to make our daily quota (a concept that George didn't seem to understand) I found myself getting stressed and almost a bit resentful of my new partner. But a few days into our partnership, during our first lunch together, all of this changed.

After spending several minutes searching for a spot of high ground to check my phone messages, I joined George on the edge of an apple crate where he was eating a big chunk of homemade bread. We were well behind schedule, so I was eating fast and starting to do the math in my head of how many more chest pouches would be needed to fill the next crate, when I heard George bite into a crispy Pink Lady and take a deep sighing breath. "This is the best job ever," he said, with the sincerity of a child. "Fresh air, fresh apples, green grass, blue sky… Best job ever."

I couldn't see his eyes (in fact I'm not sure if I ever saw his eyes on the other side of his gold framed, Top Gun style shades), but I wouldn't have been surprised if there was a tear hovering there. I looked at him for a long moment, taking in what he said and I realized that while we were there doing the exact same work together, George was having a totally different experience to me. I was working hard, stressing out, picking as fast as I could, going home exhausted and frustrated, feeling like I should be doing something else… and he was driving three hours a day, picking half the amount of apples and experiencing moments of enlightened rapture. I was definitely missing something.

After lunch I watched George picking for a while… gently handling each apple, looking at it for a moment or two before he placed it in his pouch and reaching for the next.

He might have been pissing the foreman off, but he was sure doing something right. We finished the day at sunset and I remember glancing back at George just leaning back, smelling the air as I drove the tractor back up the hill.

The next morning was misty wet and raining so most of the team took the day off. George had made the trip across town unknowingly and I didn't have the heart to abandon him, so I stuck around to work with him. I decided to leave my phone – and as many of my other thoughts as possible – in the car for the day, and for once really bring my full presence to the task. Almost instantly, the day began to feel a bit different. The apples seemed to come off a little easier from their branches and my steps through the long, wet grass just seemed a bit lighter. George and I lost sight of each other for a while, each working our own rows on foot. Despite the rain, it felt good to be there, surrounded by all this life and growth and energy in full fruition. I felt inspired by each tree's ability to give forth so many ripe creations (hundreds of apples and thousands of seeds!), and how each individual apple had the capacity to give birth to a whole new family of apple-giving trees. What a model for sustainable living! I wasn't rushing, I wasn't forcing anything, I wasn't really even thinking... but somehow the pouches and buckets were filling.

About midway through the morning, it started bucketing down really hard. I ducked under a mature Granny Smith to seek a bit of shelter. As I lightened the load of her limbs, I stepped quite close to her trunk. Suddenly a warm, almost tingling feeling came over my body. The air seemed to get a bit thicker and I felt this sort of calm come over me that I hadn't felt for a very long time. I took a deep inhalation of sweet apple-tree-air and looked up to realize that the limbs of the tree were all wrapped around me like a giant, tree arm hug. I started laughing and I glanced around to make sure the foreman wasn't coming, and then I slowly put my arms around the trunk of the tree and just hugged her right back. Several seconds (maybe minutes) passed and not a single raindrop hit me, but my face was wet with tears. I swear I could feel her pulse. Only then did I truly arrive in the orchard.

From that day forward, my time in the apple orchard was absolutely cherished and remains a heartful highlight on my path. Some days George and I made our daily quota, some days we didn't. He never really understood what it meant, and I no longer really cared. Strangely as I relaxed, so did the foreman. He stopped counting apples in the bin and I stopped counting my phone messages. And as luck would have it, we finished the picking season just before the first frost... right on time. And just a few days after our final day of picking, my next writing project began. Right on time. Last time I saw George he was talking about getting a job on an oilrig for a few months so he could be out in the ocean. He had heard it was good pay but difficult work with tough crews. I can just imagine him out there amongst a group of sea-weathered oil riggers, tearing off a piece of his homemade bread, taking a deep breath of clear ocean air. "Ah. Best job ever."

*

One of the most powerful tools we have as storytellers is the power to shift PERSPECTIVE in the eyes and minds of our audience. Indeed this is one of our most fundamental roles, responsibilities and opportunities as we bring our pen to the page... to reveal not just what happens (that's just news), but rather to give our readers/audience a unique perspective of what happens, in such a way that it shifts or shapes the way they experience it.

In a broader sense we do this every time we tell or write a story – we give meaning and perspective to an event simply in the way that we capture it in our words. I have heard it said that nothing (no event, circumstance or situation) actually means anything, except for the meaning that we choose to give to it. A broken leg can be a career-ending injury or the greatest turning point of a person's life. How we perceive our reality actually becomes our reality, and determines what goes down in the history of meaning.

Have you ever walked along the beach at sunset and noticed how that same setting sun is experienced differently by each person out there on the beach? The little kids are transfixed by their orange reflections in the rock pools. The traveler is racing with the last light to set up his tent before dark. The couple holding hands have just decided to get married and this is a moment of pure magic they will always remember. The man on his mobile phone trying to close a business deal doesn't even know the sun is setting. One moment, many different realities. This is the power of Point of View. Or as they call it in the film world, POV.

One of our first steps as writers is to decide what Point of View our story will be told from. Will we see it through the eyes and mind of the character we are witnessing or will we watch the story unfold as an observer from the outside? Will our story be told in first person POV ("*I* arrived at the beach just in time for sunset..."), second person ("*You* climb inside the cave and suddenly come face to face with a lion...") or third person ("So *he* turned back in the direction from which he had come and bolted back outside")? Will we tell the story like a fly on the wall, observing only what can be seen and heard from the outside (cinematic screenplays are written this way), or will we position our lens beneath the surface to hear the thoughts and feelings of our characters? Each of these perspectives offers a different doorway into what's really going on and in truth, they give us different versions of the story itself.

Generally we will pick or find a perspective that feels most natural to write from, and that will usually be the perspective that will most serve our story. But sometimes shifting our POV can help us see things in our story that we may have otherwise missed. Often if we are feeling challenged or stuck as to which direction a character must go next, or how a scene wants to play out, if we are able to shift our own perspective, we suddenly have a whole new insight into the scene/moment/story.

WRITING EXERCISE:
THE POWER OF POINT OF VIEW

Today we are going to explore the power of POINT OF VIEW in a fun and simple way, as an extension of our previous lesson about the STAKES.

Your mission – take the simple story that you wrote in our Nature of Stakes section (and that you may have enhanced in our Power of Details section), and re-write the experience through the EYES and MIND of someone else. If you wrote it initially in third person 'about' the boy/girl ("he went to the shop..."), or in first person through his eyes ("I woke up..."), try telling the story from the perspective of someone else in the story - the boy's mother, friend, his dog, the shop keeper or even a tree on the sidewalk watching the whole thing unfold. Climb right into the skin and voice of someone else and see if you can bring a new layer of meaning to your story by seeing it through a different lens. Notice how powerfully this simple shift can alter the look, feel and even the message of your story.

By shifting our Point of View in simple ways we free ourselves to see the world of our story through new lenses, while expanding the unique perspective we each bring to the symphony of life. ENJOY! I'll see you in Chapter 6 as we move toward the emotional center of our story and claim the Elixir of the hero's path!

CHAPTER 6:

Your Innermost Cave

The Storyteller's Creed:
I believe that imagination is stronger than knowledge,
That myth is more potent than history,
That dreams are more powerful than facts,
That hope always triumphs over experience,
That laughter is the only cure for grief,
And I believe that love is stronger than death.
*– **Robert Fulghum***

The Gift of Shadows

"You gain strength, courage and confidence by every experience
in which you really stop to look fear in the face."
– Eleanor Roosevelt

*

On a journey in the South Island of New Zealand, I had been given a quest to spend three sunrise mornings in the depths of a huge cave at the end of a remote beach. I had visited the cave in broad daylight with my family, but I had never been there in that darkest hour before the dawn, and I had certainly not been there alone.

I have always found that New Zealand has a raw sort of enchantment to it... A haunting beauty that both fills you and leaves you with a slight ache. A longing. This was definitely the case with the cave. It had an alluring power that drew me in and yet it held a gaze over me that whispered of its memories and seemed to question my motives as I approached. The cracked and jagged 30-foot ceiling in the opening chamber seemed to carry with it the eyes of all who had gathered there before me... from ancient Waitaha elders and Maori tribesmen, to starving explorers and local college ravers – and many in between. Their chanting rhythms, their silence and shouting, all seemed to wind its way back into various shadowy alcoves, pockets and stony dens, well out of sight... both beckoning and challenging me as I entered. I had always been quite a happy person, and most certainly presented this on the outside, but there was something percolating beneath me at this time that wasn't quite settled. A restlessness, a yearning for something more that I had been nervous to explore. So I had come here to find out what was on the other side of my pensive grin. I had come here to learn about my shadow.

The distant sound of breaking waves echoed softly into the cracks of the smoke-blackened wall as I stepped into the cave on the first day. Sheltered from the ever-shifting Aotearoa wind, a slight dampness filled the air. A shiver shot up my spine. I knew I was in the right place.

I stood in the main chamber looking around, adjusting my eyes to the pre-dawn light. The first thing I noticed was that from the relative lightness of the main chamber, I could see clearly into other areas that were also capturing light, but I was unable to see any of the darker, shadowy spaces. Much like trying to look out the windows of a lit room at night, my eyes could only see into those areas that matched where I was standing. Mustering up a little more courage, I stepped into an enshrouded alcove for a moment and made my first discovery. As my eyes adjusted to the darkness, I *suddenly found that I could see the whole cave much better – both light and dark spaces equally. As a well-conditioned optimist who tends to gravitate away from shadowy spaces in the direction positive possibility, this was a powerful realization. To see that these particular shadows did not harm or hinder my view, but on the contrary, they expanded it! Day one, and already I was getting answers... but I knew there was much more lurking...*

The second day called me to venture deeper into the unseen chambers of the cave and further into this realization. I spent the morning edging into dark spaces, adjusting my view and then taking another step. By the end of day two I had comfortably acquainted myself with all of the main rooms and nooks and was feeling quite proud of my shadow discovery. I wanted to believe I had already claimed my prize and discovered what I came for... but just like the quiet restlessness in my belly, I knew there was more. There was one area I had not yet mustered the courage to explore – a passage leading off the main chamber, deep into the 'innermost' section of the cave network. I had noticed the beginning of the passage in daylight, but had discounted it as an unapproachable area as it would require me to crawl and shimmy my way under a very low section of the stony ceiling for an extended length of time into a completely unknown and definitely un-seeable area, beyond the reach of any light. For whatever reason, I left the second day with the creeping feeling that I knew my task for the final morning... I was going to have to find and feel my way back into the pure pitch blackness... deep in the innermost chamber of that cave.

As I stepped toward the cave just before dawn on the third morning, only a slight hue on the horizon lit my way inward. There was a mist on the ground that almost seemed to be coming from this great craggy cave mouth, as if from the restless dreams of a sleeping dragon. A dragon that was quite possibly waiting to devour me in the center of this cave, never to be seen again. I tried to laugh this thought off, but it – and others like it (including bandits, murders and rogue feral animals) – swam spirals in my mind as I crouched onto my hands and knees and began to feel my way into the darkness. With hands outstretched to meet the walls, I inched my way deeper and deeper in. Soon I was on my stomach squeezing under the jagged roofline. My mouth now pressed close to the soot and sandy floor, my eyes anxiously searching for something, anything, to adjust to. My ears, aware of the rapidly fading sound of waves, began pitching themselves into the silence and eerie sound of creaking stone and dripping water before me... Several meters of sand crab shuffling and the ceiling gradually began to recede again, eventually opening to a small room in the very heart centre of the cave. The ocean's surge and the rising light of day were nowhere in this place. Only the dripping of water on stone amidst pure, impenetrable darkness.

I had no idea of the dimensions of the chamber or what (or who!) else was in there. My breathing was shallow and my pupils eclipsed the blue of my eyes in efforts to adjust... but my efforts were futile. I could see nothing. I was scared. I felt anxious and exposed. I felt like ants were crawling inside my skin and murderers were moving in. I could feel the walls closing in around me, full of all the haunted spirits and wounded beasts that had ever been to this hellhole dragon's lair. I wanted to scream and run and shake this whole thing right off of my body... To scramble out of there five times faster than I had crawled in and throw myself into the ice cold ocean. But somehow, instead of sprint-crawling away, I forced a shaking breath into my lungs and chose instead to dig myself a little deeper into the sand. If this was what was lurking in the shadows of me... this is where I needed to be. Even if it killed me.

I took a deep breath into my fears and nervous imaginings, and with it I felt my belly begin to relax. I took another and my shoulders gently dropped. I closed my eyes (which was no different than having them open) and took one more breath. My whole being began to settle into this bed of tiny stones and shells. Into the earth beneath it.

As I began to relax, I became aware of a deep stillness in the cave. A stillness that only the very centre of a mountain could know. A stillness that knows without seeing, and sees without looking beyond itself. A stillness that wants for nothing. Yearns for nothing. A stillness that rocks restlessness to sleep like a sweet child on a rainy night. I felt this stillness in my body... and a great peace washed through my being, as though it passed from the open hand of Mother Earth herself. Held gently in this womb, I felt as safe and peaceful as I have ever felt outside on the beach, in the grass, with a loved one in the night. In this moment of absolute darkness a light switched on inside of me. A light that I did not even know had been missing.

I was completely content, connected and present. There was nowhere else I wanted to be, but from this place I could imagine going anywhere... being, expressing anything! I opened my eyes, and just as I did, the first ray of the sunrise must've reached over the ocean horizon, because it stretched and bounced its way through the angles of the cave, sending a single hazy beam into the inner sanctum where I sat. The timing was incredible. The very moment that I arrived to genuine peace and light within the darkness, the light of day had come in to find me. I stood up and stretched my arms to the ceiling and the walls around me... then crawled my way out to greet the sun.

As I stepped from the depths of the innermost cave to the main cave chamber (a space that had initially seemed quite shadowy in itself!), the contrasting light caused me to squint. Everything seemed so bright and alive. I realized that while I had always been an optimistic, 'glass-half-full' type of guy, my reluctance to explore the shadows of my own innermost cave had stopped me also from seeing and experiencing my greatest light. Now I could see and feel the equal gift and power of both. I ran down to the water's edge and dove in, nearly freezing my head right off of my shoulders, but it certainly added to my aliveness... And as I stepped from the waves looking back across the beach, the rising mist mixed with the morning light, creating a rainbow directly over the mouth of the cave. I could barely believe it, but then I realized that it was the perfect reflection of my final lesson: That the ultimate outcome of pure light meeting darkness is the full expression of color.

With that I knew that at least this portion of my cave journey was complete.

*

We have answered the Call of Adventure and Stepped on the Path into the extraordinary world... We have moved through the Tests and Allies phase of our journey, past the Mid Point and our 'point of no return' commitment... As we turn the page into Chapter 6 of the *Writing the Story Within* experience, as writers we have each no doubt confronted different obstacles and moved through layers of our own resistance, uncertainty, challenges and commitment to be here. Well done! The same is likely to be true for the heroes and characters of the stories you may have written along the way. They have been called from their comfort zone into a world of new challenge and possibility... They have been thrown into the deep end and forced to learn to swim... They have slowly risen in confidence amidst the external challenges of this new world, until they have come to a point of genuine, conscious commitment on their path. Once they cross the midpoint of their journey, the stakes have begun to rise and chances are things have accelerated considerably, leading them on a steady landslide into the emotional center of their whole journey. A moment on the story path that is often referred to as the 'Innermost Cave'. This is not the climax of our story as a whole, but for our characters (and for us on the writing path), this moment often marks the internal or emotional climax of our journey. It brings us face to face with our greatest emotional challenge and deepest hidden fears, en route to revealing our highest inner truth and the full realization WHY we *really* came on this journey in the first place. Nestled within the Call to Adventure that first got us on the path, this is the moment that our personality self has quietly tried to avoid, while our soul has been drawing us toward it from the beginning.

In many stories this moment appears as an emotional low point for our characters and there is often a feeling that everything they have worked towards, all that they have learned and gained on this path is lost. But from the ashes of this apparent loss... from the depths of this deep cave, they will ultimately discover a crystal of truth, an inner key of understanding that will be so clear and compelling that it will allow our hero to rise up beyond all apparent challenge, beyond where he or she has ever dreamed of going, into the fullest realization of their potential.

Glancing at some of our classic Hero's Journey film stories, the Innermost Cave is easy to spot, because with it often comes some sense of death, dying or defeat. It doesn't have to be a literal dying, but it signifies a 'dying to' or letting go of the last of our older ways of doing things, and the necessary birthing of a new, aligned, spark of ignition.

In *Star Wars*, the Innermost Cave moment comes when Obi Wan Kenobi is defeated by Darth Vader, dying in front of his protégé Luke. In *Lord of the Rings*, Gandolf sacrifices himself to the dragon in the dwarf caves, falling away into the flames thousands of feet below. In *Kung Fu Panda*, the Furious Five land in a heap on the front step of the Jade Palace after being single-handedly defeated by the villain, Ty Lung. In *Avatar*, our Innermost Cave moment comes when Home Tree is destroyed and Jake Sully is banished from the Navi people and imprisoned by the Marines for treason. Heavy stuff! The Innermost Cave doesn't have to be so epically tragic as these examples (as you read in my own cave story, it doesn't have to be tragic at all), but I point these big ones out so we can familiarize ourselves with the essence of this story beat and what it sometimes takes to bring our hero to a place of genuine and lasting self-discovery.

On one hand we can perceive each of these story moments as a crisis beyond reconciliation. Loss beyond recovery. And yet, as the story unfolds, we will eventually look back and recognize this moment as a catalyst for a major turning point – perhaps the most major turning point in the inner make-up of our characters. A shift in circumstance that will ultimately give our hero no choice but to truly step up and <u>become</u> the change they have been building towards. While this moment may signify great discomfort and seemingly insurmountable challenge, it comes with good reason – to fully ignite the flame of our hero's true purpose for being.

It is here that our hero's unspoken fears are flushed to the surface, bringing up feelings of vulnerability, helplessness, loss of control and despair. But from the soil of surrender will emerge a quiet seed of power calling them to take full responsibility for their actions and to claim their role in the bigger picture. To open their eyes here in the darkness in order to discover the Elixir of personal truth that awaits them just on the other side of struggle… An Elixir that will be needed to emerge from this cave and to bring their journey to full and positive fruition. Here in the depths of the Innermost Cave is where the seed of our story's ultimate resolution is planted.

Even a story as simple as the one shared in the beginning of this chapter has an Innermost Cave moment. In my case here, it happens (you guessed it) right in the depth of the innermost cave! If you read the story again you will see that each of the major story phases we have touched on so far are represented in the experience. I answer the call on the first day, truly commit on the second day and am drawn into the innermost cave on the third. There, I encounter fear and deep unknown, before sinking in deeper, surrendering and finding an inner light amidst the darkness. That light is my Elixir, drawing me out, challenging me to carry this newfound gift back into my life. This is another example of how the Hero's Journey naturally finds us when we tell (and live) our stories in life. I didn't plan to move through those phases, and I didn't even plan to include them all in the writing of the tale. It just came out that way in the telling, because that's the way it was lived.

The events of our life are continually calling us to new adventure and experience. Why? Ultimately, quite simply, in order to lead us to these moments of deep inner realization… Allowing old aspects of who we thought we were to die away, while making room for the higher truth that is ready to shine through.

Whether you are writing (and living!) an epic trilogy or a children's fable, every story must ultimately bring us to a single point of emotional clarity – as heroes, writers, readers and viewers. There may be many layers of gifts, lessons and messages along the way, but this is the moment of deep personal truth that matters most. This is the inner sun of your story that will reach in through the cave and find you in the very moment that you discover it within yourself. The Innermost Cave is not a place to be feared or to avoid, but rather to be embraced. It is here in the shadows of our deepest searching that we discover the purest power of our highest light.

WRITING EXERCISE:
ENTERING YOUR OWN INNERMOST CAVE

IN LIFE
Consider a moment or chapter in your life when the events of your experience challenged you so deeply that for a brief time it appeared that all was lost. That everything you had built up towards had been taken from your grasp, or (as in my cave story) you were drawn into a place of such unknown that you literally had to surrender your reference points of reality into the shadows of the moment. A moment that would ultimately lead you into a realization of truth within that enabled you to rise above any and all obstacles in your path in order to do what you knew had to be done. Take a few minutes to describe in detail what has brought you into the Innermost Cave, what it felt like to be there and what deeper realization the moment ultimately catalyzed. Feel the power of the shadow, and ignite the spark of inner light with the quiet discovery of your own Elixir. If your whole life story revolved around one essential emotional discovery, what would that be?

IN STORY
After you've taken time to connect with an Innermost Cave moment in your own experience, take the next step by transferring that energy into your story or hero on the page. If you were to boil the fundamental emotional purpose of your whole story

down to one essential truth or discovery, what would that be? What might the hero of your story have to go through in order to truly make that discovery in a way that will stick with him/her as they venture forth? In modern conscious story telling, it is easy to shy away from these deep moments of challenge because we want so much to deliver the bright message of our journey, but if we are to fully appreciate the light (in the way that I did coming out of the cave in New Zealand), sometimes it helps to shine it into the shadows first. Even if (as was the case for me) those shadows are all figments of our own imagination. Our Innermost Cave moment doesn't have to be propelled by a devastating, good vs. evil, battlefield moment (as is the case in the above mentioned films). It can be subtle and deep, because the Innermost Cave is ultimately about the deepest inner truth of our hero. Our job is simply to provide a compelling pathway to lead them there. This is why it is so powerful to connect with your own experience first. Then you won't have to rely on massive external props and big budget battles if you don't want to, because you will be writing the moment from a subtle place of genuine knowing deep inside of you. I know you've been there... Write from that place and we'll go there with you every time.

Take this energy into your story today and write a scene or moment that brings us and your hero into the Innermost Cave. And if your story and hero is you (i.e. if you are writing autobiographically), well then employ the learning from this section to honestly explore your Innermost Cave moment in ways that will bring us, the readers right to the emotional truth of the journey you feel most inspired to share.

IN YOUR WRITING

What sits at the very center of your calling to be here on the path of Writing the Story Within? Yes, you want to write your story, and yes, you are committed to emerging with a great piece of work to share with many... but why? What lies beneath this vision? What unexplored impulses and veins of truth may be waiting in the shadows, ready to reveal themselves as you surrender yourself fully to the page? What would it look like for you to bring yourself into the Innermost Cave of your own writing journey? What might you have to let go of in order to go there... what elixir might be waiting there to meet you?

The Innermost Cave marks a pivotal moment in our story-writing journey. While it may initially be perceived as a death, letting go or release of one way of seeing/being, it ultimately gives birth to a higher, truer path. This is a skin-shedding moment for the snake, a beak breaking rite-of-passage for the young eagle, an antler shedding for the buck. A moment of genuine vulnerability giving forth to a new level of strength, personal power and realization. This is the moment where we truly must let go of one rope, so that we may glide through the air unimpeded and grab a hold of the next...

Enjoy the Innermost Cave of your writing experience... and welcome to Chapter 6!

"Most of the shadows of this life are caused by our standing in our own sunshine."
 – *Ralph Waldo Emerson*

Show, Don't Tell

"Don't say the old lady screamed – bring her on and let her scream."
– Mark Twain

When we have a meaningful experience, breakthrough or discovery in life, one of our human tendencies is to want to share it with those around us. It could be argued that sharing the gifts of our experience is actually one of the fundamental reasons for having the experience in the first place. But sometimes in our haste to tell all that we've gleaned to those who were not there, we can come across as preachy, and if we're not careful, we can end up alienating the people we want so much to share with. Or even worse, we end up feeling like we're trying to justify the experience, almost giving away some of the magic in attempts to translate it to others. The intention is right, but our audience may not yet realize they are ready to have the same breakthrough we have just had. It's easy for us to see why they *need* this information, so we just want to hand the gift right to them… and if that fails, ram it down their throat!

I learned early on in my ski career, that in my efforts to share my biggest breakthroughs with those who did not really have ears to hear, I would often come away feeling less empowered about the events myself. Eventually I discovered that there were those few who I could talk in detail with about my experiences (those I knew had been there themselves in one way or another), and to the rest I would simply smile in humble response to their enquiry about my weekend and say, "It was great, thanks, how about yours?"

What I ultimately discovered was that the surest way to share any new gifts acquired on our path is simply to demonstrate them in WHO WE ARE. To follow Ghandi's advice and simply "Be the change we want to see in the world." If we have made a new discovery, if we have made a new breakthrough, yes we can talk about it, but the greatest gift to all will be found in how we choose to *live* this new discovery in the moment-to-moment story of our life. And from there, how we guide others into doing the same.

As we delve into the Innermost Cave of our story experience and gather the clarity to launch our way toward the Climax of our writing journey… today we will explore a simple, yet profound writing principle that will elevate our stories from interesting to magnetically engaging. From 'telling a tale', to 'genuinely sharing an experience'. The principle is something of a mantra in the world of film/screenplay writing. It goes like this:

"SHOW, DON'T TELL."

It can seem a little bit of a strange concept at first because we naturally think if we are using words that we will most certainly be 'telling' our story from start to finish. But if we scratch a little deeper, we'll discover a multi-layered gem in this concept. The principle of 'Show, Don't Tell' means quite literally that whenever possible – and even when it doesn't seem possible – we need to strive to demonstrate our ideas, messages and the thoughts/feeling of our characters through they way they act, rather than simply telling our readers what they are thinking. While a fair amount of novels are written in such a way that we get an inside view into the minds of our characters, when we write a screenplay, we do so in a fly-on-the-wall sort of way, describing the action based on what our viewers will *see* and *hear* in the moment. This whole 'Show, Don't Tell' concept is not always a big focus in the novel writing world, but in my view it really should be, because it challenges us to get visceral, to use our senses and to climb right into the moment we are writing. The process of doing this automatically brings us (and our readers) from our heads, into the heart and body of the experience. And while at first it can feel a bit like trying a new move on the dance floor, ultimately the path of 'Show, Don't Tell' leads us to sharing our story in more compelling, engaging and connectable ways.

So how do we start doing this? Quite simply by writing as though we are looking through the lens of a camera, filming the characters we are writing about. The camera is like an objective observer, so we have to find a way to portray whatever is happening in such a way that, by looking and listening through the lens of the camera, we know what's going on for our characters. Instead of saying, "Jane is sad and embarrassed," we might have to dig a little deeper and say something like, "Jane dropped her head and looked away, hiding the red of her cheeks and the tears that were now blurring her vision." You can't just say, "Billy was hot and he wanted some ice cream." You've got to climb right down there on the street with Billy and say, "The sweat drops on Billy's upper lip quivered into a smile with the chiming sound of the ice cream truck rounding the corner. Tightening his 5-year-old grip around his mom's wrist, he jerked her frantically toward the curb." By simply painting a picture of what's actually going on, we don't have to say "sad, embarrassed, hungry, hot, excited." We get all these things – and so much more – by seeing and experiencing what our characters see and experience in the moment.

While some films use narration to enhance our understanding of the hero's inner world, and while almost all films use dialogue to fill in some of the other gaps, the primary information we take as a reader and viewer will come from what our characters *do*, and how they act/react in certain situations. Even if your story or writing is written from deep inside the mind and heart of your characters, this is still an incredibly powerful practice that will bring your prose to life and engage your audience each step of the way.

As a delightful visual example of 'Show, Don't Tell', I suggest watching the movie *Microcosmos* – a compelling narrative of the tiny insect world within a field. No dialogue or narration is used, but the story is complete and the 'scenes' of different insects in their daily plight are totally engaging and emotively charged. There is a love scene between two snails (I'm not joking) that is one of the most touching and beautiful love scenes I have ever seen in cinema, and there is a scene of struggle with a dung beetle pushing a small spherical turd along a rocky path that carries all the suspense of a Hollywood thriller. Bottom line, there is almost always a way to effectively demonstrate what we are trying to share without spelling it out. Our job as writers is to do this in a way that it makes our readers and viewers feel how our characters feel. We do this by showing, by creating a doorway for them to live the moment we are writing.

THE ORIGINS OF 'SHOW, DON'T TELL'

In the Australian Aboriginal culture there have always been 'Song Men' who are sent out expressly with this purpose of discovering new songs and stories to bring back and share for the benefit of the whole. They spend time on their own in the natural world, listening and communing with the great 'creation song' unfolding all around them, and when they have received what they came for – a new story or *song-line* to help guide the next step for their people – they return to their tribe. Their first step is to sing and share the story of their journey. Then through dance, they re-enact and express physically what happened to them while they were gone. And finally, they will create a visual expression – a drawing, painting or artistic rendition of their experience and discovery. Something both tangible and symbolic of the whole. Through sound, movement and visual art they translate the message to their tribe, so that they can all both genuinely experience and begin living the message in their daily lives. This is our job as storytellers. To re-enact and share our discoveries in such a way that our modern tribe can fully receive, integrate and apply whatever message or truth they may draw from our story into their lives. We do this most effectively when we *show*.

If we want to tell our audience that our hero is "so nervous he can barely stand still", how might we show that same information by describing his actions in such a way that we too begin to feel nervous? We might get him standing up, sitting down, forcing a breath into their chest, checking their watch, double-checking the time with someone else. They look around fleetingly, and then sit back down again, before someone they know finally taps them on the shoulder to see if they're OK. They explode in a moment of violent over-reaction, "WHAT?! Oh, Yes… I'm fine. Why do you ask?"

As humans we are incredibly perceptive. We are constantly reading people's energy and intention just by the look in their eye, by the way they hold themselves, by the way they speak and move. We glean a very small amount of information (something like 20%) from what a person actually says. The rest of the information we gather is in the HOW. In their body language and their tone of voice, in the pace and intensity (or lack thereof) of their movement. In story, we have a lot of opportunity to play with this contrast between what is spoken and what is being experienced on the inside of our characters.

In the above example, the "Yes… I'm fine," tells us more about our character than if he said, "I'm really nervous and I'm having a hard time standing still." We've already seen the character *acting* nervous, so to hear him say he's "fine", shows us that he's trying to keep himself together and that he's also self-conscious about appearing nervous or out of control. Another way to play this (depending on the character) would be to have him be so honest that it surprises us in a different way. For example he could say, "WHAT?! Yes, I'm fine. I just wet the pants I'm supposed to be married in today. But, besides that, I'm fine. Thanks for asking." In this version, we also find out some new information about the character (he's getting married today), which adds a new dimension to the scene, but again, it does it without just saying, "Jack was nervous because he was waiting for his fiancé to arrive to their wedding." There's hundreds of ways you could play the moment and make it interesting, the point of the matter is to use the description and the dialogue itself not just to tell us what's going on, but to make it interesting and real for who this character is and what is *really* going on for them!

WRITING EXERCISE:
USING THE POWER OF DETAIL TO SHOW

One of the ways to begin accessing the power of 'Show' is to focus on the small physical details of our characters and what our senses pick up about what they are doing. Take this sentence as an example for this exercise: "The Native elder walked through the forest with such reverence that every movement appeared as a prayer of gratitude." Instead of spelling it out in this way, how might we describe the way she walks, her facial expression, what she says to the forest to demonstrate her gratitude? Where does she stop along the way? How careful are her steps not to damage the moss? Is she calm and steady or shaking slightly? Do peaceful tears well up in her eyes as her tiny hand touches the naked skin of an ancient tree and her mouth accepts a drop of dew from a leaf? What are the words of her prayer? Or is her prayer beyond words…? Show us her reverence. Use all of the senses. Let us feel it in our own body, through her experience. Write a simple scene that shows this or another moment of reverential connection with the natural world (or something else if you prefer).

WRITING EXERCISE:
USING THE POWER OF UNIQUENESS TO SHOW

Another way to demonstrate who and what is going on for our characters is to take the time to really climb into their skin and get to know them... and to observe the unique intimacies of the way they do the simple things in life. Most particularly what do they do that is totally unique to who they are? How do they react when they see an animal they love or when they taste something sour? Earlier, I shared that one of the very first unique things I noticed about Asheyana when we first met was that when she smoked, the smoke just seemed to whisk away and evaporate from her as soon as it left her body or cigarette. I'd never seen anything like it. It was like there was a vacuum just above her head that knew this smoking business wasn't part of who she really was and so it was constantly clearing the space around her. To share this about her is a way of demonstrating what's going on that's a lot more interesting than simply telling us she was smoking. I grew up despising smoking, but this little uniqueness allowed me to see through the haze and fall in love. Since then, I have observed hundreds, maybe thousands of little intricacies about the way Ash does things that make her unique and that beautifully 'Show' me who she is. The way she shoves her feet out from the covers each morning in silent plea for a massage. The way her voice goes high and sing-songy and she squats down just like a child whenever she meets a new cat, lizard, bird or dog. The way her face sharpens and her eyes glaze over like cutting steel when anyone she loves is being threatened. Everything she does has a flavor to it that is totally unique to her. If I were to simple follow her for the day I could describe each of her activities in a way that made them completely her own.

My invitation to you is to take some time to observe the people you love today and describe in detail not just what they do, but how they do it. Or if your family doesn't like you stalking them, go to a park, restaurant or cafe (some place public) for a little while and just watch. Tune into a few different people as they walk by, and notice that they don't just walk... They amble, jog or hobble past... describe their actions and how they carry them out in such a way that we get a glimpse into who they are in the process. Use your descriptive words as colors in the palette to paint the tone and energy of a person. If he's a big man, maybe we could know this not by saying, "He's big", but by showing us that "he stretches the seams of his XXL jumper as he cinches his belt to reach the second hole." If she has an air of beauty, we know this not by saying, "She's beautiful", but by seeing "the double-take reflections in the eyes of those who watch her as she moves with unknowing grace through the room..." You get the picture. Show, don't tell. Pick a few 'characters' from your real world today and write a simple description of a few simple actions or moments, showing us what's really going on.

If there is a scene in your story that you have been working on, perhaps take another look at the actions and reactions of the characters and see if you can bring new depth to their behavior by showing us rather than telling us what's happening.

Showing forces us to think beyond our head and reach into the flesh of even the most ordinary moments to retrieve a hidden pearl. Step into your world today and see what it *shows* you, then climb into your WSW journal and show us what you experience!

"If you tell me, it's an essay. If you show me, it's a story."
– Barbara Greene

"Don't tell me the moon is shining; show me the glint of light on broken glass."
– Anton Chekhov

The Hourglass of Focus

"Concentration, in its truest, unadulterated form,
means the ability to focus the mind on one single solitary thing."
*– **Komar***

While each story can be broken down into a whole series of distinct sections (several of which are featured as chapter titles in this book), in a very basic sense, the Hero's Journey story form can also be divided into three primary phases – The Call, The Answer/Initiation and The Return. These phases follow the basic flow of 'Beginning, Middle and End' and run quite parallel to the traditional 3-Act story form with its first, second and third Acts. The Call is the beginning section of our story where we meet our hero in his/her ordinary world and we set up our story with the Call to Adventure. The Answer is the middle of our story where our hero crosses over the threshold into the extraordinary world, meets tests and allies, passes the point of no return and journeys into the Innermost Cave to claim his/her Elixir. The Return (which we will get to in the following chapters) is where our hero must venture back into the ordinary world with the gifts and discoveries of the journey.

In the same way that the overall story can be divided up in this way, so too can each scene or moment of a story be sectioned into these three primary areas to capture a sense of progressive flow. As we are exploring the Innermost Cave section of our story in this chapter, today we're going to discover a simple technique for progressing the energy and focus of a single scene, in a way that mirrors this overall structure, enabling us to lead our readers right to the very emotional centre (or 'Innermost Cave') not only of our story, but of each and every scene. This exercise is based on a combination of a few of the key elements we've looked at so far, and I like to call it the 'Hourglass of Focus'.

The Hourglass of Focus gives us a simple pathway for focusing the power of detail in a way that zooms in and magnifies our lens specifically around the area of most importance for our scene, and to use that 'moment' of intense focus to then open back out into a deeper meaning or message. It allows us to gradually layer details in such a way that progressively leads us to the center of our scene, without getting bogged down or missing the chance to really deliver our message. The key is to create a rhythm of detail that opens our readers to what's coming. One that engages them completely in the moment in a physical sense and leaves them ready to hear and connect with our perspective of it. The Hourglass of Focus isn't a rule or technique I've learned as much as a way that I have observed truth often emerging in my own and other people's writing. So dig in and explore it for yourself. The Hourglass of Focus goes like this...

PART 1 – THE SET UP (TOP OF THE HOURGLASS)

We begin our moment in a general sense at the top of the hourglass, setting up the details of our scene/world/moment from a wide-angle-lens view. We see and sense the many details of the scene, but we see them initially from this broader perspective – gazing across the landscape, so to speak. Imagine, for example, arriving at a park and 'taking in' the scene as a whole for a few moments. We notice the light, the trees, the breeze, who's there, who's not there, etc. In the top of the hourglass we 'set up' the moment in a sort of holistic way, using our senses and glimpses of detail to get an initial sense for the moment – enough to make it real, genuine and unique, but not enough to weigh it down.

PART 2 – THE FOCUS (CENTER OF THE HOURGLASS)

As the sand funnels in closer to the center of the hourglass it hones and narrows its focus. We draw in more and more specifically until there are only a few grains of sand going through the tiny hole in the middle. In the middle section of our scene, we bring our focus closer and sharper into the center of WHY we are really here in this scene in the first place. Every scene has a fundamental purpose, and here in the center of our hourglass we zero in on it. The middle of the hourglass and the focus of our scene is like the Innermost Cave of our story – it brings us to the deepest point of emotional truth in that particular moment. In our park example, we've arrived, we've walked around until we've found a certain place to be, and we find our attention drawing very closely to something specific – a bird, a flower, a blade of grass, someone we know. Something that brings our focus to a point and does so completely for a moment or two, becoming a metaphor for the whole reason we came here.

As we connect with this one single thing and give it all of our focus, we find that our experience here at the park begins to take on a more specific meaning or purpose. It's that moment when a specific thought that you're having is suddenly matched by the song of a bird, a shift in the breeze, or the glimmer of a drop of water on a leaf... and in that moment, you are so present, so purely drawn into the specifics of this experience, that it gives you a doorway into some greater understanding or perspective about life. It is in this absolute focus in the NOW, that suddenly you get a glimpse into all of time... It is in this focus on one very specific thing (a blade of grass, grain of sand, drop of dew) that you suddenly feel connected to all things...

PART 3 – THE PAY OFF (BOTTOM OF THE HOURGLASS)

Having dipped into the very center of the Universe for a moment, the hourglass then begins to open back out again, and the grains of sand that were drawn so intensely into the center are now liberated and released back into the open space. So it is with our story or scene, by drawing into the absolute core of our scene's purpose – into some simple microcosmic or emotional reflection of the whole – we emerge with a view or a perspective of this outer world that we otherwise may not have had. It is through this journey to the very centre of this moment that we are catalyzed and inspired to come back out and share the insight gleaned. Each scene is like a mini hero's journey and this our moment of coming out of the cave and with our elixir.

An example came to me a couple of years ago during our last day in Byron Bay before leaving to go overseas for 12 months. A special moment unfolded down at the beach in a very 'hourglassy' way. I will share with you here.

The three paragraphs below are essentially divided into the three main sections of the hourglass. See if you feel the natural draw, focus and release of the moment.

*

It was just on sunset and too late for a walk by most accounts, but for some reason I felt drawn to drive down to Wategos beach and walk out over the headland to the easterly most point. It was cloudy and almost dark... but I had to go. I was alone on the trail except for the occasional jogger going the other way, the chiming flutter of paired-up wagtails finding their evening perch... and the wind. She was everywhere. Like a seasoned mother. Not overbearing, but ever-present. I came out of the trees and stepped onto the crimson-lit knoll, taking in the magic of one of my favorite spots on Earth. This thin piece of land that divides open ocean from crystal clear bay. Wild sea to my right, small glassy waves on my left, and me standing in the center, on a soft bridge of sand, grass and stone. Anchored to the Earth, connected to the sky, surrounded by sea and the fire of life.

It had been a busy day of packing and logistics, so it would have been quite easy to miss my invitation, but as I glanced down into the shallows and spotted the pod, I was very glad that I hadn't. A family of three dolphins surfing and playing so close to shore I could have walked out to greet them. Shiny black backs arcing through waves in perfect curves, mirroring the swell shapes they rode. Graceful acceleration, unhurried rhythms. I could feel the "Pppwwoooooshhhh" of their breath in my own chest as they surfaced... And as their movements slowed with grace to meet the twilight, so did mine. Whatever to-do list this walk was avoiding floated right out with the tide. Whatever path we were being called on tomorrow didn't even exist. Here, for once, here for now, I am home.

I'd been floating around town the past three days tangled up in details, fluttering this way and that. Somehow each day they'd found me – at different beaches, at different times. I'd look out and catch a glimpse from a parking lot or a footpath. I'd catch myself thinking, "I've really gotta go take a moment just to be... but when?" Here they were again. And finally, gratefully, I'm here too. Brought to this moment by a family of three, carrying a message for my family and me. That in the gap between wild waves and glassy bay, there is place... an open, quiet, playful space. Sometimes it looks like a stone, sometimes it looks like a patch of grass or an old car, a park bench or a fig tree limb. Whatever it looks like from afar, what it's really called... is the moment. This is where the dolphins live, this is where they meet us and remind us of our own infinite capacity to trust and breathe and ride with joy, the magic waves of life. "Pppwwooooshhhh". Here we go.

This was just a spontaneous expression of a simple moment. It wasn't planned to fit into a mold or shape but you can see how naturally we drop into this hourglass form. It just sort of happens if we let it. The general leads us into the specific, the macro leads us to the micro and then it opens back out again – with something new to bring along with us.

*

WRITING EXERCISE: DROPPING THROUGH THE HOURGLASS OF FOCUS

Take a moment right now to stand up and walk out your door. Go for a proper walk out to some place you love if you have time, but otherwise, just step outside. Take a breath, open your senses and move in whatever direction you feel 'called'. Let your steps lead naturally into a moment. Any moment. Whatever moment may be right for you to experience on this day, at this moment, right here and now. Don't bring an agenda, just bring yourself and be guided from the surface of your experience into the very center of a very specific moment of engagement... from the general into the very focused, into the center of your own hourglass. Don't force it or put any major expectations on the moment, just see what grain of sand may be waiting for you, calling to you, for whatever reason. Allow yourself to focus in on a single moment or object in your environment and then let it drop on through to the other side.

When you're ready come back inside (or sit down on the spot) and write what you experience, capturing the Hourglass of Focus in whatever way you feel called.

Going There Emotionally

"No tears in the writer, no tears in the reader.
No surprise in the writer, no surprise in the reader."
– Robert Frost

When I first started developing stories for film, I was under the impression that as the storyteller it was my job to act as a sort of puppeteer of my narrative. To cleverly construct the pillars of the story and then to lead my characters through the scenes and growth arcs that I had devised for them, and to let them serve the message and idea that I was brewing. I had studied story and film in a variety of ways, I had learned the science and the art of structure, I knew what was the 'right' and 'wrong' way to construct a 3-Act story, and I knew what it was like to be a human being and growing in the world, so clearly it was up to ME to chart the path and lead my readers there.

When I finished the first draft of my first feature screenplay, I was proud. It closely followed the note cards and outline I had developed and I knew it ticked all the boxes in a structural sense. Each of the key turning points of the Hero's Journey were hit at just the right time, the beats were clever and the story was solid! But when it came time to begin sharing pieces of the story with the producers and actors who were reading for the roles, I could tell something was missing. People loved the idea of the story and they connected with the characters and the beats, but they weren't engaging with the heartbeat and the emotional essence of the tale. All these elements were very real and alive for me, but as I listened to other people read the lines I had written and discuss the flow of the scenes, what I realized was that the story 'made sense' but it didn't have a pulse. It was like a nice looking mannequin. It was interesting, but not a heart gripping page-turner. Why not?

I had put all this time and energy into carefully crafting each moment to lead logically to the next. The characters had desires and genuine conflict to contend with… the beats were loaded with real and rising stakes… So what was stopping my audience from really feeling the emotional truth of the story? What was stopping them from crying at the sad moments and laughing at the jokes? What was stopping them from wanting, really wanting, what the hero wanted, just as much or more than he did? The answer was simple. Me. In my self-appointed god-like storyteller role, I had built this story from the sidelines… from the puppet-rafters. The characters were different people than me, so I thought my role was to understand them for who they were, but to remain detached enough to portray them objectively on the page. It wasn't natural for me to stay on the sidelines of anything really, but I thought that was my role. In my self-imposed detachment, I hadn't allowed myself to really 'go there' and feel the emotional essence of the story, my heroes' plights, struggles and journeys… so how the heck could I expect, or even hope, that anyone else would?

I knew something had to change. And it actually had to change fast. The film's director had organized our first big actor workshop for that evening and my job was to select 3-4 of our best scenes to work on. I had picked a couple of key moments based on my perception of how they'd play out, but now I was reading back through the eyes of others, and I felt like the words had about as much depth and emotional substance as the paper they were written on.

I was at a crisis moment, and for me it really was one of the first real 'Innermost Cave' moments in my professional writing career. I had gained skills, learned techniques and I had earned the commission to write this screenplay with my ability to vision and structure the story and capture ideas into compelling prose. I knew the characters, I knew the beats of the story, and I had put an immense amount of time into creating a great 'looking' script, but now something deeper was needed. It was showtime and I needed to find within me a way of writing that would actually move people when they read it. I needed to find a way to connect at a heart level with my characters and their story so that it would propel actors, readers and viewers into genuinely emotive experiences. I began to realize that if I really wanted them to 'go there' emotionally… I was going to have to go there first… and fast!

The first scene we were going to workshop that night was a break-up scene between two young lovers. It was a moment of powerful vulnerability and hurtful misunderstanding and on the pages of our story outline, we knew it had potential to really pack a punch. But so far, it was more like a slap in the face with a butterfly wing. My trained impulse had been to write what I thought each character would say, given their situation, but this had lead to a fairly predictable unraveling of events and a less than fulfilling outcome for the scene. As I sat there considering the details of the circumstances that lead to this moment of heartbreak in the story, trying to 'figure out' how to write the moment in a more authentic way, I suddenly realized that while I had never experienced the exact *circumstances* of these characters in my own life, I had in my own way experienced all of the underlying *feelings* that were driving it. I knew the feeling of being misunderstood, of feeling betrayed and of having my heart broken.

So instead of trying to write the scene with puppet strings from my characters' point of view, I took a few minutes to remember and connect with one of my own experiences that mirrored those feelings, and when my own emotional cup was full and flowing, I started to write. Rather than try to figure out who said what to who and why, there in the board room of the production office, with actors warming up in the other room waiting for their scene, I simply channeled the very real energy of my own experience into the characters of my story and then let that energy guide the moment. As the characters reached the emotional crux of their exchange I hit the pinnacle of my own connection to my memory. A tear rolled off my cheek, landing on my keyboard. I stared at it for a second in surprise… then kept on writing. I didn't have to think about what would happen next, who would speak or what they would say. Somehow by tapping into my own truth and experience, I had opened a vein of connection to the emotional truth of my characters, and from there, they simply showed me where to go. The specifics of their lives became like the outer dressing or props on the stage that we were sharing, bound by our mutual emotional truth.

With very little effort from me, the scene revealed itself and the words came through faster than I could type them. I had spent hours and hours working on this scene over the past few weeks and I had probably written about eight different versions. None of them were right. Here in the board room, from a place of simple and truthful connection, I wrote the whole thing fresh in about 5 minutes, printed it off without proofing it and handed it to the director and producer – both of whom welled up into tears while reading. I took a deep breath and walked back into the boardroom to re-write the other three scenes needed for the night. We needed them in about thirty minutes. At this pace, with this new approach, all I needed was about 15.

Needless to say, the actor's workshop went great and in the next few weeks the whole script was re-written from this newfound place of connection. With that draft, we won the next round of support for the project, including key cast members, and took the next step to fully realizing the vision for the film.

For me, it remains one of the most powerful Elixirs of discovery on my professional writing path. True to any great 'Innermost Cave' moment, the immense pressure of the situation called me to a point of emotional truth I had not previously allowed myself to go to in my writing, and through surrender to the moment I found a higher path. This was my first real glimpse of a truth that has stayed with me and influenced my writing and teaching ever since: that one of the most direct paths to making our writing ring true for others comes with our willingness to first make it personal, intimate and connected to our own unique experience. Through our connection to the intimate, we access the Universal.

WRITING EXERCISE:
GOING THERE EMOTIONALLY

Think of a time in your life when you felt truly excited and grateful. When something happened or emerged on your path that made you feel utterly overwhelmed with appreciation. Take a moment to recall what lead up to this experience and remember – in as much detail as possible – how it felt to have this feeling rising up within you, causing you to smile, laugh, scream, sigh or cry. Remember how it rippled into your connection with others, how it bolstered your faith and perhaps ignited a new sense of purpose and meaning in your life. Spend a few minutes saturating yourself with this moment and feeling it in whatever way you can. Write about it. Feel it in your body. Recall your thoughts at the time and how they influenced the way you stood and moved and spoke. As much as possible, allow your memory of this moment to permeate every cell of your being. Really live it inside, right here and now. Stand how you were standing, breathe how you were breathing, move how you were moving at the time. And once you've really connected to this energy of excitement and gratitude, take a moment to imagine a parallel moment for one of your characters in story. If you don't yet have a story with characters, or if your characters and story are YOU, start by simply writing the emotional truth of this moment as though it were a scene and you were writing about yourself.

For an extra challenge, write the same emotion into a scene, which stars a 7-year-old girl or a 90-year-old man. Drawing upon the same emotional wellspring, describe the circumstances of their lives and then lead them, in your own way, into a moment of unforeseen gratitude and excitement with the same resonance of that which you experienced. It's like laying the same base line beneath a different melody. When the notes are clear and true, the song will rise and reveal itself to you.

If you're having fun, try the same exercise with different emotions – with love, anger, hope, sadness, fear and courage. All of these we have experienced and many of them will rise up in our stories, so our task is simply to find our own personal reference points of truthful connection to the feeling and let that fill our cup and guide the way.

Beneath the external details of our own unique experience, there exists a stream of emotional truth that is shared by all. Knowing this, we have the capacity to connect, relate and write from a genuine sense of authenticity whether we are telling our own story or someone else's. This doesn't take away the need for real research and learning the 'rules' and details of the world we are writing about (particularly if it is not our own) but it does relieve us in most cases from trying to figure out how characters will react emotionally in a given moment. If we have taken time to get to know who *they* are, and we have a line of connection to our own emotional experience and similarity… and if we are willing to 'go there'… we can bring a sense of emotional truth to virtually every scene we write.

Enjoy the power of Going There Emotionally. It's a bit like Method Acting for writers, and it may surprise you how powerful it is. You just may find that it is the difference that makes the biggest difference in bringing the scenes of your story and steps of your hero to places of deep emotional truth for all to share.

> *"The credit belongs to the man who is actually in the arena, whose face is marred by dust and sweat and blood; who strives valiantly; who errs, who comes short again and again, because there is no effort without error and shortcoming; but who does actually strive to do the deeds; who knows great enthusiasms, the great devotions; who spends himself in a worthy cause; who at the best knows in the end the triumph of high achievement, and who at the worst, if he fails, at least fails while daring greatly, so that his place shall never be with those cold and timid souls who neither know victory nor defeat."*
> **–*Theodore Roosevelt***

Who Am I... Really?

"Reputation is what men and women think of us;
*character is what God and angels know of us." – **Thomas Paine***

*

There is a story of a lion cub whose parents were shot by poachers when he was only a few days old. Unaware of this tragic event, the young cub remained in the empty den for a day or so waiting to be fed, before eventually stumbling into an open field where he came upon a flock of sheep. He wandered among them, tiny and quite helpless, until he was eventually taken in by one of the female sheep who had recently lost one of her lambs... to a lion. The sheep mother's udders were full to the brim with milk, but without a young one of her own to feed, they were quickly becoming swollen and sore. So she offered them to the baby lion, he suckled away, and instantly a bond formed between them. The lion grew up with the flock as his family and naturally came to believe himself to be one of them. With no other frame of reference and no one to tell him otherwise, he was – as far as he could tell – a sheep, just like the others. Sure there were a few minor differences (the length and shape of his claws compared to their hooves, the growling and purring sounds of his voice compared to their "baahs", and his almost uncontrollable desire to chase birds, mice, crickets and pretty much anything else – including other sheep – that crossed his path when he was feeling playful... or hungry). But he never harmed another sheep in the flock, and he while did find himself at times staring out across the horizon with a sense of longing, yearning perhaps for something more, he could never quite pin point what that 'something more' might be, so he continued to grow up, quite convinced that whatever differences existed between he and the others in the flock were just little things that made him unique as the sheep that he was.

One day, an old male lion came into the area looking for food. Male lions rarely hunt alone (in fact they rarely hunt at all!), but occasionally they find themselves without a family and in need of fending for themselves. This lion had been a leader in his pride for many years, but recently a younger, stronger male had driven him out, so now he found himself on his own in search of food... and friendship. He was wounded and quite old, so he was grateful to come across the sheep, for he knew they were among the easiest to catch and kill. But as he positioned himself downwind and quietly approached the flock, he suddenly caught scent of what smelled to him like another lion... Could this be an ally to help in his hunt? Or perhaps a challenger to compete with in his quest to find himself a new pride? Sneaking up a bit closer, the old lion peered through the grass to discover a strangely unexplainable site... There in the plain light of day, an adolescent male lion was standing right in the middle of the sheep herd. What was strange about it was that none of the sheep seemed to notice… or even mind that he was there. Stranger still was the fact that the young lion seemed far more interested in chasing butterflies than hunting down any of the young lambs or sheep around him. Eventually the youngster did crouch down and pounce on a sheep about half his size, but he just as quickly pounced right off, revealing his desire was not in fact to eat the lamb, but simply to play with it!

Then the strangest thing of all happened. A hungry young hyena came into the area stirring the sheep into a frenzy. The hyena was nowhere near the size or strength of the young lion, but as the flock of sheep bolted across the field seeking refuge, the young lion was right there amidst them, cowering with his tail between his legs. This infuriated the lion elder, who could no longer sit back and watch this strange scene unfold, so he charged out into the field, giving forth a mighty roar. This sent the hyena running for the hills and caused all of the sheep to pick up the pace and bolt toward a thicket… All except for one.

The young lion had been frantically running with his wooly family, but something in that guttural roar struck a chord deep within him. As the flock scattered into the shelter of the thorny underbrush, the young lion stopped in his tracks and turned to face the elder.

The old one approached the youngster with stern scrutiny, circling him a few times to make sure that he was real, before nudging him in the scruff of his neck and leading him to a nearby waterhole. As the two approached the pool and stood beside each other, the young lion caught his first real glimpse of himself in the water's reflection. He was dwarfed in size by the elder, but there was no mistaking their likeness. In this moment he realized that he was not at all who he had thought himself to be. He had loved his sheep family dearly, but he had always felt somehow different. Now he knew why. Now he knew who he really was. While he surely had much to learn from the elder about what it meant to be a lion, he knew in this single moment by the waterhole that he could never again go back to being a sheep. He might become the first of his kind to protect instead of hunt those sheep (this perhaps he could teach the elder!), but he was a lion, there was no mistaking this. He was not put here to be fearful and to cower at the site of danger, but to stand in his power as the king of the land and to become all that he was truly born to be.

*

Of all the missions, quests, jobs, tasks and careers that one may choose to explore in life, perhaps the oldest and most enduring quest – through the ages and through various phases of our lives – is to simply, truly, "Know Thyself". Enshrouded by the fabric of our memories, relationships, beliefs, preferences, fears and aspirations, there is a deeper stirring, a yearning, to know a Self that exists beyond the specifics of our life circumstance. Beyond what we may currently perceive as possible. Beneath the surface of almost every activity and endeavor exists the fundamental question that each person (in life and story) must ultimately come to terms with... *WHO AM I?*

We may find ourselves tangled in relationships and situation that feel strangely misaligned, and we may talk ourselves into staying there, into staying small, into being other than who or what we truly came here to be. Our true essence may elude us for a time, but it will never go away. In the end, we cannot make a lion into a sheep. And when we catch a glimpse of our true being – through searching, quiet discovery or a mirror held up by a friend – a light comes on within us and begins to grow. This is the light of who we really are.

Many of our characters in story begin their journey with certain expectations of their own abilities and certain perceptions of their identity based on their current life in the ordinary world. When they cross the line into the extraordinary world of their journey, the rude awakening that, "This ain't Kansas anymore," may come as an initial shock to their system. But as their broken expectations give way to a willingness to experience things anew, they begin expand their ability to experience life in this new world... and in doing so they discover and awaken dormant capacities and aspects of themselves. Confronting pieces of who they always thought themselves to be, they make room for what and WHO is really ready to come through. In essence, this process of breaking down what appears to be, in order to discover a higher truth is what story, song and poetry is all about. We have been baptized by the fires of life and here we stand with a fresh view into the wellspring of our true self, ready to share what we've found. It is from this heightened state of being that our hero in story emerges from the Cave. It is from this state of being that all future action will be generated. This is a moment of true awakening for all of us in story and in life.

No matter what the nature of our writing may be, in order to ultimately arrive at our aspired outcome, we (and our characters) will almost always be required to expand our sense of Self along the way. We can change every action, effort and all that we are doing, but the most profound and lasting shifts will always come from a growth in who we are 'being'. So as we emerge from the Innermost Cave and prepare to cross back into the world with the torch of true discovery, the following enquiry is a fun and progressive exploration of the age-old question, "Who Am I?"

By taking time to deepen our connection to who we really are, we inevitably expand the possibilities of everything we do... and create!

I suggest that you first explore the enquiry below for yourself, simply answering spontaneously with each piece that comes up. Don't over-think it, just jump in and see where it takes you. When you're ready you can circle back and guide the characters of your stories through the same line of questioning...

WRITING EXERCISE:
WHO AM I?

OPENING PERSONAL VIEW: How would you describe yourself now? Describe what comes to mind when you consider your strengths and weaknesses, your gifts and passions... Your essence and your path... Who are you?

PUBLIC VIEW: When we watch a film story, one of the most powerful ways we get to know the characters (second only to how they act) is by what other people say about them. In fact we often initially trust what others say more than what the characters say about themselves. If we took a survey of the people you know, people who work with you and people who see you behind the scenes of life, how would they describe you? What would they say of your strengths and weaknesses, passions and gifts? What would they say about what you most have to learn? How would they describe you?

BIRD'S EYE VIEW: Understanding that different people see different sides of who we are, but that everyone is limited to their own unique perspective, what if we could rise above opinion and look down upon our personal identity with a more objective overview. Start by looking at the actions you take each day, the way you move, the way you interact with people and situations in the world. If we had a secret camera on you throughout the day, what would we see? How would we perceive you to be, based on your external actions and reactions in the world?

INNER BIRD'S EYE VIEW: Now look a little deeper and imagine that we have a similar bird's eye/secret camera view, but now we are watching your inner landscape – your thoughts, feelings, beliefs and inner dialogue on a given day. What would we see in here on a day-to-day, moment-to-moment basis? How does this internal world of you line up with – or contrast – the external life you are living? What is the inner bird's eye view of you?

STRIPPED BACK VIEW: Now put aside your current life roles – your family, friends, colleagues and social obligations. If you were pulled away completely from your current situation in life and plunked into a totally foreign community (perhaps washed up on an island and taken in by an indigenous culture) who knew nothing of your past or current reality, how would they describe you? What characteristics would they find endearing? What would they want to teach you? What gifts and skills would they recognize and seek to draw out in you?

CHILD'S VIEW: *Reaching back as far as you can into your childhood, what did you want to 'be when you grew up'? Why? What characteristics or qualities were appealing to you about that job or identity? If that child could see you now in your current life, how would s/he describe you? What would s/he love about your life? What might s/he strain to understand? What message or wisdom might s/he have for you?*

PARENT VIEW: *How would your parents have described you as a child? What gifts, potential and greater wishes did they have for you? How would they/do they see you now? What have they learned from you and what would they still love to teach you?*

THE HERO'S VIEW: *If you could see yourself and your life through the privileged eyes of your true and highest Self – someone who sees and believes in your unique, unlimited potential – what would you see? Imagine seeing through the eyes of someone who knows the journey you are on... someone who has walked this path to full, triumphant completion. Someone who knows your waking dreams and unspoken aspirations and sees them as realities waiting to be unfolded. Who are you in the eyes of one who sees all possibility, who knows your highest truth?*

WHO ARE YOU IN TRUE HEROIC FORM?
I AM...
Play with this, have fun with it... and I fully invite you <u>not</u> to hold back! The greatest challenge and first potent step to experiencing the fullness of who we are, is our willingness to dream it, to see it, to speak or write it into being. YOU are out there (in there) waiting for you to arrive, to claim your true heritage and step on through... When will now be the perfect time?

As we close this section and enquiry today, I invite you to think of a time when you have experienced this true heroic self in action in your life. Perhaps a moment where you were trying something new and caught a glimpse of what magic was awaiting you on the path ahead. Perhaps in a moment of deep soul searching where at the bottom of the well you discovered a golden spark of new possibility. Perhaps a climax moment when all the pieces of your journey came together. These breakthrough moments that often feel like fleeting miracles offer doorways not only to what is possible in the world, but what is called for within each of us. They are showing us a glimpse of the hero we really are. Pick a true I AM moment from your experience and take a few minutes to describe it here now.

We can explore the question of "Who am I?" from a myriad of angles and perspectives. They each give us insight into the ever-evolving make-up of our true character and allow us to open beyond our often-limited perspective to see the bigger picture of our path and journey. If we can connect at this level (or even close to it!) with the heartbeats of the subjects of our writing, the truth of who *they* are will naturally guide each story decision we have to make and permeate the page in ways that illuminate the hearts and minds of our readers. So be it.

Congratulations for completing Chapter 6 and the Innermost Cave of your *Writing the Story Within* journey! Take a deep breath, make yourself a cup of tea and we'll see you back here for Chapter 7 as we 'cross back' over into the ordinary world with the elixir of who we really are!

> *"You came into this life with your piece of the puzzle, and this world would not be complete without you and your contribution to the whole cosmic process...*
> *Yes, you do have a mission, and you can fulfill it only by being yourself."*
> **– John Randolph Price, The Jesus Code**

CHAPTER 7:

Crossing Back – Your Journey Home

Do not go where the path may lead,
go instead where there is no path and leave a trail.
– Ralph Waldo Emerson

The Power of Decisions

It is said that sometimes you have to lose yourself to find yourself. This is one of those ideas we often try to avoid on the path of both living and sharing our stories… but somehow it still seems to find us! And while the shadows of the forest path can certainly be a bit uncomfortable, when we are willing to follow the signs and keep taking steps, whatever loss and confusion we endure is almost always paid back in full with the gifts of what is found, discovered and claimed on the other side. In story, when our heroes enter the Innermost Cave, there may come moments when they (and we!) wonder if they will ever make it out. The challenges seem insurmountable. The hole they have often dug for themselves feels too deep to get out of. But in the center of this spiral, when all seems lost and our hero has come to a place of genuine surrender, somehow a spark of new possibility is lit from within… A clear and simple truth born inside of them that has a way of elevating their view and vision beyond all apparent conflict, back into the wide-open field of possibility. With this growing flame in hand, our hero has what s/he needs to rise from the Innermost Cave and Cross Back into their ordinary world with the power to transform it into an extraordinary place! This is the gift of where we now find ourselves on the story path, as we commence the Journey Home and rise in rapid form toward our story Climax.

*

About 18 months ago, my family and I felt a strong call to leave our home in Byron Bay, Australia and venture out for a time. We had loved living in the 'Shire' and could fully envision a long-term future there, but for a few reasons things just weren't really working. There was a growing schism between the life we came there to live and what we were actually experiencing. Particularly in our work, we had reached a space of stagnancy that made us feel that a genuine 'shaking of the tree' was needed.

We began entertaining the thought of moving over to the United States for a while. For Ash there was some official motivation around satisfying her US green card requirements, for 10-year-old Josh there was the prospect of adventure and friendships in a new land, and for me, there was a subtle sense of needing to reconnect with my roots and birth land… and with an entire world of people and experiences I had known as life prior to my arrival in Australia. I had left the US 17 years ago on what I thought would be a 1-year adventure on my bicycle and skis, and while we had been back to visit many times throughout the years, in a deeper sense, I had never really 'returned' from my trip. Not to live, anyway. Now almost two decades later, I realized there was within me a circle that had never fully been closed. A journey that had begun but never consciously finished. And a handful of friends who were still out there asking, "Hey, when's Chip coming back from his trip?" I had been in

Australia all this time –with cars and farms, my beautiful wife, son and animals of all sizes – but in some sense, I had never consciously resolved my life in the US… I had just kind of packed it in a box with my ski clothes and forgotten to look back. So as we were moving the boxes of our life around a bit anyway, I figured it might be a good time to take a good look inside.

While the clay of our US impulse was still quite wet and changeable, I put a call into Flight Centre to see what our options were. It just so happened they were having a nearly half price sale… which finished that afternoon!! Quite synchronistically, we had just received an unexpected chunk of money that fit the fares almost exactly, so within a few hours of sparking our initial vision, our plane tickets were purchased and we were starting to pack!

Our aim was to have all the essential pieces (car, home, work projects, school, etc…) fully organized before arriving to the US, but in the end it took almost all of our energy just to tie up life in Australia in time to leave. And while on one hand the whole concept of moving continents seemed quite outlandish (literally), every time we paused to ask, "What exactly are we doing?" another piece of the puzzle seemed to appear. It was as though each single step we took was matched by an open door of equal measure, so we just kept taking simple steps, right up until the moment we climbed on the plane – out of breath, with only an inkling of where we were heading.

Normally when we fly into the States we go first to LA, but for reasons I am just now beginning to appreciate, the tickets we purchased for this particular trip, brought us straight to the San Francisco Bay area, the hometown of my birth.

I had received a call from my old college roommate about a week before we arrived with an offer to help him start a new business in the Bay, so we landed with a certain sense of purpose. But when my buddy's business deal unexpectedly fell through about two days after our arrival, we found ourselves feeling lost in what now seemed to be a foreign land.

America is an amazing blend of both dreamers and of doers. There are enough people to support the most peculiar niche, and for every idea that's sprung from the consciousness, there seems at least 12 varieties to choose from. That goes for everything from cereal brands to flavors of Kambucha mushroom tea. As a visitor, it's like a giant buffet with infinite tastes and textures to choose from. As a new arrival seeking to make clear life choices and find the best place to BE… it can be dizzying to say the least.

Even in the surf town of Santa Cruz, 2 hours south of the city – where we thought we'd find a slightly larger version of all that we loved about Byron Bay – we found ourselves feeling tangled in a labyrinth of elusive paths, confusing variables and traffic.

So much traffic. Finally, after several weeks of digging and searching, trying to match our hopes and skills with people, projects, places to live and schools for Josh – a stroke of synchronistic surrender lead us to a home in the redwoods 30 minutes out of town. Josh could walk to the local elementary school and Ash and I could take some time to figure out what to do next. A highly entertaining film may one day be written about the next few months of our journey, but suffice to say, events played out very true-to-form with the 'Tests and Allies' phase of the hero's path we were living. We made some great breakthroughs, discoveries and a few new friends, but overall it felt like we were standing on a giant hot plate and someone was gradually turning up the heat. I made repeated trips up to the city to explore projects and opportunities, but each was like a mirage... shining from afar, but evaporating as soon as I got close enough to see what was really there. We were grateful for our home in the trees, but we sensed that it was just a stopping place, a perch to gather courage for the next step. Our financial reserves were running dangerously low and I knew that if we wanted to stay in America much longer, we needed to find something more solid to commit to. In the absence of any external opportunities in what I had always thought of as the 'land of opportunities', I realized what we really needed to commit to was OURSELVES.

I had launched a new online program the previous year in Australia called Moving Mountains (a month long hero's journey experience for the SELF), and it was coming around again in a few months. So as we reached the energetic 'Mid-point' of our journey, we crossed the Point of No Return by committing to stay at least long enough to launch the second annual Moving Mountains program to a new level in the States. With that idea came an almost instant impulse to move north to Ashland, Oregon, where we knew we had close friends and a creative team ready to work with us. Within about 15 minutes of thinking this thought, we had found a great house online in our favorite part of town. And within two weeks, we arrived in Ashland with our psycho kitten Princess and a U-haul moving truck full of furniture we'd acquired in Santa Cruz.

As soon as we landed in this little mountain hamlet, things started to fall into place in a whole new way. And as per the rising tempo of this phase of story, things also began to accelerate. The stakes were higher (we were now launching a business) but our energy and clarity of focus rose to match. The next few months unraveled in a positive blur with bold new 'mountains moved' (the Moving Mountains program went great, with people chiming in from all over the world), unique new friendships formed, enchanted schools discovered and an overall sense of settling into the creation of a good feeling life in the States.

But amidst this babbling brook of positive new experience, remained an inner feeling that this too was a temporary stop on the road. It was as though we were placed here on assignment, on a 'need-to-know' basis, and the details of where-to-next were only revealing themselves through our connection to the present moment. We had pushed our one-year plane tickets out to the very last possible day of departure and we found ourselves somewhat tormented with the question of do we stay and continue building a long-term life here in the US or do we return to Australia and truly claim it as our home. For as long as we had lived there, we had always wondered if maybe we should be somewhere else. We had traveled extensively, and while each new land had woven new golden thread into the fabric of our being, we were all feeling a yearning to put a stake in the ground, to simplify, to be willing to stop and truly say, "This is home."

During the month prior to our scheduled departure we began to search deeply into our lives and our hearts to feel the highest path. Each day was like a tennis match of pros and cons – with new possibilities emerging every step – and while I could feel a deep inner calling within Asheyena to have her feet once again on Australian soil we both felt somewhat tormented by a feeling that this journey was not yet fully complete. But with non-refundable tickets pulsing just around the corner, and a sense of unease about letting them go… we came to what felt like a stalemate. We had exhausted every angle and still the path was unclear.

One afternoon we were walking along the river in our favorite park just out of town. As we contemplated what seemed like irreconcilable variables, the river we walked along revealed to me a path I had not yet considered… Watching the single current come to a section of land where it divided temporarily around a small island, before reconnecting just a short way down the path, suddenly I saw a new option. Before I had a chance to second-guess it, I spouted it out loud as we walked. "What if you and Josh go back to Australia on a 'scouting mission', and I stay here for a short time to tie things up and wait for final clarity to settle in?"

We are a very tight family and definitely prefer to move as one, so this was a strange option and not one that we had considered. But for some reason the river made me feel a sense of calm about it… as though there were pieces in the US that still needed to be collected, and this path would allow important pieces to unfold. Perhaps in time we would know why. Similar to our 'Midpoint' decision to move up to Oregon, this impulse brought another burst of acceleration, and within a week I was dropping the rest of the Richards pod off at the San Francisco airport, saying goodbye to my own plane ticket and trusting that as soon as all was clear we would have the power to do what needed to be done next!!!

When I returned to Oregon that night and stepped into our hollow-feeling home, I realized where I was really stepping was into my own Innermost Cave. Strangely, I got the sense that when Asheyana and Josh landed back in Australia, they too would be stepping into theirs!

I have now been here a week on my own and feel as though I have been partially living my life and partially watching my experiences within my own private hero's journey cinema. Each day I have stepped a bit deeper into the cave of my own self-exploration and each night as I connect with Ash, I hear her words on the other side of the world doing the same. Seeking for truth within herself. Drifting off to sleep in different lands, we both listen for the quiet truthful whisper calling us HOME.

As the days pass I begin to understand why I have felt a sense of division in myself about whether to be here in the US or in Australia… it is quite simply because I now have DNA in both lands. Family and tribe in both lands. History and memory in both lands. Blood, tears and laughter in both lands. I have felt pressure to make a decision to be in one place or the other, but in a deeper sense there will always be a part of me in both. There will always be things and people that I love in both places. As I begin to relax into this realization, I suddenly see myself not as a locked-in inhabitant of one or the other, but as a bridge between the two. An ambassador for the global village we are all moving toward in a greater sense. This is quite a liberating feeling, but with it comes another realization that carries a focused urgency. I have been spending my days in the trees and rivers, falling more and more in love with the surrounding lands of Ashland, but when I come back to the house in the evening it feels empty and sterile. It no longer feels like a home because my family is not here to share it with me. The bedroom is too hollow to sleep in, so I set up a mattress on the back deck under the stars where at least I'm reminded of camping out with Josh. I may be a global citizen, but my home, my true home is wherever my family is. What I want now more than anything is to build a home sanctuary where we can pour our love for each other directly into the land. To build a foundation for sustainable living that others can share in and learn from. And with this realization it comes to me that while being in the US has served a great purpose in completing the circle I begun 17 years ago, in reconnecting with dear loved ones, in planting seeds and building pillars of alliance for years to come, now it is time to cultivate the soil for a physical home base from which we can all thrive in coming years. A base to grow food pathways for others to come and share.

I scan my heart across the globe to feel where this may be and in the same way that we felt called to leave the safety of the 'Shire' about 18 months ago… I suddenly feel in my heart that it is calling us back. As I drop into this realization here in the pine trees and mountain streams of Oregon, unbeknownst to me, Asheyana and Josh have been doing the same in the clear ocean waters of Australia… and suddenly the path forward becomes clear to us all.

Writing these words today, I now have one week to complete my draft of this book, sell our car and much of our furniture, send boxes of what we love back to Australia and find a temporary home for our kitty. On one hand it feels like a big stretch, maybe an *impossible stretch for the normal rhythms of life. But this is not a normal moment. This is a leaping from the cave moment. A Crossing Back moment. And while I predict that I will sleep very little in the coming days… I know there is an energy now coursing through me, rising in me, propelling my actions into a focused direction that was not there before. There is a fire that has been ignited from my time of reflection, and now as we anchor our decision to return with full commitment to Australia, I will do so with a grounded sense of determination. With clarity of purpose and a knowing that for every bold step I take, the path will rise to meet me. Knowing that this moment was always going to come, where the elixir of our journey would motivate our return in the deepest sense, the truest sense, to who we truly are and all that we came here to be in the world. I will embrace my remaining time here on this great land, savoring sweet moments with my brothers and parents… taking the time to properly close the circle I opened many years ago, knowing that in doing so I am freeing up tremendous energy for a whole new journey to begin. Here we go!!!*

*

As we follow the path of story from beginning to the end, there will always be several key moments that call for new levels of growth, clarity and decisive action. Moments that require conscious decisions to step into foreign territory and commit further to our path. The way our heroes and characters respond to what comes at them, the decisions they make and the actions that stem from those decisions, ultimately dictate the flow of their journey and their destiny in the story. And while their direction may shift and turn many times throughout the tale, if we look at the archetypal form of story as a whole, we will find that most stories hinge on the power of three or four major decisions. Like support posts of a great story bridge, these moments of key decision making lead progressively from one to the next and act as pillars to hang much of the story's action upon. As an audience we are drawn to these moments of decision because they speak to our own call for clarity in the way we arrive at and commit to key decisive moments in our life.

In the first phase of our story, our hero will almost always be required to make a blind faith (often reactionary) decision simply to answer the Call to Adventure and Cross the Threshold into the extraordinary world of their journey (also known as Turning Point #1). At our Midpoint, or point of true commitment, they must make a more consciously aware and responsible decision to burn the bridges of their past and stay on the path… to commit to seeing their quest through to completion. Several story beats later, as stakes rise and our heroes emerge from the Innermost Cave with the Elixir of their true Self, they must make a third decision. One that is based on absolute clarity and conviction. Their first decision put them onto the path quite blindly, the second key decision kept them there with a sense of determination. Here at our moment of Crossing Back (also known as Turning Point #2), our hero's decision must come from a place of deep inner knowing and authentic, 'generative' empowerment. I say generative, because from this decision our hero will be required *generate* a whole new possibility into existence.

Whatever stakes have risen since the Midpoint, whatever challenge now faces our hero as s/he draws toward the Climax of the journey, it will call for a level of focused, committed, creative action that will stretch them (and us) way beyond anything they have ever experienced. From the depths of their Innermost Cave our hero made a decision, and here in the Crossing Back, they will begin to physically express the power of that choice in the world.

As we emerge from the Cave and step on the path of what Joseph Campbell called 'The Road Home', the notion of 'Show, Don't Tell' (discussed in Chapter 5) becomes particularly relevant, not only for us writers, but for the heroes of our stories. In every great story there is a moment where the hero must come to a deep and transformative realization about who they are and what is most important to them. Here our hero's realization is put into action. Often bold action, well beyond what our hero may have even thought of doing in the past. The reason this action must be so bold is because it must fully reflect the internal breakthrough our hero made in the Cave, *and* it must be strong enough to match and rise above the power of the challenges at hand. Everything our hero has learned on the journey must now be harvested in viewable, tangible, physical form. This Crossing Back moment will catapult our hero into a rapid ascent toward the story Climax (Chapter 8!). But it all starts here with the power of a simple, empowered, expansive decision. Actually, it started with a deep internal discovery in the heart of the Innermost Cave (Chapter 6), and what we are now seeing is the first outward expression of what was gathered there.

In Chapter 4, we introduced a story moment called the 'Early Win' that often comes for our heroes shortly after they have stepped on the path. This moment here – our crossing back moment – often comes as a direct 'payoff' to the Early Win. For example, in *Avatar*, Jake Sully's Early Win comes amidst a pleading argument with warrioress Netyri, when hundreds of tiny seeds from the sacred tree float down and land on him, giving us all a 'sign' that Jake is not just another human in a big blue body… he is somehow special and will play an important role amongst the Navi people. When Jake emerges from his Innermost Cave of banishment from both the Navi and the Marines following the devastating destruction of Home Tree, he comes with a clear focused decision that he must do whatever is possible to save the sacred world of Pandora. This decision catalyzes an idea and line of thinking within Jake that is way beyond all preconceived limits… AND it's perhaps the only idea that would give him a chance at full redemption. Jake telegraphs this moment to us, the audience, when he says, "Sometimes your whole life comes down to one insane moment," as he leaps off the back of his banshee dragon onto the back of Taruk, the biggest, most feared and formidable beast in all of Pandora. Jake's dialogue is a textbook description of our Crossing Back moment, and the absurd extremity of his action fits perfectly with the theme of this phase of our hero's path. Extreme times call for extreme measures and if ever there was a moment for our characters to take bold, decisive action, this is it. Our Crossing Back moment is a declaration of our hero's commitment to doing the right thing at all costs. Anything short of pure embodied truth will simply not be enough to achieve the impact necessary to do what must be done. Anything more than this and – at least in Jake Sully's case – our hero would likely die in the process of trying.

Decision inspires vision. Vision infuses action. Action aligned with vision, creates miracles. It is said that miracles are the most natural expression of who we really are. And miracles are what are often needed at this moment of the story for our hero. There can be no half steps, no partial truths, no hidden agendas or hesitancy. Here is the moment to express all that has been learned acquired (and more) in one clear decisive action that will shift the tides and enable our characters to move with great power and clarity toward the Climax of their journey.

By tapping into the nature of DESIRE (Chapter 3), we connected with the inner wants and needs of our characters. As our characters begin to take steps toward that desire we came into contact with the nature of CONFLICT (Chapter 4) and what elements (internal, external and intimate) may rise 'against' or stop our heroes from reaching their desire. In Chapter 5, we added STAKES to the mix, turning the heat up to create a primal and progressively building story fire. In Chapter 6, we stripped our heroes of all that they'd gained so far, in order to lead them into the Innermost Cave and the emotional center of their journey. And while these moments of deep searching and even deeper digging can appear as painful and impossibly difficult for our hero, what we ultimately discover is that whatever crisis or challenge they are thrown into is just the perfect match to light the torch of their greatest Self discovery. In this light, even the most antagonizing forces can be see to be working on behalf of the greater good of our characters. Even the most powerful 'bad guy' or greatest fear is ultimately a doorway to the hero's greatest gift.

Once this gift has been claimed by our hero, the next and final step is to bring it back to the world s/he came from. The road ahead may not be easy – in fact it will most likely challenge our hero and all of their allies in ways they have never experienced before, but here on the path there is clarity. And with clarity there is power. Now is the point of full return. The Crossing Back has begun.

THE WRITER'S JOURNEY HOME

On the writing path, this moment of decisive, empowered action can be an incredibly powerful driving force in our work… and it can be a little tricky to come to. When you are working on a project that requires daily effort and consistent, disciplined focus, it can be easy, over time to lose some of the creative fire or luster for the piece. You may have pushed past the Point of No Return and proclaimed your commitment with great focused effort, but by the time you hit that three-quarters mark, it sometimes feels like you enter a sort of 'no-mans-land' where you can almost smell the finish, but there's still a considerable amount of ground to cover. This is a dangerous place to hang out for too long (a bit like hanging around in the Innermost Cave for too long), because it's here that almost-finished projects can quite easily be placed aside in favor of that sparkly new idea that's just surfaced. It can be quite alluring to think that maybe this project just needs some breathing space. Don't be fooled… this three-quarters-finished place is a place of clear, decisive action. And if it feels a bit flat, like you're waiting for someone or something to inject the moment with a bit of fire and momentum, what you will discover is that who you are really waiting for here is YOU. You have journeyed this far, which in and of itself is a huge achievement. Now is your time to take a breath, call for help if need be, and write yourself across the line. Harvest the power of all that you have learned and discovered so far on the path. Harness the clarity that comes from reflection. Honor the gifts that you came here to share and step boldly onto the Road Home.

WRITING EXERCISE:
THE POWER OR DECISION (YOU AND YOUR HERO)

Step 1 – Consider a time of searching in your life, where through introspection or external pressures, you were lead to a moment of clear and empowered decision. A moment of deep inner conviction that came from within and propelled you into bold and decisive action. Write about the moments leading up to your decision and describe the energy in your actions that lead from it. How did your clarity of focus and the decision you made influence the power and commitment of your steps on the path? What extraordinary actions emerged and how did they impact your world?

Step 2 – Consider the deep discovery that you and/or your hero came to in your Innermost Cave moment in the previous chapter. What would be the ultimate outward expression of that internal breakthrough? What is the most extraordinary action you could imagine taking to demonstrate your (or your hero's) deepest inner truth? Write a simple scene describing this action.

Step 3 – As a writer and a storyteller, now three-quarters of the way through your Writing the Story Within experience, what decision could you make this week that would completely alter or transform your approach to your writing for the better? What clear commitment could you make to yourself, that in following through courageously, you will chart a path of great creative breakthrough and service to the stories that want to come through you? Write what comes for you and prepare to act boldly in the direction of your highest committed clarity.

Now is the time of Crossing Back!

"If the light in your life has changed to yellow, I recommend you floor it.
It's safer than the alternative."
– Jeb Dickerson

"Freedom lies in being bold."
– Robert Frost

When Bad is Good

Beyond the realms of right and wrong there is a field. I will meet you there.
– Rumi

*

There was a farmer who cared obsessively about two things… his son and his Donkey. Having lost his wife in years previous, the farmer's son and his donkey were the last living beings in the farmer's life. One he loved beyond measure as his closest (and only) living relative and the other he relied on exclusively for his livelihood as a farmer.

One night a great storm came through the farmer's valley, blowing open the stable gates. The driving wind and rain frightened the farmer's donkey, causing it to bolt off into the mountains. Upon discovering this the following morning, the farmer was distraught beyond words. Who would till the soil? Who would carry the grain and pull the cart into town with their crops to sell at the market? The farmer felt cursed and thought that surely his life would be ruined.

Two days later as the weather cleared, the donkey returned, and with it, it brought four wild horses. A great stallion and three breeding mares. The farmer was thrilled beyond words. Now he would be able to expand his crops and grow his livelihood in ways that he never dreamed possible for himself and his son. He felt very blessed.

Two weeks later, the farmer's son was training the stallion and the boy fell off the horse's back, breaking his leg on impact. "What a tragedy!" thought the farmer. The boy would be unable to walk for weeks and wouldn't be able to play with his friends or help out on the farm. What could he and his son have done to deserve this terrible injury and misfortune? The farmer had no clear answer… and again, he felt cursed.

A week later, the farmer's country went to war and all the young men were drafted to go off and fight. Because of his broken leg, the farmer's son was left behind and spared from fighting in a battle that ended up taking the lives of many. The farmer was grateful beyond measure. His son was safely at home where he belonged, and would be well enough to help tend the crops and care for the horses. Once again, the farmer felt greatly blessed.

And the story continues…

*

This Zen story can be told in a few different ways, but in essence it demonstrates our tendency to attach meaning, feeling and judgment to the events and experiences of our lives. To see and judge things at face value – as good or bad, positive or negative – based on the immediate short-term, isolated impact on our life.

To me, this story demonstrates two things (well, more than two but we'll start here). Firstly, it shows us that things are not always as they seem, that the tide is always shifting, the wheel is always turning and that sometimes (most times) what appears as a challenge, flaw or crisis, is actually the doorway to a new possibility. Sometimes what seems like a dead end or the very worst thing that could ever happen, is actually the very best thing – in disguise.

The other thing that this story demonstrates is that the general flow of life's currents is always, whether we realize it or not, moving life-ward… moving in the direction of positive becoming. Like the river is always moving toward the ocean, we too are always moving one way or another toward our ultimate union with our own limitless Source. Sometimes the river rushes, sometimes it falls, sometimes it seems to stay still for a while… but it is always moving, always seeking to draw us where we need to go in order to BE that which we truly came here to be.

As a storyteller in the modern world with a desire to deliver positive messages to the masses, it can be easy to shy away from the extremes of the ebb and flow in the river. But what we need to realize, is that the journey to get there, and the steps that our heroes must take along the way – through the veil of what may 'seem' bad, scary or negative, into the open field beyond – is a great and powerful gift not only to our hero but also to our readers and viewers. It shows them that life is not always as it seems and that if we are willing to suspend judgment long enough to see what's on the other side of a seemingly challenging moment, we will almost always find ourselves uncovering an unexpected treasure, gift or doorway of new possibility.

The Chinese character above is the symbol used for the word 'crisis'. It is actually made up of two separate symbols put together. The first symbol means 'danger' and second symbol means 'opportunity'. In story this is truly how crisis is experienced by our heroes. Yes, it will push them beyond what they ever thought possible – but in truth, isn't going *beyond what they thought was possible* what they want anyway?!

When we are open to discovering the good within the bad, and empowering our heroes to genuinely move through conflict and rising stakes to find their higher path, we cut a trail for every reader and viewer to see how this may also be possible in their own life. If the story is truthful and compelling, when the audience watches the hero emerge from the Innermost Cave with fire in his eyes and a torch in his hand, they are not really only watching the hero… they are watching the possibility of themselves in areas of challenge within their own lives. They take the emotional breakthrough of that scene and placing it like a filter over their own experience. As we show them what our hero must do to claim his centre and find his way home, our audience begins to envision and forge a path for themselves. By discovering the gift within apparent conflict, we may all learn to begin trusting life a little more… to let go of our tendency to attach labels of good and bad or to judge things at face value, so that we may recognize the reflection of higher truth that rests at the center of all things, drawing us ever closer to our own truth and higher connection to Source.

The martial art of Aikido talks about this notion in its philosophy to 'accept the hit as a gift', recognizing that the striking force coming at us from our attacker is neither bad nor good, it is simply energy. Energy that can be aligned with and channeled in positive directions if we know how to work with it. In this sense, the greater the energy coming at us, the greater the capacity to transform that energy into good.

When I first really got this, it completely transformed my perception not only of story, but also of the challenging people and situations in my own life. Suddenly I began to recognize even the toughest situations and individuals as invitations for me to find a way to find and harness the good. Imagine if the whole world thought this way! Suddenly great crisis and challenge on all levels – environmental, societal, government, etc. – could be seen as our greatest doorways of opportunity to truly rise up into the heroes we all came here to be. Perhaps that is what's happening and as storytellers we have the gifted role of helping to pave the way.

As we catapult ourselves in the direction of our story Climax, one way to infuse our characters' steps along the path is to ask the following two questions:

"What's the very worst thing that could happen?"

"How could that actually be the very best thing?"

WRITING EXERCISE:
WHAT'S THE WORST THING THAT COULD HAPPEN?
(AND HOW COULD THAT BE THE VERY BEST?)

Think of a time in your life (or in the life of one of your characters) and consider the above questions. Consider a moment when something happened that felt like a major crisis. A seemingly insurmountable obstacle, challenge, diversion or stumbling block… Something that you never would have consciously wished for… in fact you would have done anything in your power to avoid it. But moving through, somehow this crisis lead to a positively unexpected breakthrough and bold new experience on your path. This could be a big life changing moment, or it could just be a simple thing. It could be something from the past, or a moment in your current reality that is in the process of transforming before your very eyes.

Spend some time writing about this event in your past or present circumstances that seemed or seems like the worst thing that could possibly happen. Then, look at how this negative experience could actually be seen as the very best thing that could happen. Move through the journey to see what gifts await on the other side when we choose to keep our eyes open to both the danger and the opportunity within life's apparent crises.

I am struck by how important storytelling is among tribal peoples; it forms the basis of their educational systems. The Celtic peoples, for example, insisted that only the poets could be teachers. Why? I think it is because knowledge that is not passed through the heart is dangerous: it may lack wisdom; it may be a power trip; it may squelch life out of the learners. What if our educational systems were to insist that teachers be poets and storytellers and artists?
What transformations would follow?
– **Matthew Fox**

When Less is More

"Writing a story or a novel is one way of discovering sequence in experience, of stumbling upon cause and effect in the happenings of a writer's own life."
– Eudora Welty

During a recent *Writing the Story Within* mentorship program, one of the participants sent a great question in response to our lesson on The Power of Detail (Chapter 5), wondering how do we know when it's too much? The following is her question and my answer, which comes at a perfect time on our path here. Just as specific details offer a valuable key to giving our writing a genuine heartbeat and grounded connection, there is a point where description can become an obstacle to that very same sense of connection we are seeking (too much of a good thing...!). As we 'Cross Back' over the threshold and prepare to race toward the Climax of our journey (Chapter 8), we need to be able to travel light and move fast. Unencumbered by excess energy or even details in our descriptions. The following is one student's question and my somewhat detailed response!

QUESTION: *How do we know when it's too much description? I used to watch children paint at kindergarten and they painted the most magnificent things but then they would add one little bit too much paint and the whole thing turned into a blob of mud on the paper. How can we describe the things we want in detail without going overboard?*

ANSWER: This is quite a subjective question that would yield different answers depending on who you asked, but in my opinion you just about answered the question in the asking...

As a parent watching a child paint, you can sort of sense when the painting is complete, at least in your eyes. But of course we each have a different sense of the sense of completion. Your might think the painting's finished and your child is just getting started. Maybe she's going for a deeper shade of textured mud than has ever been created on canvas before. It's a bit like decorating a house – how many nick-knacks, pictures and lampshades do you need before you start overloading or taking away from the ambiance of the room? The Zen minimalist will have a different answer than Grandma. Digressions aside, the bottom line with your writing is that you want to have just enough detail to make the moment real and penetrating, but not so much that it draws our attention away from the moment itself as we try to process all the words. In my experience, if you are open to it, you can usually *feel* when enough is enough.

In the film-writing world, where the form leans well in the direction of the Zen minimalist, LESS is almost always MORE. A good screenplay draft is almost a bizarre form of poetry. It's like the blueprint of a house, with only the most necessary lines included, that somehow still manages to deliver all the right energy and impact for the builders (or, in this case, filmmakers) to follow. What a novelist might take 3-5 paragraphs (or pages) to say, the screenwriter often has to do in 3-5 words or a single line. Particularly when drafting a 'reading draft' of a script (the one you'll give to the actors and studios to get them involved in the project), you have to find a way to deliver maximum depth and power while keeping that thing light and moving. "Less is More" becomes the path.

I remember attending a Robert McKee Story seminar in Sydney during the early drafting stages of my first feature film. I remember hearing Robert say that when all was said and done and the story had been effectively refined, every single word in the finished screenplay would be handpicked and chosen deliberately. If you chose to use the word "the" in a sentence, it was because that word "the" was absolutely essential to the story at that exact point. Nothing extra. Nothing wasted. I remember thinking, "OK Robert, now we're going a little overboard." But low and behold, I can still remember combing through the final shooting script several months later and quite literally pulling out single words like "the" and "a" when they got in the way of a smooth and potent read. I remember looking at our final page-count and being shocked to see how much we had culled things back. We lost a few gems along the way, but overall, each time we put ourselves through this process we were left with a better read.

I have always enjoyed descriptive writing, so I used to find it excruciating to write these meaningful, in-depth sections in my early drafts, only to have them shaved down to a basic haiku in the end. But as I settled into the craft I learned there is also a power in brevity, and I have found my own way of balancing the flow so that I'm free to write the way I naturally write without ultimately perceiving it as a waste of time. Even now, I often give myself the luxury of deliberately over-writing the first draft of a piece. I write everything that comes to mind and wants to come through about a person or a moment, and then once it's all out on the page, I give myself the challenge of honing the essence of the entire page into one or two lines that somehow say the same thing. If done well it doesn't feel like a compromise, but rather a concentrated, full-dose version of the original. The marrow of a bone.

What may start as a page-long description about a big tough guy walking into the room, ends up as quite simply, "He was built like a brick house with a cast iron face and hands the size of bowling balls," or something like that.

The goal is to find a way to be both very specific and also very economical. To this end, I find metaphors and similes to be particularly powerful in getting the most out of "Less is More" descriptions. When we compare one thing to something else, it provides a springboard for our mind to leap forward and then fill in the blanks. What kind of guy has a cast iron face? Instantly you are sent on a journey into your own experience and perception of cast iron and faces and where those two items may have met in your own life – or not. By drilling into these little descriptive nuggets you're both providing concrete detail and giving your reader a great gift... the opportunity to interpret your words and make them their own.

So the key is to use just enough detail to bring us to the absolute center of why we are here, but no more. It's a balancing act and a sliding scale that is constantly fluctuating. You might have a sentence or two of deep specifics and then open it up with a couple of very short, even one-word sentences. Then back into the more detailed focus again. I like to vary the rhythm and flow of my descriptions like this to let them breathe and open new spaces in the minds of the reader. You will find your own rhythm too.

Often, as I described above, it can be helpful to give yourself the opportunity to begin with no limits, describing every detail to its tiniest microcosmic form... using this detail to bring *yourself* to that center place of really knowing what you are writing about. And then once you are there and you have it all laid out on the page – no stone left unturned – you can begin to comb back through with your highlighter, refining, honing and focus your thoughts around the ones that pack the most punch. Not diffusing the power or energy of your description, but focalizing it. Allowing the elegant solution or perfect metaphor that somehow says it all to emerge... in just a few words.

Sometimes it will take me a whole page or more to write myself into clarity, and only by the last sentence or two will I really drop into the heart of the matter. Even if all the other words end up on the cutting room floor, and all I use is the very last sentence, it will have been worth it if that sentence really sings. If I don't get to that centerpiece nugget, then no amount of descriptive words will be enough. We know our description is too much when it's used to talk around an idea without ever bringing us to the core.

So have fun with your description. Go for it and let it flow freely onto the page. Then take a deep breath or two and come back fresh, honing into the essence of what you are really trying to say. Give yourself the challenge to refine it into a single crystallized nugget and that will leave you room for those sections that may need a bit more length or space to breathe.

WRITING EXERCISE:
WHEN LESS IS MORE

Try this today... Step into your world (or the world of your story) and pick a person or character to focus your attention on. Reflect upon all of their attributes (inside and out), their history, their present circumstance and their dreams and aspirations. Allow whatever descriptive words or sentences come to you to flow upon the page. Give yourself several minutes to write with no limits... describe this person in as much detail as you can. Who they are, how they dress, what they look like, what they love, what they do and how they do it.

When you're done with your initial outpouring, step away for a few minutes and allow the words to settle. Then when you're ready, come back and begin to comb through and identify the words and phrases that stand out the very most for you... drill into the essence of what those words really mean to you, and allow yourself to begin culling back the rest... For the purpose of this exercise, see if you can hone your descriptions down to a single sentence or Zen-like expression – while faithfully capturing the essence of your character. You may not get every detail, but if you are true to the core energy of your character and willing to think outside the square, you will likely emerge with a single sentence that not only gives us a unique and genuine glimpse of the core of our character, but it leaves us eager to find out more.

"Storytelling reveals meaning without committing the error of defining it."
– Hannah Arendt

"Don't tell fish stories where the people know you;
but particularly, don't tell them where they know the fish."
– Mark Twain

When Yin Meets Yang
The Balance of Stillness and Action

"So divinely is the world organized that every one of us, in our place and time,
is in balance with everything else."
– Johann Wolfgang von Goethe

In Asian philosophy, the concept of **yin yang** (or 'yin and yang' as we call it in the West) is used to describe how polar opposites or seemingly contrary forces are often interconnected and interdependent. Light and darkness, night and day, ebb and flow, sun and moon, birth and death, summer and winter. Yin and yang are complementary opposites that interact within a greater whole, each playing its part in the dynamic rhythm and natural system of life. As one quality reaches its apex, it naturally begins to transform and give rise to the opposite quality. As the sun reaches its peak each day (yang), it begins its descent toward the horizon triggering the rising of the moon (yin) on the other side. As the seedling rises from the earth into full fruition (yang) in the height of summer, it will then produce seeds and begin to die back in time for winter (yin). Yang is thought to encompass the male qualities of logic, outward expression and movement in the world, while yin represents the feminine qualities of intuition, receptivity and stillness. Yang is doing. Yin is being.

While our Western cultures like to categorize the light and dark side of objects and experiences as positive or negative, right or wrong (and then do everything we can to avoid the dark/negative/wrong parts!), the philosophy of yin yang is less judgmental and more inclusive of the whole. It doesn't see these two polar opposites as separate rivaling forces, but as two sides of the same coin. Two essential, co-existing parts of the same overall picture. We cannot have a wave without a trough. We cannot have action without rest. Everything has both yin and yang aspects, and while yin or yang elements may manifest more strongly in different objects or at different times, they are in truth constantly interacting, never existing in absolute isolation.

In recent times, our modern Western world has become increasingly yang-driven. Technology that perhaps was initially designed to give us more time has instead created more pressure to perform faster and do more in fewer hours. The treadmill is moving at ever-increasing speeds and the majority of the Western world feels great pressure to keep up. So much so that it often takes some sort of unexpected event to stop us in our tracks and force us to take a genuine breath of yin back into our system. Sometimes we can delay the shift from yang to yin for a certain amount of time – talking ourselves into days, months or even years of one track yang-focused effort – but eventually, if we are not conscious of bringing balance into our own world, our world will find a way to bring balance back to us.

We all know the feeling of being out of balance in one direction or the other (feeling overwhelmed by our intuitive inspirations with little or no outward follow-through OR feeling over-run by task and action, with little regard for the more subtle rhythms and messages of life). Some people get a cold or the flu right on the tail end of a highly focused project. Some people get a major injury as soon as they retire from their life-long career. In my world as a rising athlete, it took two major surgeries (plus a minor one) to slow down my yang focus and begin recalibrating my yin. The Universe is happy to provide whispers when it's time to shift from yang to yin (or back again), but if we do not heed the call, it will eventually start speaking a little louder.

As writers we can at times feel stuck on one side of the yin yang balance or the other... We may either spend too much time in the yin of our creations – reflecting, receiving, dreaming and quietly churning without following through and expressing these inspired visions on the page (for example when we have no external pressures or deadlines to push us) – or we may shift into our yang (perhaps brought on by pressures in the professional world) and push through with our outward expressions, doing and creating without taking time to fully tune in to our deeper creative wellsprings. While bursts of pure yin and pure yang may at times be required in every project or creative endeavor, in the long run, our greatest work will never come from an isolated expression of one without the other. The ultimate balance comes when we allow the natural flow of these two vital forces to work in confluence with each other... Intuiting and reflecting at our deepest levels (yin), then boldly acting and following through with commitment and outward perseverance (yang).

THE YIN AND YANG OF STORY

Just as the energies of yin and yang must find their greater balance in our life, the same is true in the lives of our characters and the stories they express. In a general sense, our stories must always find a balance between more inward reflective scenes/moments and outwardly expressive scenes, between the moments that challenge and the moments that nurture our characters, between moments of positive growth and expansion and moments of pulling back and dying to what used to be. Moments of newfound intimacy meet moments of solitude and separation. Running meets resting. Speaking meets silence. Yang meets Yin.

In the structure of our story, we will find we have a general flow between scenes that are more yin-based and scenes that are more yang, often alternating one to the other. Most scenes or sequences will carry a dominant charge of either yin or yang, and will usually be followed by a scene or sequence of the opposite charge. As writers we want to be conscious of this, creating powerful swings between both polarities without overloading or needlessly repeating either yin or yang. Too much action or drama without at least some small moments of pause and reflection and we will wear out the attention span and emotional energy of our audiences. Too much reflection and idle talk without action - we will become stagnant and our audiences will go to sleep. And while much of our current film industry often pushes the envelope in the realms yang (particularly in the action-adventure genres), a well-crafted story will always give us moments to catch our breath and integrate – in order to fully digest what's happening and embrace the deeper currents of the hero's path.

We all know the feeling of being energetically pummeled by non-stop action and we also know what it's like to watch paint dry when a story moves too slow and stagnates. The key is to embrace the ebb and flow, peaks and troughs, and to keep the exchange alive between yin and yang. Sometimes we may have a whole sequence or section of our story that really pushes the boundaries of yang and this is fine. We can stack it up like this, building one action scene on top of the next. But if we do, we need to be sure that we let the scales balance at the end of this sequence and let our heroes and audience take a breath or two before we leap into the next section. Otherwise, no one will have the energy to go on. Likewise, sometimes our heroes will go through extended periods of in-action, stillness and stagnancy, and this can be very powerful (particularly if we the audience really want them to move, but they cannot bring themselves to it). But what comes from this quiet time must eventually give birth to some new level of genuine yang expression. Otherwise we will all leave feeling less than fulfilled.

In an overall sense, if we follow the flow of yin and yang through the major story beats we have covered so far, we will often find that the Call to Adventure comes as a yang moment that imposes itself on our hero, forcing them into a short time of yin-based reflection to debate and decide if they will answer the call. Stepping on the Path into the extraordinary world of their journey requires yang again, but as they are thrown out of their comfort zone they must humbly learn a new way (yin) before making a more conscious commitment at the Midpoint (yang), which ultimately drives them into the Innermost Cave (yin). From there, they will rise up from the ashes of their darkest yin moment, into clear bold action (yang), Crossing Back over and launching into the final 'Act' and the Climax of the story, where our characters will in most cases be called upon to express the combined energy of both yin and yang in order to truly achieve the higher purpose of their journey. Overall there will be a flow back and forth between these energies, section-to-section, scene-to-scene, character-to-character, and the final resolution of our hero will most often require a genuine sense of integration – embodying and expressing the balanced energies of both yin and yang.

Overall, if blended with the story map we have referred to so far, this flow between yin and yang might look something like this:

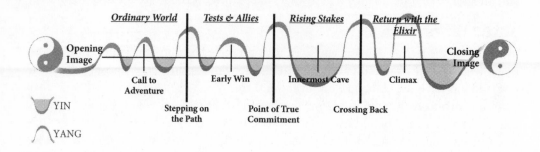

Regarding our characters themselves, we will normally find a general migration throughout the story from one primary energy to the other, often climaxing with a balanced integration of the two. If we are dealing with a hero who enters the story in their yang (extroverted, action-oriented, pushing outward in the world) their biggest growth or shift in the story will often come in the form of an event that requires them to slow down, drop in deeper, grow still and receptive for a time (yin). In *Avatar*, even though Jake Sully's Navi warrior training is quite active, this is highlighted by the gradual shift in focus from action to connection (yang to yin) in the natural world of Pandora.

Likewise, if our hero arrives into the story favoring their yin (holding back, receptive, seeing truth without necessarily acting upon it), their shift will often require them to swing into their yang, and learn to express themselves more boldly through their actions in the world (as is the case with Po in *Kung Fu Panda* and Frodo in *Lord of the Rings*). Whichever way the balance (or imbalance) swings for our heroes in story, it will often become subtly apparent with our initial Call to Adventure and will usually reach a peak in the second half of the story – particularly in the time period between the Innermost Cave and the Crossing Back.

While this is just a glimpse into the power of yin and yang, we can see that our awareness of this potent exchange of primal energy provides a rich and fascinating doorway to the inner truth of our heroes, their stories and the stories of our lives.

"What I dream of is an art of balance."
– Henri Matisse

WRITING EXERCISE:
THE YIN AND YANG OF LIFE AND STORY

THE YIN YANG OF LIFE
Take a moment to describe a day in your life and to tune into the natural flow of YIN and YANG. Which energy guides and infuses the majority of your daily activities, decisions and endeavors? Where is your yin and yang in balance, and where (and why) is it out? Which aspect expresses itself more dominantly than the other?

THE YIN YANG OF WRITING
Where is the swing of yin and yang amidst your current daily writing rhythms? Are you pushing too hard to get yourself out there without taking time to gather inspiration for your work, or have you perhaps been gathering your creative fires deep within for too long now and so they are ready to move through you more powerfully onto the page (and beyond)? How might you allow the scales to shift into balance, letting the energy of yin and yang guide your steps in more meaningful ways for a better-feeling, more fulfilling outcome?

THE YIN YANG OF STORY
Write a scene or moment (from either your own life, from your story - or both!), where the hero is forced/drawn/brought into a moment of shift from one polar extreme to the other. From big bold action (yang) into stillness (yin)... or from stillness /stagnancy (yin) into dynamic action (yang). Capture the very moment of this shift in your writing - what leads to it and how it comes about. Is it consciously chosen by your hero or is externally imposed? What dormant energies and new possibilities emerge when the balance of yin and yang are restored?

In nature, life and story, there is a natural flow between the energies of yin and yang. Sometimes we are in harmony with yin yang balance, and sometimes, depending on the demands of the moment and the habits we have developed, we may slide way to one side or the other. Many of our greatest teachers, artists, inventors and leaders have been known to spend concentrated time of solo reflection (yin), followed by concentrated time out in the world with people (yang) – teaching, sharing, giving. Fill the cup. Empty the cup. Fill the cup. Empty the cup. This is the way the rhythm rolls. If we respect and flow with it, it infuses all that we do… and all that we are.

As we raise our awareness of the vital creative forces of yin and yang within our own being, they will naturally find their rhythm and greater flow in our heroes and our stories. Enjoy this exercise and I'll see you tomorrow for our next step on the path!

When Heroes Speak
(A.k.a. Learning to Listen)

"Nature gave us one tongue and two ears
so we could hear twice as much as we speak."
– Epictetus

When I first started writing in the film world, dialogue was a bit of a mystery to me. Through a lifetime of detailed journaling, I had mastered my own approach to descriptive narrative, but I hadn't spent much time writing scenes of people speaking. When you look at a screenplay format, you quickly realize that most scripts are about 80% dialogue... so my experience was about to change.

At first, a lot of the dialogue I wrote sounded right in my own head, but to others it often appeared 'over-written' (too much) or as they say in the film world, 'on the nose' (meaning the dialogue was too directly stating the message of the scene - spoon feeding the audience). The director and I decided we didn't like the term 'on the nose' (too degrading), so we decided to use the term 'young' instead to describe dialogue that hadn't yet fully dropped into place. The word 'young' was not only more encouraging, it was a much more accurate description to me, because often when we first write a line of dialogue we are still in early phase of scene exploration. We are searching for the best way to express what we have to say, we don't quite know how to do it, but we don't want to forget the impulse, so we just blurt it out straight, like a child would. If we shut these early impulses down because they don't 'sound right' yet, we risk losing a whole lot of magic that is nestled within our youthful efforts to bring them through. Taken in the right light, these young scripted scenes serve a huge purpose because they actually help us find the essence of what we are seeking to express in the scene.

There's a creed in the film industry that says, "If the scene is *about* the scene, you've got a problem," meaning that characters rarely just come out and say exactly what they think or feel (particularly adult characters), but sometimes in the early drafts, you may need the scene to be about the scene, because the truth is that you are still looking for it yourself! If you cut yourself a bit of slack, your dialogue can be a great path to lead you there.

If the first draft states plainly what the message or essence of the scene is, it is then your task to begin to allow your characters to speak more naturally and artfully – giving them unique voices and genuine subconscious patterning to dictate and guide *how* they say (or avoid saying) what they really feel. The ultimate aim is to use each piece of dialogue not just as a voice for the message of the scene, but more importantly, to reveal the characters themselves... Who they are beneath and beyond the words they are speaking.

Artful, authentic dialogue is worthy of a book on its own, but for today I'd love to share just a few essential keys that have really helped me transform the spoken words of my stories from one of the most challenging elements to one of my greatest joys and passions in writing. I used to dread the feedback that might follow a newly crafted scene of dialogue, but now I embrace the opportunity to connect with my character's unique voice as one of the most enriching experiences on the story path. The very cool thing is that it's a lot easier than one might think. In fact 'thinking' is what often gets in the way. So here are a few hot tips to help you take your spoken exchanges with characters to a new level.

1. GOING THERE

When I first started writing dialogue, I could hear the words the characters were speaking in my mind, and in *my* mind those words sounded great. I could hear the emphasis and intonation just the way they were supposed to be delivered, and to me, I was nailing those lines! But for some reason this same clarity of voice wasn't coming through to those who were reading the material. What I quickly realized (along with the fact that everyone reads differently!) was that there is a difference between going into the minds of our characters and going into their hearts. When we write what we *think* our heroes would say, more often than not we will end up with a scene that *makes sense*, but doesn't necessarily register any emotional charge for our readers.

In my experience, one of the first steps to writing truthful and engaging dialogue is similar to writing genuinely engaging scenes (as discussed in Chapter 6). That is simply to begin by allowing ourselves to really 'go there' emotionally as we write. If we can sit before a scene and connect with a time or moment in our own life that we have had a similar/ parallel experience, or at the very least experienced the same emotional charge as the character, this is a great place to begin – and often our closest line of genuine connection to our hero. I often take time to write about my own experience first and the kinds of things I actually felt and said at the time... then, with the emotional charge of my own experience bubbling over, I simply transfer that energy across to the scene I'm writing. I speak through their voice and language, but with an emotional truth that comes from my own experience.

I've found that if the scene is sad and I'm crying when I write it, people are usually crying when they read it. If I'm excited, laughing or inspired as I write the dialogue, then so is my audience. This was my first big step to writing truthful, impactful and engaging dialogue. Simply giving myself the permission (and responsibility) to really 'go there'. I invite you to do the same this week in your writing.

2. LISTENING – INSIDE AND OUT

As previously mentioned, when I first started writing stories, I thought it was my role to sit energetically 'above' my characters and to move them about like puppets, serving my needs to deliver different story beats… But what I soon realized was that my real job was actually to serve them.

It takes a certain level of openness to recognize that our characters don't just exist in our heads… they are living energies with their own journey to experience and share. They have their own purposes to live out on our pages. On one hand it is our role to craft them and to give them shape, texture, history, dreams and gifts. But once a genuine spark has been lit, if we are willing to quiet our mind and genuinely connect to their hearts and voices as living beings, it is both humbling and inspiring what they will tell and show us.

Meeting Balthazar (Listening on the Inside)

In the past I may have read that last paragraph and smiled at the idea without really believing it, but when I was working on a major film project a few years ago, I had a series of experiences that genuinely blew my mind and took my writing to a whole new level. I was working on an opening sequence, which was going to include a bit of narration from a sagely mentor figure called Balthazar – one of the Three Wise Men (or Magi) from the Biblical story of the birth of Christ. I had been working on the scene for days and I could feel that it wasn't quite right. It needed to go to a new level of expression, but I couldn't quite 'figure out' where it needed to go or how to take it there.

Sleep-deprived and pushing rapidly toward (or maybe past) my deadline, I finally broke down expressing my frustration to Asheyana, hoping she could throw me a rope and see something in the scene that I hadn't (which she and Josh often do! In fact several of Josh's ideas resulted in the very best scenes of that story). Ash was busy and didn't want to read my opening sequence *again*, so she looked at me, and – as she also often does – made a simple two-word suggestion that completely changed my outlook and approach to the scene – and a *lot* of other scenes and moments since.

"Ask him," she said matter-of-factly, as though telling me to ask a farmer for a spade.

"Ask who?!" I said, hands gripping onto my imaginary hair.

"Ask Balthazar. If you want to know what he would say, why don't you ask him what he wants to say."

She returned my bewildered gaze with a detached smile that seemed to say, "Go on. You'll figure it out." Then she walked out of the room.

I sat with this for a moment. Who was I to summon the spirit of Balthazar, the great

Magi, to share his words directly with me? But the more I thought about it, the more I realized how presumptuous it was for me to even try to write a scene about him any other way! Particularly if my intention was to honor his voice with an expression of genuinely engaging truth. He may have passed away 2000 years ago, but I knew his spirit must be out there somewhere… maybe he'd even appreciate the chance to speak his story. I wasn't sure if I was a worthy scribe, but with most other research avenues exhausted, and with very little steam left in my own mind/body/creative vehicle, I figured my best shot was to go straight to the source.

The Magi were known for their connection to the stars and the natural world, so I grabbed my journal, went outside and walked around barefoot in the grass for a while. After several minutes of quiet pacing, I stopped in the spot that felt right and just stood there in the quiet of the night. I closed my eyes and took a breath and put an inner ear to the sky… Almost instantly, an image came into my mind. I was in a cave. There was fire… a sacred fire and a circle of stones. There were others there, gathered together in some sort of meeting and I was just sort of watching it all happen. The image was totally different than anything I had conjured up on my own prior to that moment. The details and geography were different… and the energy was different. From this first image, other pictures started to rise, and a whole sequence began to play itself out on a sort of movie screen in my mind. And low and behold, as I sat there with my eyes closed and feet sinking into the dew, I started hearing a voice.

I had been writing scenes for the Balthazar character for several months by now and thought myself quite connected to his presence in the story. But this was totally different. The voice was deep and clear. There were no questions about word choice or cadence. They just came through, and as they did, I just started scribbling them down. This was Balthazar's voice, and he was telling me a story.

It was a story that had taken place many years before the story that I was actually writing, and as he told it, I was there watching it unfold. I wasn't thinking what was supposed to come next. I was just watching and listening and transcribing what I was seeing and hearing. There was a power in the words and a sense of realness in his voice unlike any that I had written before, and yet it took very little effort to write it. It was as though the words were simply passing through me and my whole job was just to stand there in the grass and let it come on through. I finished the scene and not only did I love it… but I felt a real sense of invigoration and aliveness in my body… and the beginnings of a genuine sense of kinship with the energy of Balthazar.

To this day I don't know whether it was really Balthazar coming through to share his tale or whether it was just my own deep yearning to connect to the character at a deeper level, but what ensued was a relationship that nurtured my craft and fueled many scenes with a whole new sense of truth and depth for months to come. So much so that at first they were difficult to integrate into the story because they felt so different to how the scenes had been written before. Some of them were noticed straight away, and others, strangely enough, were submitted 3-4 times before people suddenly started saying, "Wow, I love what you've just done with that opening scene," as though it was first time they'd actually 'seen it'. Maybe it took that amount of time for this new level of truth to settle in.

Over the course of a few months, most of these Balthazar scenes found prominent places in the story, and for me, they served as energetic pillars and reference points whenever I felt lost along the story path. Balthazar's voice was like a truth comb running through the narrative.

The biggest gift for me as a person was to experience a genuine sense of connection with what the very real energy of a living being that existed somehow outside of our normal frame of reference. As a writer, this was both humbling and rewarding, and it showed me that one of our greatest opportunities is to embrace our role as a conduit for the living energy and voice of our heroes. Not to fill their mouths with words that we think they should say, but to quiet ourselves enough to listen and to humbly serve and share their call. It may feel like a stretch of the imagination at first, but if you are willing to open your mind and heart to listen without judgment or locked-in expectation of what your characters are supposed to say... you may be surprised what comes through (bring your journal!).

Hitting the Streets (Listening on the Outside)
Once you've gotten a sense for the inner world and *essence* of your characters (the part of them that runs deeper than the specifics of their life), the next step is often to get a sense for how that essence plays itself out in their real world. To take that clear emotional charge that we are now connected to, and to ask ourselves, how would this energy express itself through this person in this environment? What makes their voice unique? Again, you will be amazed.

When we track into how people actually speak, we instantly go beyond the mind's ideas of words, into the river of truth. And the truth is, people don't always speak like we think they do! By allowing ourselves to be a fly on the wall and actually listen, we come into a new level of connectedness to the vernacular and unique expressions of the characters in our lives and our stories. A great way to begin doing this is to simply go out and listen to someone who thinks, feels and speaks like your character.

As an audience we smell authenticity a mile away. Anything less than the real deal and we will simply begin to disengage. It's a bit like my experience eating Mexican food in Australia. Having grown up in the western states of the US (and having made several trips to Mexico), there is a certain cellular experience that comes with a truly authentic fish taco or burrito. Strangely enough, that experience just seems to get lost in translation when repeated on the other side of the Pacific. All the ingredients are right and the presentation looks great, but there's just something missing in the texture and taste. It's a subtle thing, but it's been enough to make me choose *not* to eat Mexican food in Australia, even though I love it. Until recently when I discovered a restaurant owned and operated by – you guessed it – someone from Mexico!

As writers, one great way to short-cut this challenge is to begin by writing from the center of our own experience (or at least from the centre of our own imagination, as in the case of the *Harry Potter* series). We may not think our life is particularly interesting, but the truth is that a story well told from our own natural perspective (as experts of our own life) will almost always be more compelling than a story told about a world we haven't 'lived in' and don't fully understand. If and when we choose to write about a world that is different than our own reality, along with creating a connection to the characters by 'going there' emotionally, one of our key responsibilities is to go there physically. We have to find a way – at least in a homeopathic sense – to 'experience' the world of our heroes as authentically as possible.

When I was hired to write my first feature film (*One Perfect Day*), the backdrop of the tale was in the classical music arena and the modern youth dance party scene – two worlds I knew virtually nothing about. Based on my emotional connection to the story characters and their internal journeys, I could write the basic scenes, but when it came to nailing the dialogue, there was only one place I could go – and it wasn't Google or Wikipedia. I had to spend time talking with, being with, listening to and recording the actual thoughts and words of the types of people I was writing about (classical musicians, composers, DJs, teenagers, etc…). I decided that rather than try to craft unique voices for my characters, I should just find their approximate mirrors in the real world, spend time in their environment, ask them similar questions and listen. This was a massive breakthrough and took a ton of pressure off my back. Once I stopped trying to be the source of my characters' voices, and began to allow myself instead to be like a scribe or translator, cross-pollinating the actual words and ideas I was hearing on the street with the details and spoken words of my characters, not only did I make a bunch of amazing new friends, the dialogue in our story took a quantum leap overnight! Suddenly the words and voices of the characters started coming to life on the page. Readers who had been particularly critical of the dialogue in earlier drafts, were now telling me how engaging, unique and truthful my characters' voices were. All I was really doing was listening closely, sampling the words and expressions of real people, and then allowing those words to weave into the heartbeats of my characters and the fabric of my scenes.

As with most things in life, the less we try to 'be clever' and the more we allow the genuine heartbeat of the moment to guide us (be that an external heartbeat of someone we're talking to or the internal voice of a sage from long ago), the more our creations ring with truth… and often end up being quite clever after all!

The following is the Chinese symbol for the word 'listen'. To me it captures much of what we have explored here in effective listening (inside and out) to the voices and essence of our heroes. All of the elements below come into play when crafting authentic dialogue.

"To Listen"

EAR

YOU

EYES

UNDIVIDED
ATTENTION

HEART

3. READING BETWEEN THE LINES

As a pretty straightforward and direct person, one of the other things I had to realize when I first started writing dialogue is that there is a big difference between what is spoken and what is really being said. We are a very strange species and probably the only animal on the planet that consistently speaks partial truths, often using words to mask, instead of express, what we really feel… We express in varying degrees, not only based on our emotional state, but on our lifetime of training from society and our family about what is and isn't appropriate/acceptable/fair/right to speak about. Oftentimes we say, "Yes" to things that we don't want to do, and we say, "No thanks" when really we want to say, "Yes, please". We say we're doing "Fine" when really we are struggling, and when we have the very most to say – when we are bubbling up inside with emotional overflow – we often say NOTHING at all.

This is a very powerful thing to realize as a writer. Finding the best and most truthful way to let our characters express what they really feel without just having them blurt it all out on the page is an ever-present mission… unless of course our characters are children!

Children often do say exactly what they think and feel regardless of the consequences, regardless of who they may offend (the movies *Big* and *The Invention of Lying* both offer great portrayals of what would happen if we spoke more innocently and directly as adults). Young children know nothing but the truth, so they are simply clear beacons of it. In our stories, children can sometimes be used in this way to expose truth that the adults around them may otherwise be unwilling to breach. In life, they do this quite effortlessly everyday, and with their honest perspective often comes great wisdom.

Here's a funny story… Several years ago, my little boy Josh was asked to be in a film that James Twyman was making. James' initial vision was to create a sort of fantasy adventure feature film about a group of special children being called from various places, to come to Mt. Shasta in California for an ancient, sacred meeting about the future of the world… These kids were being summoned by great elders to help.

We were on our way over to the States from Australia at the time, so James met us in Hawaii to film Joshy's part. He wanted to do a few simple scenes of Joshua asking me about Mt. Shasta and expressing his mysterious inner call to go there. Josh was five at the time and understood the intention of the scenes, but every time James rolled the camera and began a scene with the question, "Why do you want to go to Mt. Shasta?" Josh would sit there thinking for a moment and then he would quite simply say, "I don't want to go to Mt Shasta. You just want me to say I do." He was happy to be in the film, but to act or say anything that wasn't his truth was completely a foreign concept to him. This made filming a little tricky to say the least (lots of funny bloopers), but the very cool thing is that it actually caused James to rethink his approach to the project. To his credit, James has a wonderful way of responding to the pulse of the moment, and in the end, he changed the whole focus of the film away from fantasy adventure, into a pure documentary that explored the uncompromisingly truthful gifts and messages of today's children!! It's called the *Indigo Evolution,* and if you watch it, you'll see Josh in there just being himself – no acting required.

The point is that kids are very clear and direct, but, as adults, we often mix and blend our truths with subconscious patterns and hidden agendas, so it can take us much longer to actually get to what we really want to say. As an audience, we watch this internal pathway unfold, ever conscious of both what the characters are saying, and what they really mean underneath. We know from their actions and body language what's really going on, but their words often have a totally different way of getting there. This can be agonizing to witness, but it keeps us on the page and in our seats – because we all know the feeling.

There's a moment in the film *The Pursuit of Happyness* where Will Smith's character, Chris Gardner, is standing on the street with the big boss of his company (the company he's desperately trying to impress) and the boss asks if he can borrow five dollars for a taxi. Chris opens his wallet and we know this is the last five dollars to his name. We know that without this particular five dollars he won't be able to eat or feed his son that night. He is so close to getting the job, but right in this moment he has absolutely nothing, and the boss has no idea… He stares at the bill, swallows, then offers it up with a smile, "Sure. Here you go." This friction between what is spoken and what is really going on for Chris is a powerful doorway and an example of how what our characters don't say often tells us just as much about them as what they do.

One of the most powerful scenes in my first film was loaded with dialogue in the script, but the final scene as it was shot had no dialogue in it at all. The actors workshopped the scene and the lines worked great, but once they dropped right into their characters on set, new possibilities began revealing themselves. Ways to demonstrate the energy and feelings of the lines without actually speaking at all. The dialogue wasn't wasted. It was simply used as doorway into a different way of expressing the same idea. One that felt natural for the actors while delivering the essence of the scene as it had been written.

In many ways, the key to writing great dialogue is quite parallel to writing a great story. We need to bring ourselves into the emotional truth of the character/scene we're writing (a.k.a. Go there)... We need to quiet our mind to hear what is really going on (a.k.a. Listen)... And we need to deliver that truth to our readers in a way that they never would have expected it.

By taking time to get to know our characters inside and out and by immersing ourselves in their world (whether that world exists in our own mind or out on the street), we put ourselves in a powerful position to allow their words to reveal not only what they want, but *who they are*. Sometimes this means we load up the scene with all of our character's energy and intention, and then they say nothing at all... But often in saying nothing, *everything* is expressed.

WRITING EXERCISE: LISTENING AND LETTING THEM SPEAK

Step 1 – *Go out into the world with your journal today. Park yourself someplace interesting, where you will have the opportunity to hear what people say, how they express themselves and what energy is shared with and without their words. Record snippets and pieces of dialogue that jump out at you. Capture unique turns of phrase and colloquialisms. Pieces of dialogue that are telling of who they are and where they come from... then write a simple scene around it.*

Step 2 – *Pick a scene from your story or from your life and follow the three keys above. Allow yourself to really go there emotionally, to listen (externally and internally) and read between the lines in order to craft a scene that expresses the truth of your characters in a way that we would not have imagined. For fun, see if you can get your characters to say the opposite of what they really mean, but do it in a way that makes us realize their deeper truth!*

Enjoy the extremely rich environment of your characters' words today... allow them to infuse and inform and even surprise you. As much as this is your writing project, it is their story you are telling. By taking time to come to your own center within it and surrendering to the pulse of the moment, you will be sure to share your heroes' heartbeats in ways that are both intimately connected and universally engaging.

Woohoo! Congratulations for completing Chapter 7. Catch your breath, get a snack and I'll see you back here for our courageous leap into the Climax of this heroic journey!

CHAPTER 8:

Your Story Climax
(Bringing it ALL Together)

*"We want a story that starts out with an earthquake
and works its way up to a climax."*
– Samuel Goldwyn

The Hero's Return

We have answered the Call to Adventure and crossed the threshold from our ordinary world into the extraordinary world of story. We have moved through Tests and Allies to the Midpoint moment of true commitment on the path... We have journeyed to the Inner Most Cave and through a time when perhaps all seemed dark and lost, before claiming the Elixir of our true Self and the inner gift of our journey. With this new discovery and clarity of focus, we have crossed back into the world from which we came and we are ready now to walk (run, leap or dive!) with full strides and newfound truth embodied, carrying the torch of transformation with us.

Today we come together to explore the role and energy of the CLIMAX of our story. That moment in time where all the skills and lessons we have learned in the physical realm (through the Tests and Allies phase of our journey) must be combined with the deeper lessons and gifts we have acquired in the emotional and energetic realms (in our Inner Most Cave), to ignite a solution and triumphant resolution to our journey. One that both solves the external issues we have been faced with and resolves the internal yearning and calling that drew us into the journey in the first place. The climax often presents the most complete and comprehensive challenge to the hero and in doing so it gives the hero the greatest opportunity to fully anchor and express all that s/he has gained, learned and BECOME on the path.

*

It is said that life imitates art... and vice versa. I have certainly found this to be true at times, and it comes as no surprise that as I write this chapter in the book, I am myself immersed in just such a moment. With my family now safely back in Australia, I have been left in the US to culminate our experience here and to galvanize all that I have learned into the completion of not only a mountain of external details (from shipping containers and migrating kittens to selling cars, cleaning the house and completing creative projects) but also coming to center and closing the circle in an energetic sense with friends and family, mountains and rivers that we have journeyed with while here. Meanwhile, Ash is doing her best to put a new stake in the ground for our life back in Australia and this is no easy task either (getting cars running, finding a new home, contacting schools, and planting seeds for new projects that are yet to be born). Together, via Skype, we meet, share our burdens and help heart-storm solutions... When I look to the hours in the days that remain and factor in all that must be done, I know that there is no possible way to do it all. But as I step into this day I also do so with a quiet, hopeful smile, knowing that this realm of impossibility is actually where the hero has been nudged and drawn to from the very beginning. And when he (or in this case, I) reaches a point where even with absolute commitment, alone he will not make it, he is forced to open up his lens and see a higher path. One that involves, includes, empowers and aligns with others.

I have heard it said that, "Accepting help is a gift to the giver." This is not an excuse to freeload, but a way of recognizing that when we are committed to our highest path, there will always come a time when we have reached the limit of what we can achieve on our own. And in this moment, if we are open, we will see that while we each have our own great journey to walk, the greatest fulfillment of our true self-expression will come when we are unified with others for a higher good.

In my efforts to move heroically through my last days on US soil for a while, I know that out of my own necessity I may be calling on the heroic spirit of my neighbors and friends. There are many variables and unknowns but I have already begun to notice that each step I take with clear intent, opens the way for others to do the same. My challenge embraced becomes another's gift to harness. Case in point: I need to sell our Nissan Pathfinder before I leave. But before I sell it, I need to use it for everything else I have to do up until the moment I climb on the plane. It's a special car and it has been very good to us, but it also needs work and love to go the distance. How am I going to sell the car and achieve everything else that needs to be done with it until I leave? And how can I do it in the most peaceful and efficient way? My mind searches for answers. I think of Craigslist and eBay and the bulletin board at the Co-op… I don't have time for this. I need a clear and decisive answer. Nothing comes to mind so I plant the question like a seed and enter my day, doing everything else I can in the meantime while it grows. An hour later I drive past my friend Jon's house. I don't have time to stop, but I do anyway because Jon is a good friend and soon I won't be able to stop by and see him. Next stop – flyers, Craigslist, etc… but for now I'll just take one moment to connect. I step onto Jon's balcony, and take a breath to separate myself from my to-do list, and before I have a chance to say a word, Jon asks me what I'm doing with our car when I leave. I tell him I'm not sure, that I really need to sell it. He frowns, thinking and tells me he's looking for a car for his son… One that they can put a bit of love into with the knowledge that it will go the distance. He asks if he can take it for a spin. Um, sure. Absolutely. An hour later Jon's paid me cash for the car and given me the keys to his truck to use until I leave (even better for my moving needs). In a few days, his son Patrick (also a good friend) will drive me to the airport in my own car that's now his – complete with shiny detailed dashboard and 'new car' smell. Both of us thrilled at the climactic result.

Yesterday another friend invited me to a picnic in the park to say goodbye. Picnics are high on my list of things that I don't really have time for this week, but strangely that quiet voice inside again urged me to drop by. When I arrived, a small group was gathering in the shady grass of a mighty oak. I was introduced to a few of my *buddy's friends and colleagues, we chatted lightly for a while eating sandwiches and fruit. As I was leaving I struck up a conversation with the founder of a US-based transformational consulting firm that happens to be growing rapidly in Australia. It just so happens they are looking for a handful of people with very similar skills and passion to mine, to help deliver a series of groundbreaking workshops within large organizations Down Under... Hmmm. Within a few minutes we've made plans to meet up the following day to explore the possibilities of working together... (Unbeknownst to me at the time, our conversation would escalate to a meeting with the Australian Director and within a couple of weeks a wonderful new opportunity would begin to materialize, awaiting my return to Australian soil.)*

This is the way this story climax continues to unfold. Subtle messages requiring bold, decisive action, surrender and allowing, followed by more of the same and another flying leap! Bit-by-bit the pieces come together. Still so much to do – more than possible I am sure – but these are the realms of the hero, are they not? So I will do my very best to stay present and see how else impossibility gives way to new dimensions of positive experience.

*

As heroes in the making, we enter the story path somewhat blind to what it holds for us. Driven perhaps by faith, daring or simple urgent need, but as we begin, we have very little knowledge of what is to come. During the journey our awareness grows. Through experience we slowly come to understand, to gain knowledge, skills and wisdom. The final step of our journey as we enter the Climax of our experience, is to go from understanding and knowing the truth to being the truth. Our truth. We must move beyond awareness of concepts and ideas into the embodiment of ourselves as the hero of our own path. We are the ones we have been waiting for.

At first we were **students** – reluctant, resistant, challenged by our preconceptions of ourselves and the world around us. We then became **initiates**, stripped of what we thought we knew, infused with new skills, perceptions and understanding. As we claimed our true commitment and ventured from the Cave we entered the realms of the **master**, knowing who we are and what must be done. Now, in the Climax of our journey, we must express this mastery with and among others, and in so doing, become **teachers** of the living truth we have acquired.

We have experienced our point of departure, we have crossed the Point of No Return, and now we have alas come full circle to where our return is granted and won through the full expression of who we have become.

This is the power of the Climax. We all know well how this energy plays out in most film stories. It is the time of the big speech, the final battle, the desperate and complete declaration of love, honor and commitment. It is that moment that the hero may have feared the very most all along, but this is her chance to fully express what she came into this story to express. In some ways this moment can be seen as the greatest test. But in truth – much like my Aikido instructor told me when I went for my first official belt grading – this isn't really a test, it's more of an opportunity to outwardly claim and demonstrate to *yourself* all that you have learned so far.

In a lot of Hollywood films the Climax comes down to a 'save the world' moment, where if the hero is successful in his last ditch effort, he will save all of mankind, but if he misses this chance, all will be lost. While it isn't necessary to consider the end of the world in every story we tell, the gift in Hollywood's maxed-out version of the Climax is that it shows us some keys to making our own Climaxes truly satisfying to the hero, the reader, the writer and the audience. I will list a few elements here that to me make it all worthwhile.

ELEMENTS OF AN EFFECTIVE CLIMAX

1. As mentioned above, the Climax must combine what has been learned on the outside (new skills, etc.) with what has been learned on the inside (new Self discovery and perspective).

2. The Climax, perhaps more than any other turning point for the hero, must involve decisive, pro-active focus by our hero. When the hero enters the Climax of the story on their terms, with a plan (which may of course change), with heart, mind, spirit and body focused on a clear and specific aim.

3. The solution of the Climax will always stretch the hero beyond anything s/he has ever done before. I know we've said this before about other story beats, but this is the real enchilada. There may be familiar issues and challenges, but the stakes and players are all operating at a whole new level.

4. What is fought for and achieved in the Climax must in some way be for the higher good of all. The Climax may be triggered partially by the personal need or desire of the hero, but the ultimate resolution of the Climax must also benefit those around him/her.

5. The Climax must give the hero an opportunity to directly face and in some way defeat/dissolve/rise above his/her greatest fear from the past. The hero will usually move through a series of challenges in the Climax, often in ascending order, rising steadily toward the biggest, baddest, most difficult challenge of them all.

6. At the 'Climax of the Climax', the very peak moment, we and our hero will often come

to realize that while we can and must do our very best to win or triumph in this situation, one of the greatest gifts of the hero path is to realize that we are not alone. Many fulfilling climaxes are both empowering and humbling for our hero for they give the hero a glimpse into the bigger picture, in which they are just one small piece. Often in the moment when the hero has pushed as far as humanly possible, some unexpected element will come to help push him/her through just that little bit more and that makes all the difference (consider the movie Avatar… Jake calls on the help of all the other tribes and this allows them to make a powerful initial attack on the human army. But when the humans push back with full force and it appears that the native people will be defeated, at the fragile moment just before complete surrender, something happens… Eywa, the spirit of the natural world comes in to help, sending all of the giant animals and creatures in to assist the natives in driving back the humans and saving their world). As an audience we are reminded that there are forces both seen and unseen that rise to meet us when we are truly committed to our path.

7. While the Climax often entails a sense of personal sacrifice, the deeper truth I like to think about when considering the Climax in my stories (and chapters of my life) is to ask myself the question, "What do I love and care about so much that I would be willing to die for it?" and then to take it one more step and ask, "Knowing that, how can I now set about the task of LIVING for it?"

These are just a few key elements of a well-crafted climax that must come together in order to leave us – the writer, the reader and the audience – satisfied and fulfilled.

In my opinion, while more and more stories are now exploring alternative ways to resolve the greatest challenge of Climax, too many still resort to a stale and overtly patriarchal approach of pitting good against evil and having them duke it out to the death. Life is almost never this black and white, and yet many of the stories we continue to pump out to the masses carry the message that when things get tough, the only solution, the best solution, is to make the other person wrong and fight it out.

One of the reasons I feel committed to both writing stories and to mentoring those who have stories to tell, is because I am inspired to be part of creating a new wave of story that is more inclusive of higher solutions to our planet's issues and challenges. Stories that activate new visions of the possible within our readers and viewers, opening synapses in their minds and hearts to recognize the greater creation story that we are all here to share and contribute to.

Sometimes if I watch a film and I am not satisfied with the Climax or the ending, I will take time to consider (and even re-write) how else it could have gone… how might things have unfolded to arrive at a more complete and fulfilling resolution for all involved? We each have the power to re-write our own story too… in fiction and in life. To stop ourselves midstream and ask, is this pathway leading to the ultimate desired outcome of this tale? How might we come to a place of completion that's even more rich and fulfilling than this? If we can be bold enough to dream it, to speak it and to write it into being... this is often the first step to calling true fulfillment into the fabric of reality.

WRITING EXERCISE: THE POWER OF CLIMAX

Take some time to explore the essence of the CLIMAX in your STORY, in your path as a writer and in the pinnacle moments of your LIFE.

Step 1 – What moments have you come to in life that have called you, by absolute necessity, to step into and BE something more than you ever thought possible? What area of your life may now be rising to such a time of Climax?

"What do you love and care about so much that you would be willing to die for it?" Knowing that, "How can you now set about the task of LIVING for it?"

Step 2 – Consider the same for your characters in story. What scene or sequence would represent the ultimate honor to your hero's path, by offering them the greatest possible challenge – thereby calling upon every ounce of internal discovery and external resource to fully realize their high potential? Who/what might come in to help and join them when it matters most? And how might the Climax of your story not only provide a solution to your hero's greatest challenge, but do so in such a way that it ripples out for the good of ALL... Bringing some new light or balance... some new possibility into the hero's world?

Step 3 – You have arrived here on the writing path. You are standing here at the threshold of Climax in your own Writing the Story Within *experience. Whether you have written your own major story work each step of the way, or whether you have just been tracking along with the exercises, gathering tools and visions for the days to come... However you have chosen to arrive here, you're here. Well done! How might you now step forward into the Climax of your own* Writing the Story Within *journey and fully express your true heroic self on the page (and beyond). What would be the most fulfilling Climax of this writing path you are on? How might you honor yourself and the Muse within you to bring it all together for the good of all?*

Now is the time.

This is the power and the gift of our story's Climax... it calls our heroes to synthesize everything they've learned and to bring their very best to their experience, while simultaneously allowing the greater forces within and around them to guide and propel their steps to full fruition!

This is your moment. Right here. Right now. To live, to write, to be the full expression of who you came here to be... If not now, then when? If not you, then who?

Now is your moment of power. Now is your time to shine. Are you ready? Of course you are. Otherwise you would not be here right now reading these words (even if you skipped a few pages to get here). OK then, enough said. Let's get in there and take our next step on the path.

Consciousness of Character

*"A picture must possess a real power to generate light, and for a long time now
I've been conscious of expressing myself through light, or rather in light."*
– Henry Matisse

I have often thought that what makes a story truly worth telling is the underlying gift or message that it brings to its readers or viewers. It need not be overt or preachy, but it must in some way build a bridge from one way of looking at or experiencing life, to another. Even stories that are crafted purely for entertainment, do so best in my opinion when they at least open a doorway for us to explore some aspect of our path anew (even if it's simply to make us laugh about something we wouldn't normally find funny). In our quest to build this bridge, it is almost always our heroes who deliver the primary gift of our story. Sometimes with words, sometimes with actions and always with the overall arc of who they become during the course of their journey.

As we travel through the writing of our story we will naturally deepen our connection to the characters and subject of our writing. We will become aligned with their heartbeats, their desires and the pulse of their steps on the path. One of the great discoveries that we will make is that they are not static, one-dimensional beings. They are living, growing and evolving energies. By the very nature of life and story, they must be.

While our hero may remain essentially the same person from start to finish, the true gift of a character-based story is the opportunity to share and witness change and transformation while it is taking place. As we watch and experience our heroes move through phases in their own growth and discovery, we inevitably find ourselves watching and experiencing those parts of ourselves that are ready to do the same. And if you are open to receiving the messages that stories may have for you, you will be delighted to discover these gifts and gems are everywhere you look – even in films and stories that may have no overt similarity to your life or conscious message for you. As you begin to view stories through the lens of the hero that *you* yourself are becoming, you will naturally begin to draw from each story just exactly what you need, even if the story is not even remotely similar to your path.

It is a running joke in my family that often after we have watched a film together (from drama to slapstick comedy), there is a high chance that I will want/need to go for a walk or swim or sit someplace quiet and digest what's just happened. It doesn't seem to matter whether it's an animation film about surfing penguins, a period piece set in medieval times, or a slapstick comedy set in Las Vegas… if it's a good story built on archetypal rhythms, as I watch the characters in their journey, I am also watching myself in mine. The more in tune with the hero's path you become, the more you will develop an ability to see beyond the details of the story itself, to the deeper rhythms of life that are unfolding within it.

If we have an intention to deliver a positive message or higher truth with our writing, one of the temptations is to want to present our characters in their best and highest light from the very beginning. To bring them into the story all polished and evolved and then to let them carry their great gifts to the world as they go. But what we must remember as story tellers, is that our primary role is to build a bridge… to give our readers and viewers an experiential map of change and transformation so that they not only get the message of our tale, but they also get to see how we got there, so they can apply the same energy of discovery to their own life. If we are too eager to deliver our story's message, or too anxious to present our hero in his/her best light, we can miss the opportunity to engage and build an effective bridge for our audience. While it can be natural to shy away from those shadowy bits, flaws and deep inner challenges that our heroes may need to face, by giving our heroes the opportunity to work through all aspects of themselves and the full extremes of their journey, we create the greatest doorway for others to connect, relate and learn from their steps along the way. In the same way that we often say "the journey is more important than the destination", the steps that our heroes take along the way are often more important than where they finally end up. As an audience we of course want a fulfilling resolution, but in order for this to be possible, we must be authentically connected to each phase of the path along the way.

The stories we relate to the most give us an honest view of the human condition and they lead us on a journey to discover new perspectives of our own experience. With this in mind, one of the best ways to develop, track and guide our characters, is to gain an understanding of how we humans move through phases of growth and consciousness.

Several years ago I was exposed to a simple model for understanding four of the primary levels of human consciousness. It resonated very deeply in my own life at the time, and since then I have really enjoyed exploring the model with others and also applying it to the progressive phases of character development in story. This is not a definitive guide to human consciousness (or character development for that matter), but within the context of our exploration here, I find that it provides a potent tool for building authentic, transformative character arcs within story… and you might also get something from it for yourself as well. Each level leads progressively to the next, requiring our characters to simultaneously gather a new level of truth and let go of or release an old pattern or way of seeing the world.

Synchronistically, the Four Levels of Consciousness we will lay out here match up quite perfectly with four of the main story phases we have outlined throughout the *Writing the Story Within* experience. In fact, if you were to map the entire story form onto a single line, you could basically cut it into four even sections (as pictured below), and each of these sections would represent one of the levels of consciousness we are about to discuss.

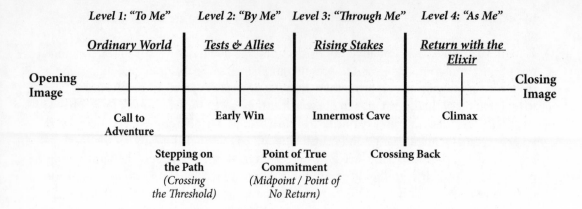

When I'm writing a screenplay I will often keep a map just like this one nearby and use it to track my key story beats as though I'm on a family road trip. When I make an unexpected turn (which happens in road trips and story), the map is there for me to recalibrate and adjust other beats to keep the balance. On the bottom half of the map, you'll see the nine key 'story moments' that we've explored in this journey (each of which are chapter titles and/or sections of this book – no coincidence). On the top half of the map, you'll see the overall storyline is divided into four main sections. Above each of these, I've listed the coinciding Levels of Consciousness we're about to explore!

Follow along with the map as we move through the Four Levels of Consciousness and see if these stages of story and consciousness resonate for you!

FOUR LEVELS OF CONSCIOUSNESS (IN CHARACTER, STORY AND LIFE)

Level 1: 'TO ME'
The first level of consciousness that we often experience in life – and that which our hero often embodies in the Stage 1 (Ordinary World) introduction of our story – is what we call 'To Me'. It is an early level of awareness where we and our heroes have the perception that life's events are happening 'to us'. Like a child new to the world or someone who has not yet learned to take full responsibility for his/her actions, we are susceptible to the forces of nature and life around us. Perhaps because many of our heroes enter their story at this level of consciousness, quite often our Stage 1 story catalyst or 'Call to Adventure' (as explored in Chapter 3) is perceived as an event or experience that happens 'to' our hero. A lightening bolt occurrence that penetrates our hero's ordinary world, knocking them off balance, causing them to react. In this first level of consciousness, our tendency is to feel as though we are victims of the circumstances of our life. We are on the unexpected receiving end of the incident, accident, injury, job assignment, baby on the doorstep of our life. We may have desires and visions for a higher path of our own, but at this stage it really appears as though 'life is happening to us'.

Level 2: 'BY ME'

After reacting to the circumstance of our Call to Adventure, after resisting and blaming others for what has happened, eventually we/our hero will come to a place of new dynamic action. A place where we are ready to move from pointing fingers outside of the self as a victim of circumstance, to being more of a generator and creator of reality. We are forced to take responsibility and begin to take our life into our own hands. In order to move from the first level of consciousness to the second, we (and/or our hero) will have to claim a new sense of PERSONAL EMPOWERMENT, and we/he/she will also have to let something go. Like rising to higher altitudes in a hot air balloon, we must not only cultivate more energy, we must also drop a few sand bags that have been weighing us down. In the case of moving from Level 1 to Level 2 of consciousness (from 'To Me' to 'By Me'), what must be let go of is BLAME. Whether we are right, wrong or fully justified in blaming others, there comes a time when we (and our character in story) must step beyond the realm of blame, beyond the realm of the victim and begin to create something new. We must set aside what has happened and set ourselves upon the path to going where we truly want/ need to go.

The 'By Me' phase of consciousness lines up perfectly with our hero's crossing from the ordinary to the extraordinary world, as they step on the path and begin the journey to learn new skills and gain new allies. During this phase of the journey, our characters will at first be humbled and thrown into the deep end of the new, but this is usually what is needed for them to make a change and start stretching themselves to take responsibility for their experience. This is our Tests and Allies stage of the journey where we slowly get to discover that we are more capable than we realized we were, that we are not victims but rather creators of circumstance. As we embrace our new abilities and responsibilities within the extraordinary world of the story we begin to get a glimpse of the hero we really are. This is not handed to us on a platter but must be worked for with the sweat of our brow and claimed 'by' our steps and progress on the path.

In story, this is a building or rebuilding phase for our characters, where their actions must be grounded, real and self-driven. Breakthroughs in this arena leave them (and us) with the sense of, "I did it! I can do it!" And from the space of 'By Me' the hero emerges with a sense of ownership about the world and circumstance she has created/earned/caused/ achieved… this is a powerful step on the path.

WRITING EXERCISE

Think of a time when – perhaps out of necessity – you rose out of feeling like a victim of your circumstance and became an active participant and creator of it. When perhaps you had been given a challenge that seemed beyond your ability, but as you took determined steps and harnessed new skills and confidence, you began to gain a sense of mastery over the situation. Take yourself right to a moment of 'By Me' experience and describe the events. What lead you into the sense of your personal power in the situation, how did you express it? What results did you achieve and how did that make you feel?

Level 3: 'THROUGH ME'

When we have worked hard at developing skills in any activity or endeavor (from music to sports to mathematics), there is a moment when we cross over from a feeling of consciously pushing to earn and achieve each step and notch on the stick, to entering a sense of grace and flow with what we are doing. We may have been trying the same thing over and over for quite some time, when suddenly it is as if something inside shifts, and we go from playing the music to feeling as though the music is actually playing through us. We go from being the surfer surfing the wave, to feeling the energy of the ocean coursing through and guiding our movements upon it. From being the writer writing the story, to feeling as though some greater intelligence or creative essence (the Muse!) is actually elevating our thought patterns and expressing itself through us on the page.

As with our leap from Level 1 to Level 2, in order to move to our 3rd Level in Consciousness we must again be willing to both claim something new and let go of an aspect no longer needed. As we move into 'Through Me' consciousness, what we will claim is a new sense of CONNECTEDNESS to what we are doing, but what we must be willing to let go of is our sense or need of CONTROL. As we begin to recognize that this song, this wave, this story is bigger than we are, we begin to align ourselves more humbly with that greater energy, trusting its flow to carry us where we need to go.

When we enter 'Through Me' consciousness we will go from feeling quite significant in our own achievements to feeling a new sense of humility about being part of something greater than ourselves. In our hero's journey story form, this third level of consciousness often emerges in the second half of our story, where our heroes have crossed the initial threshold into the extraordinary world, and they have moved through the Tests and Allies stage, developing new skills to survive in this new world. Now, following their Point of True Commitment at the Midpoint, our characters must begin to demonstrate what they have learned in ways that really matter, not only to themselves but to the world around them. In many cases, this section of the story will see our heroes coming up against higher levels of challenge that will literally force them to reach beyond their own individual skills and abilities, into the expanded realms of human (and other) potential. Ultimately the hero will be drawn into their Inner Most Cave, where through surrender or exhaustion of their own personal abilities, they will open themselves to the higher energetic forces within. Losing control may cause them to face their own mortality, but in doing so, they begin to harness their capacity to reach beyond it. This is the doorway from our 'By Me' experience of the world to our Third Level of Consciousness, 'Through Me.'

WRITING EXERCISE

Think of a time when you had been practicing or working on something to the point that you began to feel a shift in your experience. Perhaps subtle at first, perhaps clearly pronounced, a moment in time when you went from focusing your energy and doing the task at hand, to quite literally feeling as though the energy of the activity was moving through and guiding you. This feeling of the music, the ocean, the skateboard or the muse moving 'through you'. *Take yourself right to that moment and describe in detail what lead up to the moment, how it felt, and where it leads to in your experience.*

Level 4: 'AS ME'
When we let go of blame and move from our perception of life as something that happens 'To Me', we begin to discover our true power in a life that happens 'By Me'. When we let go of the need to control, we move from our perception of life happening 'By Me', to discovering our connection to the greater powers of life itself moving 'Through Me'. As we travel through the Third Level of Consciousness and experience this sense of flow on a consistent basis, eventually, perhaps when we least expect it, we will come to a fourth leaping-off point and the simple but profound realization that we and this greater energy that is moving through us are actually the same thing. That whatever is moving 'Through Me' is also inside of me… To move beyond the experience of life occurring 'Through Me'

we must be willing to claim a sense of UNITY (also known as ONENESS), and to do so (or rather 'be' so), we must simply be willing to let go of our sense of SEPARATION.

Moving into the Fourth Level of Consciousness, we let go of our perception of the infinite nature of the Universe as an energy that moves around and through us, and we open ourselves to experience this infinite nature in and 'as' our very being. This is the purest expression of who we really are. I and the greater forces of the Universe are ONE. The music, the ocean, the story I am telling are not only moving 'Through Me' and guiding my expression... they are moving 'As Me', the living expression of who I Am.

When we and our heroes enter the 'As Me' phase of consciousness, we begin to recognize ourselves as a note in life's great song, as a ray of the sun, as a drop in the ocean... at once unique and fully expressive yet also perfectly blending as part of the whole.

In many stories and hero's journey experiences, the Climax calls for a level of almost supernatural Self-expression from our characters... the type of unity of movement that only comes from a deep sense of inner alignment with the greater forces of life. This is a place of both absolute mastery and absolute humility as our hero comes to the peak of his/her personal expression, and in doing so, unifies with that same space in others and dissolves into the greater force of life within and all around them. We all know these moments when, through conscious focus or complete surrender, we feel as though we have touched, and expressed, the energy of God/Spirit/Infinite potential in our actions and our being. 'As Me' Consciousness is the space our heroes must often come to – at least briefly – as they move through the Climax of their journey.

WRITING EXERCISE

Consider a time or moment in your life when the elements of your endeavor converged in such a way that you felt a genuine sense of unity and oneness with what you were doing, who you were with and the world around you. A moment when you felt the veils of separation drop between you and the great creative energy of life and for a time experienced yourself AS a part of this energy. Not just an acknowledgement of something greater 'out there', but of the presence of that something greater in and as <u>who</u> you really are. Take some time to drop into this space and describe the experience in detail... Where it came from, what it felt like and what emerged from the moment.

__EXTRA CHALLENGE:__ Now that we have touched on the four levels of consciousness and begun to see how they play out in our lives, see if you can think of a single event, experience or area of life in which you moved from Level 1 'To Me' up through each of the different levels and layers, finally arriving to a place of genuine unity and Level 4 'As Me'.

__DOUBLE EXTRA CHALLENGE:__ Now do the same for the hero of your story! Explore his/her different phases of consciousness throughout the Acts of the story you are creating and what events lead him/her to let go of what must be released in order to step up and claim the next level of being. Track their journey from start to finish and see if you can recognize the key moments of shift in their consciousness. Where do they begin their journey and where do they end?

Do the same with a few films this week and see how the Four Levels of Consciousness weave through and inform the actions of your favorite heroes in cinema.

While not every story will bring the character through each and every level of consciousness, and while every hero may not fully realize their own Level 4 'As Me' state of being, it is powerful to bring this level of awareness to our writing so that if there is a chance to lead our stories, our heroes and our audience into their own experience of a genuine shift in consciousness, we can follow a natural progression that opens the doorway from one to the next. We know what must be claimed and we know what must be released as we rise from 'To Me' to 'By Me' to 'Through Me' and ultimately enter 'As Me' Consciousness. This is the journey of transformation in story and in life. It is not a stagnant model but a dynamic pattern that grows and evolves in each 'now' moment as we do in the various phases of our life. It is not a destination, but a journey. In one sense we may never fully 'get there', but in another sense there is actually nothing to 'get'. The highest form of consciousness is our purest form of being who we already are.

Having come through this exploration I am left with a different visual sensation for what our map of story could look like… Keeping it in one straight line doesn't quite capture the full dimensionality of the journey, so I will attempt to draw this story path a little differently now, suggesting the infinite spiraling potential of this pathway into higher consciousness and the stories that are ready to be shared along the way!

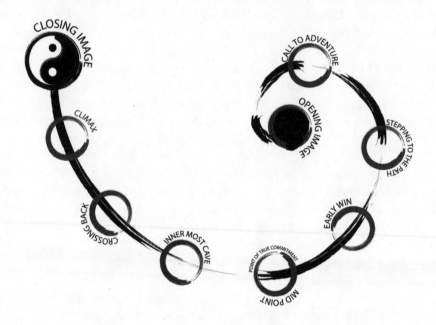

"Each one of us is Life personalized. We are each Life as a person; therefore, each one of us contains within himself all the intelligence, the power, the faculties and the instruments for the expression of Life. Each person has the ability within himself, the power and the intelligence at his command to express Life in peace and happiness, in abundance and satisfaction… To know that Life became you for a purpose and that you occupy a place no one else in all the world occupies…"
– Dan Custer, The Miracle of Mind Power

Crafting the Scene
(The Micro in the Macro)

"We cannot choose where to start and stop. Our stories are the tellers of us."
– Chris Cleave, Little Bee

In the same way that we will come to see our heroes as the carriers of our story's message, we will also come to see our scenes as the carriers of our heroes. Each scene is like a stepping-stone in the river of our story. The current is strong and winding. The stones are round and wet. At times wobbly, at times a stretch to reach and leap from one to the next. We can't go backwards, but occasionally the river winds around herself in such a way that we catch a glimpse back to all the shining stones we have journeyed across so far. We can't see too far ahead, but every once in a while we catch the scent of ocean air, letting us know we are heading the right direction. The river unfolds in ways we may never have imagined, and yet when all is said and done we look back upon the river path – perhaps with a sense of awe – and we know it was just exactly as it needed to be in order to bring us to where we have come. And every stepping-stone on the journey was somehow essential to our passage.

Modern audiences are savvy, clever and quick to assess characters and situations. Even (or especially!) kids are incredibly adept at filling in the gaps and putting subtle pieces together to make a whole. As people, we do this continually throughout each day – entering the scenes of our life, assessing the mood and manner of those we connect with, making micro-adjustments in our behavior along the way to enable us to continue moving along our own story path. The amount of information we read, take in (and give) just in watching someone walk across the room is astounding. We're not always right in our assessment, but we're constantly doing it. Filling the gaps and making up stories. In my home town of Byron Bay, when I see a guy with white finger shapes on the outside edge of his sunburned back, I instantly know he's a fresh arrival to the sun. I imagine him trying to reach those hard-to-reach spots with sunscreen on his first day, thinking he's done a good job and heading out into the heat. I can feel the tenderness and peeling that may soon be to come and I think back to the first day of a family holiday when I was a kid, arriving maroon-colored to dinner after choosing not to use sunscreen that afternoon. Drifting back to this guy on the street, I hear him laugh and say a few words to his friend and now I know he's from Europe… from the sounds (and looks) of it, northern Europe. This makes me think of my own last trip to Europe and of a future journey that Ash wants to take… I have never spoken with this guy but in just a few moments of watching him I take in what I see and begin filling in the gaps with my view of his story… while connecting it back to my own! As an audience in story we are like sleuths. Our minds crave this sense of engagement where we have must pull the pieces together and see them as a greater whole (while making subconscious connections back into our own world). To make a leap from one moment to the next and, through subtle cues, fill in the gaps between them. As we journey down the story path, there is a fine line between depriving our audience of essential information (which they hate) and spoon-feeding them with too much (which they sometimes hate even more). Walking this line is an intricate dance, and begins as we begin to focus in on the structure, flow and placement of our scenes.

We could probably write a whole book about the art of crafting effective scenes – in fact several people have – but for now let's just take a moment to explore some of the essentials. In doing so we'll realize that we don't actually need a whole book to learn and study scene structure, because in a strange sort of way, we're already holding one! Allow me to explain...

THE MICRO AND THE MACRO

The first cool thing to realize about writing effective scenes is that just about everything we have learned so far about story as a whole applies on a micro-cosmic level with the creation of our scenes. Much like many other beautiful phenomena in the natural world, at their very core, stories can be seen as fractals.

> **frac·tal** *n*
> *An irregular or fragmented geometric shape that can be repeatedly subdivided into parts, each of which is a smaller copy of the whole.*
> (Encarta® World English Dictionary © 1999 Microsoft Corporation)

Like drops in the ocean or particles of clouds, stories can be divided into smaller and smaller components. Each piece carries a complete energy all of its own, while sharing fundamental principles and many similar attributes to the whole. This is true for the overall story structure down to the individual Sections/Acts (which are made up of a series of Sequences), down to the individual Sequences (which are made up of a series of Scenes), down to the individual Scenes (which are made up of a series of Beats), down to individual Beats (which are made up of a series of singular Moments) down to single moments. Now.

In the same way that every story has a beginning, middle and end, so too does every scene. In the same way that every story is essentially propelled by the desire of our hero, so too is each scene driven by the wants or needs of the character(s) within it. And much like the Hero's Journey form as a whole, our characters enter each scene with a specific 'call to adventure', they often must cross some threshold of what is comfortable in efforts to take steps toward achieving their desire, they experience challenge, conflict and stakes, ultimately leading them to the heart center or crux (a.k.a. inner most cave) of the scene where some shift or change is required to break through and get what they really want. In a sense, each scene can be seen as a miniature hero's journey experience for our characters.

Not all scenes resolve and come full circle like a full hero's journey experience does, but within each scene are elements that feed into each other, while also building bridges to the scenes before and after.

By following your overall understanding of story into the building of your scenes, you will find that your scenes develop quite naturally. Here are a few golden keys to help kick things off and stay on track!

Scene Key #1: Start with the End in Mind (a.k.a. Know your WHY)
Early in our journey we took some time to clarify the end-result 'intention' for our story. That fundamental, feeling-based outcome or emotional take-away that we are committed to creating with our tale. What are we going to leave our readers and viewers with at the end? Knowing that our story may carry several gifts, messages and nuggets along the way, it can be exceptionally helpful to ask the question, "If I could only achieve ONE outcome with my story, if I could deliver just one message, what would that be? What is at the very heart center of this tale?" In essence, "WHY am I writing this story?"

When we take time to crystallize the ultimate emotional outcome of our story, we are left with an energetic North Star to follow, track and refer to throughout our journey of writing it. A feeling-based spine that will intuitively inform each decision and step along the way. Sure, the path will twist, wind, double back and lead us into moments and experiences we never imagined prior to commencing, but if we have our internal compass set for where we are eventually going to arrive, we will find ourselves naturally making creative decisions that uniquely lead us there. And we will enjoy the process along the way!

The same is absolutely true for the creation of our scenes. If we take the time to really clarify our intention, and discover the deeper WHY of our scenes, we will save days, weeks, lifetimes of energy searching for it in our words. In the beginning of my professional writing path, there were times when I would quite literally spend days working on a single scene without really, truly getting clear what it was about. I eventually realized that was why it was taking me so long! I knew what was supposed to happen to satisfy my story outline, but I didn't know *why*.

In every scene, every story, every life, we reach moments where clarity of purpose is essential to move forward. If we don't have it… we get stuck, we wander, we stray. When we don't know the purpose of what we are doing, the steps we take become an exploration of that question. When we don't know the underlying purpose of a scene, our writing becomes our process of searching for that essence. Sometimes this is the best way to discover what we're looking for – by writing ourselves there. But sometimes we don't have time for this. And either way, challenging ourselves to clarify our underlying intention for the scene allows us to powerfully navigate the path to get there. This doesn't mean over-engineering or planning so much that we stomp the heartbeat from our scenes. On the contrary, by setting a clear emotional imprint into our own heart before we begin, we open wide the gates for the wild horses of inspiration to gallop forth. Our path may shift by the second line… but guided by our North Star, we can relax and allow the journey to unfold, trusting that our compass is set and we will arrive just where we need to go in the perfect time and way.

Key Questions: *If your scene could achieve only one thing, deliver one clear message or leave your readers with one clear feeling or experience, what would that be? What is the single most important purpose of this scene? Why is it necessary for the telling of this tale?*

Scene Key #2: Come in Late… Get Out Early

When we tell a story, one of the keys to building characters and circumstance is knowing what happened before our story began (also known as the back-story) as well as having a sense for what's going to happen next, in the future once our story is complete. In most cases, the stories we tell are just brief cross sections of a much wider continuum. As authors, when we take time to get to know the bigger picture, our words have a way of carrying the depth and weight of that broader perspective, even if we never mention it directly. In life, we can tell a lot about someone's past simply by the way they act in the present, so with story, by being true to the moment, the most relevant pieces of past information almost always have a way of finding their way to the surface.

Armed with this wider view of the overall story (the one that stretches before and after), one of our greatest roles and responsibilities as storytellers – that can actually cause excruciating procrastination if we are not careful – is deciding where to begin, and what cross-section of the overall story to include in the telling of *our* tale.

A common occurrence in early drafts is to think we need to include more than we really do. I have worked with several writers and stories where after close inspection of the overall story, we realize that the first ten pages – or in some cases the entire first act – is really just back-story, and not needed in the telling of this tale. And while the extra information is interesting, we usually find that if we jump into the story a bit further downstream, our readers have a way of catching up and what's more, they enjoy the process of doing so.

The same is very true for the crafting of effective scenes. While our tendency as writers is to want to make sure our readers are fully up to speed each step of the way, we also need to keep things moving and trust that our audience is ready to pull their weight. To this end, one of the guidelines I like to follow when I am crafting scenes is to 'Come in Late and Get Out Early'. Sure, there are times when we will want to draw out a moment from the very beginning right to the end in full detail, but in many cases we can come in a lot later than we think, and we can get out of the scene a lot earlier that we might imagine, and our readers will still come away with everything they need. When we throw our readers in midstream they quickly learn to swim, and in most cases they love us for it. If we want to write about our heroes going to a baseball game together, do we need to show them buying tickets, waiting in line, buying drinks and hotdogs, finding their seats, watching the game, then waiting in line to get out and driving home? Or can we just describe a single moment of them leaping up from their seats, cheering and spilling their drinks on each other as someone hits a homerun? Of course there are instances when we will want to show each of the individual steps of an event, but in most cases, it is wise to govern the length of our scenes by asking, "When is the latest I can come in and the earliest I can get out and still leave the readers with the essence of this moment?"

Remember, as per Story Key #1, each scene is here to deliver ONE THING, one next step, one key message or gift to our hero. If we know what that is, we begin to sense what else is needed (and what is not) to make the moment ring true. It's also important to realize that we don't need to tie a bow around each scene. We don't need to answer every question and resolve every issue. Sometimes the gift of a scene is simply extending a question or leaving us wondering what will happen next. The great thing about individual scenes is that they almost always lead to more scenes, so letting them gradually unravel is a gift to the audience. We contribute to this mission by coming in late and getting out early.

Sometimes I will enter a writing passage right in the middle, at the very crux moment and then circle back if need be and fill in the readers as I move along. By stepping into a passage midstream in this way, it instantly calls for the full attention of the reader, and once you have that full attention you can guide it wherever you need it to go. The following is the beginning of a research article I wrote about the power of sound. Rather than beginning the article with the facts, I chose to leap right to the middle of one of my most powerful experiences ever with sound, and let that be the doorway to the research…

*

I remember the first time I heard it. I had forgotten my wetsuit that morning, so I was shivering even as I looked out from the beach. But the water was so crystal clear, it felt like it was calling me… and I knew I had to answer. As I reached the sapphire waters out past the break, I slid off my surfboard and dove down deep – something the buoyancy of my forgotten wetsuit would have made slightly more difficult. I swam down as far as I could go, where all is silent and still… And as I stretched through the morning sunrays, I suddenly heard him in the distance… His hauntingly peaceful hymn, echoing through the water. Moving to and through me. Coming up for air, I saw his breath plume on the horizon… and I dove back down to listen. This ancient song that has circled the globe for millions of years. This song that continues to change and evolve, yet is sung in unison by all within a thousand miles.

It has been said that the song-lines of whales weave a sonic web of energy through Earth's waters... that the vibration of their singing actually helps to keep the magnetic fields of our planet in balance (while aiding their navigation through it in the process). As the pulse of this Humpback sonnet encircled me, I felt the truth of this theory to the core of my being. For a moment, with my own garbled bubbling from the depths, I attempt to sing back. Then I rise to the surface with a yearning question permeating my being... How could we begin to access the primordial energy of our own voice in such a way that it could contribute to the balance of life?

*

WRITING EXERCISE:
COME IN LATE... GET OUT EARLY

Write a brief story description of the most interesting/impactful moment in your day today, including everything that happened. Write out the scene from start to finish with all of the details you can remember, including the events leading into and out of that moment, and the message it left you with. Next, re-write that critical moment focusing more purely on the 'heart-centre' or the crux of the moment. Try coming into your scene midstream, without all the back-story leading up to it. Try coming in just before (or even just after) the key moment and see how that changes your writing. Play also with your exit. Can you leave the scene early enough to make it a cliffhanger, so we have to keep on reading?

Scene Key #3: Every Scene Brings Change
To live and survive all things must grow and evolve. Nothing static lasts. At its heart, each story is a living expression of this truth, and each scene is its testament.

One of the things we have discussed throughout our *Writing the Story Within* experience is that story, in its very essence, is about transformation. The reason our heroes are called on their journeys is because they are being called to change, to grow, to transform. The reason we follow them into their story is because we are called to the same. We are each called to awaken some aspect or faculty within ourselves, to claim some gift or elixir from the path and to bring it back into our own world as a beacon of the new. Who and how our hero is in the end of our story will always in some way be different than who and how s/he was when the story begins. It must be so for this is the nature of story. Along with the pure thrill of the ride, it is the promise of growth and transformation that draws us to join our heroes on their journey. And with good reason.

On a microcosmic level, the same is true with our scenes... In order to deliver an effective scene, along with knowing what the purpose of our scene is (Scene Key #1), and delivering just the right cross section slice of the bigger picture (Scene Key #2), we have to be vigilant about asking and answering the question, "What is different at the end of this scene than when we began?" (Scene Key #3)

Something needs to have changed or shifted during the course of our scene, and more often than not, that something is what we call the 'emotional charge'. Story master Robert McKee has developed a comprehensive science around this element, but in basic terms we can track the emotional charge of our scenes in much the way we track currents of electricity – as a series of opposite charges connected to each other. In electricity, opposite charges (negative to positive or positive to negative) are needed for an energy current to flow. In a simple sense, this is how it works with our scenes. If one scene has an overarching positive feeling or result for our hero, chances are very high that the next scene will bring about a setback or unforeseen challenge of some sort. If one scene is overtly negative, then chances are high there will be at least a small concession or shift toward the positive in the scene that follows... and the one after that will flip to the negative again, and onward we go.

These same principles can often be applied within the scenes themselves. If you have a scene that starts off with a negative charge, challenge or setback to the hero, through the course of the scene that charge will usually shift to the positive. The problem may not be totally solved, but in some way the charge of the scene will have shifted. Change for the better or in some cases change for the worse (going from bad to extra bad). Either way it's change, and that's what we need to keep the story alive. If you have a character or scene that starts in one state of being and just coasts through without shifting or changing in any way, you will eventually find yourself asking the question, "Is this scene even necessary?" If it's not changing in some way, it probably is not.

Shifting and changing the emotional charge throughout our stories keeps the energy alive and moving, and it also keeps our readers fresh. Too much of one energy – good or bad – and they will get bored or worn out. With most well-crafted stories you can actually track along from start to finish, giving an overall positive or negative charge to each scene and you will see that they pretty much alternate, building upon each other throughout the entire tale. Sometimes there will be some asymmetry and irregularity in the rhythm, sometimes the charge will go from bad to worse or good to great, but the energy will constantly be shifting and changing, matching positive with negative charge. This is a law of electricity and Scene Key #3.

Scene Key #4: Pull Back the Sling Shot

When we have set a clear feeling-based intention for our scene (Scene Key #1) and/or our story, one of my very favorite things to do next is what I call, 'Pull the Sling Shot Back'. What I mean by this is to pull ourselves right back to the beginning of the scene (with a clear understanding of where we are heading) and ask ourselves, *"OK. Now that I know where we're going to end up... what is the most interesting, engaging, unique and dynamic way to get there?"* When we first start writing scenes, we often succumb to the temptation to write our characters to the outcome as quickly and directly as possible. We just get them there without any major twists, turns or tugs on their sense of character. If we don't pull our hero far enough back from where s/he will ultimately end up we may find that it just isn't that fun or compelling to get there. If there was ever a place in life where 'getting there is half the fun', story is that place. So pull back the sling shot as far and unexpectedly as you can.

The perfect place to practice this concept of 'Pulling Back the Slingshot' in our story is to do so on a microcosmic level with each and every scene we write. Where am I going to end up? And knowing that, where is the most interesting and compelling – and often uniquely challenging – place for my hero to start? Once you get into the flow of writing scenes, you will come to love this question, because it always allows for something dynamic and unexpected to enter the mix. It pulls us out of the box. Often times I will write an initial draft of a scene without thinking too much about it, simply to establish a clear end point. Then once I have that end point, I come back to the scene and pull the sling shot back.

If you know for example that this is the scene that the two young lovers kiss for the first time, that's great. You can set your compass for kissing, then pause to consider what are the most interesting challenges we could throw in the way of two people wanting to kiss for the first time? How can we pull them right back away from the possibility of kissing so no one thinks it's going to happen, and then somehow navigate the waters back to the center again? We've all seen scenes where that kiss is handed to us on a platter and (depending on the kiss!) it can leave us feeling less than truly fulfilled. But when we have had to work for it, when we have had to feel the tension of desire mounting within, meeting genuine obstacles and challenges along the way, then we appreciate arriving to the moment so much more when we finally get there. Perhaps we'll choose to begin the scene in the midst of an argument, or place the characters on an amusement park ride where one of our heroes wants to vomit, or maybe the desire is clear but friends and family keep coming in at awkward times until the whole room is full of people who aren't supposed to be there... Or maybe they don't like each other at all and their first kiss happens in a dare game or by accident when one of them trips into the other. When we pose a challenge to our heroes that even we don't quite know how to solve, then we will be forced to dig a little deeper to find the most engaging answer. At that stage we are usually on the right track to writing a compelling scene.

Pulling back the slingshot is about raising the stakes for our heroes, and it's also about 'amping up' our creativity as a writer. Asking ourselves to think beyond the dots and allow the most unique expression of our scene to come through. Once you know where you and your heroes are heading, it's a matter of asking, "Are we going to take the highway at full speed, or are we going to wind our way along the river on a unicycle?" There will be right times for both. It's about setting our sights on the story map and then having the courage to step back and ask, "What's the most outrageously unlikely, engaging and character revealing place I can start in order to reach this end point?" Ask this question and your mind will go to work finding unique and compelling answers from the back end of a fully stretched slingshot.

> ## WRITING EXERCISE:
> ## PULLING BACK THE SLINGSHOT
>
> *Write a first kiss moment from your own life, from your story or simply from your imagination. Think of the facts and where your scene will arrive, then dig as deep as you can and see how far you can pull back the slingshot in just a short space of time. Begin the scene from some place very different than where you plan to end it, and see if you can challenge yourself to find the most unexpected but enjoyably compelling pathway to get there. Take 5 minutes and do this now. Have fun, dive in. Go!*

Scene Key #5: The *And, And* Factor

It is said that you shouldn't rely on your family to be honest critics of your writing, but throughout my professional writing career I have discovered quite the opposite to be true. Ash is probably the most clear and honest person I have ever met, so when she reads my work she does so with a laser-like ability to expose holes and sticking points. Josh on the other hand, brings a different element – one I like to call 'The *And, And* Factor'.

Have you ever noticed that when you tell a story, to a room full of people, you naturally shift and shape the telling based on the subtle responses and reactions that you receive? If, as you're recounting the tale, you get some unexpected laughs from a certain moment or aspect of the story, you might pause there and ride that wave a bit longer. If you feel like you're losing your crowd or boring them, well you might find yourself skipping right to the end… or changing your focus to pull them back in. Telling stories live is one of the greatest ways to gauge the rhythm and flow of a tale… and to see if it is resonating with a living audience. In my experience, there is no more brutally honest and rewarding arena to test out stories than with kids.

Like many dads out there, very early on in Josh's life, I became a source for bedtime adventure stories. Stories that up until the telling, I never even knew existed. Sure we read books some nights, but once I started making up live tales, there was no going back. I'm not sure where they come from, but when it's bedtime and there's a bright bold kid staring at you waiting for something magic to emerge, it just so happens that it often does. Probably similar to many dads and moms out there, a lot of our initial stories began with stuffed animal props that were already with us on the bed. Deb the rabbit gave birth to a whole series of stories about 'Deb's First Skateboard', Spark the bat became the unlikely hero of the legend of 'The Great Grandfather Bat School'.

It's not always easy to muster the muse under pressure (particularly at the end of a long day), but if we take the leap and begin, we quickly learn that stories can rise out of pretty much anything. If you have a title, a character, a piece of string or the tiniest spark of an idea, from that seed a story will grow. And if your child is anything like my child, you will find that they will quite literally pull the thing from you! When Josh was really little, I always knew when my story was hitting the mark because he would be perched there with his dummy (a.k.a. 'pacifier') hanging half out of his half-opened mouth like a cigar, watching me with a wild sort of smile. This grin would encourage me to keep on going but once we were into the story there was no turning back. In fact, if I so much as paused to think of what came next, Josh would jump right in there or elbow me in the chest saying, *"And...? And...?"* There was no room for thinking, no room for reflection. We were on the story train and this train was moving. The incessant "ands" would sometimes start stressing me out and eventually I would have to stop and just say, *"Hang on a second, it's coming!"* But the gift in Josh's hyper-presence was that it kept me right on the pulse of the moment. I knew that if I wanted to keep his attention, I had to keep coming up with better and better twists and turns to the story. The ultimate climax would come when the half-cracked smile exploded into a belly laughter and there was nothing left to say "And" about. At that stage, I was usually exhausted and out of breath, and Josh was so ramped up that he was ready for the sequel.

Night after night, Josh's "Ands" kept me on the pulse, they kept me creatively moving and they forced me to continue digging deeper to find more exciting and engaging resolutions to each new tale. A few years later when I was working on a major animated kids film, Josh became my ultimate script editor. After writing each scene I would print it and bring it to bedtime. If it worked live with Josh, I knew it would work for whoever was reading it. In fact, I even started asking Josh for his advice on certain scenes I was having trouble with, and one of his clear impulses lead to the crafting of a scene that became a unanimous favorite among all readers of the draft. From the mouths of babes, and from our desperate responses to the "And, And" factor, great stories emerge.

EXERCISE:
TELL A STORY LIVE TONIGHT

If you have a kid nearby or in your household, belly up to the bedtime arena, grab the first stuffed animal you can find and see what story sparks rise to greet you. You don't have to have the whole thing planned out – or even any of it. Just begin and let the eyes and response of your audience guide the way. If you don't have access to kids, then tell a story to someone else in your world. The same response is available; it may just be covered with a few more layers. But if your story is fun and if you are connected to the moment, you will find that even the most cynical listener will quite quickly be distilled down to that childlike essence that loves a good story. Before long, you'll be able to sense the energy of "And...?" in their eyes, and you might even be able to pop a dummy in their half-opened mouth.

As we refine the shape of our story, as we put each scene to the litmus test and as we muster the courage to combine, remove and shift stones around in the current, we discover ways to give our readers just what they want/need in ways that they couldn't have imagined. We lead them on a journey they would not have expected and we leave room for them to climb inside fully engaged, connecting key dots, releasing the slingshot and leaping from stone to stone along the way... saying "And...?" at every turn!

WRITING EXERCISE:
TRACKING THE BEATS OF SCENE

Following our scene discussion, I invite you to take the following challenge this week. Watch a film with remote control in hand, and stop the story after each scene to assess what happened and how the scene moved the story/characters forward on the path. With at least a few key scenes that you really love write down the answers to the following questions:

What is this scene about and why is it essential for the story?
What does the main character of the scene want?
What does the main character need?
What is the primary want/need of other characters in the scene?

How far 'into the scene' does the scene begin (i.e. do we begin at the beginning or are we jumping in midstream), and how early does it end?

What stops/challenges the character from getting what s/he wants? How does this challenge stretch him/her to do things we may not have expected?

Beat for beat (moment by moment, action by action), what actually HAPPENS in the scene? Is every beat and moment necessary?

Can you see the pattern of the hero's journey or the basic 3-Act structure (beginning, middle end) unfolding in microcosmic ways in the scene?

Can you recognize the alternating flow of positive and negative charge? What is the 'emotional charge' at the beginning of the scene (the basic feeling as we come into the scene)?

What is the 'emotional charge' at the end of the scene (the basic feeling as we come out of the scene)?

What is the ultimate outcome of the scene?

What makes it possible for the hero to achieve a fulfilling outcome (or why don't they?)?

Can you think of anything that could have made the scene even more compelling, engaging or revealing of the character (Could they have pulled back the slingshot even further? Were you saying "And...And...?" each step of the way?)?

EXTRA STORY CHALLENGE:
Do this same exercise with one (or better yet, ALL!) of the scenes of YOUR story.

This process may feel a little time consuming at first, but as you hone into the rhythms and beats of the scenes of story, you will begin to naturally track the subtle, deeper undercurrents that drive and motivate the characters within each moment and scene you watch, read and write. As you do this with stories outside of you, you will invariably gain a deeper connected understanding and more informed perspective of your own story... and the stories you are here to share. You will be able to troubleshoot challenging scenes and add new dynamics to all key story moments... And in doing so you will add dimension to your whole story experience (inside and out!).

The Balance of Writing and Life

"The best way to prepare for life is to begin to live."
– Elbert Hubbard

*

Many years ago when I was just starting to nurture my dream to write stories for cinema, Asheyana and I visited Los Angeles with the idea that maybe we would move there for a while. As the global epicenter of cinematic creativity, it seemed like a logical place to live and be if writing movies was the dream. So I lined up a few meetings with friends of friends and contacts in the film world to see what possibilities could be stirred. One of the meetings was with the founder of a successful television production company who, at the time had three episodic shows in full production and several others in development. We hit it off straight away and had a great chat as he looked through my rather unorthodox resume, which at the time had no major film or writing credits, but plenty of life adventure and a few unique pieces of creative entrepreneurialism (ranging from short film production to ski clothing design). Toward the end of our conversation he said that if I ever lived in LA he'd love to have me as part of his team. I started to smile, thinking this was a sign and my window to express our LA living idea. But in the very next breath – before I could speak – he finished his thought by saying, "But... my greatest advice to you would be, don't move here." I was a bit taken aback. He went on to explain that while Los Angeles is indeed a brewing pot for incredible creative success, to live within that pot can be very stifling and oppressive for creative individuals. A lot of people get caught up in who is doing what project and who just sold what story or optioned what script and all the rest of the blah blah blah of trying to make it in LA, which can end up being a huge obstacle to actually creating and producing something of genuine meaning and significance. He looked me in the eye and said, "Look, if you have a real inkling to live and work your way up amongst the Hollywood scene, then by all means come. I'll help you in any way I can. But my greatest advice to you would be to go live somewhere else where you can have a life full of deep and meaningful experiences. Let those experiences infuse and inspire your writing, and then when you are ready, come back here and bring us something new and fresh. There is an ever-increasing thirst for creative originality in the world, and particularly in this town. In my experience that type of originality comes best from living an originally creative life. Go live someplace amazing... and then when you're ready, bring a slice of that amazing back here to share."

*

I have always been a kinesthetic and experiential learner, and this conversation was enough for me to feel totally great about flying back across the Pacific and re-immersing myself in Australian life. Rather than being in Australia, thinking I should be in LA where 'everything was happening', I allowed myself to relax into whatever experiences arose on my path, trusting that the richer the life lived, the deeper and more truthful the stories told would be. Interestingly enough, within a few months after arriving back to Australia I found myself being paid to write and produce pilots for television – one of which was a documentary series that eventually went to air called (believe it or not) 'Australian Life'! And six months after that, after connecting with a dynamic youth charity organization in Melbourne, called REACH, I was hired by one of its founding directors to write my first feature film (something that may not have happened had I been working away in the trenches of LA).

So what was the lesson? Well, for me it was two-fold. First of all, the greatest inspiration for story is life. Period. And secondly, the magic of the Universe is not bound by geography. If you have a clear desire and intention to write or create something (in whatever medium), and if you are willing to step out into the world with that intention and follow the path that opens with a certain level of trust, it will almost always lead you to the full fruition of your vision in ways that you could never have imagined – often a lot faster and more enjoyably than if you would have simply followed the path that your thinking mind might have initially thought you should take.

This morning I woke with an inner calling to spend the day up on Mt. Ashland, the guardian peak that sits above the town we have been living in for the past six months. I am leaving here in a few days to begin my journey back to Australia to join my family, and I have felt inspired to go pay homage to the mountain for being such a gracious host and to spend the day in quietude, writing. I had given myself a deadline to finish my book before I left, so with just a few short days and pieces left to go, I could feel the power of a day in the mountains to help bring it all through. My only concern was that the tires on our truck (the keys of which I am about to hand over) are in genuine need of replacement and so I wasn't crazy about the idea of driving on the gravel mountain roads. As I pulled up to the stop sign of the main road out of town, with this quiet debate moving through my mind, an old pick-up truck drove past, driven my friend Malcolm. Malcolm's one of a few great Aussies we've met while in Oregon and he was actually the very first person to bring me up to Mt. Ashland when we arrived several months ago. It had been over a decade since the last time I had skied, and in true Australian fashion, within about 30 minutes of meeting me, Malcolm had organized ski gear for me to borrow and set a plan to pick me and Josh up the following morning. Since finishing my ski-coaching career 13 years ago we'd spent most of our time living on the coast, embracing a rising passion for surfing and the ocean, unaware that anything was missing. But venturing up to the mountain with Malcolm the day after we met, had given me a chance to re-awaken a part of myself that had been laying dormant for years and it felt great. Like a favorite spice that had been left out life's recipe for so long that I had forgotten what it tasted like, then suddenly I caught a whiff again and everything came back. At the center of this piece of me was the pure and simple energy of FUN. So we made several trips up to the mountain together and it was an absolute delight to infect Josh with an enthusiastic bug for deep snow and mountain adventure. Now, in the height of summer six months later, I'm about to go up to the mountain and say goodbye, and here comes Malcolm driving along the road. I flagged him down to discover he was also heading up to the mountain to do some work on the Tibetan Buddhist temple half way up and he invited me to come along for the ride. This was a slight diversion from my plan of spending the whole day solo, but saved my worry for the tires and seemed somehow fitting, somehow right and almost poetically so, to be riding up the mountain on one of my last days with the guy who had brought me up there on one of my very first. Love the way this Universe works!

Malcolm's a practicing Buddhist and we've often dropped into pretty deep discussions about life and the spiritual path. He likes talking about all of his discoveries while exploring the particular lineage that he studies, and I really enjoy listening, asking questions and comparing thoughts from my own path. This day was a little different, as I already had a plan in motion and was quite focused on my writing. When he invited me to come with him to the temple and sit in the garden beneath the area where he was going to be working, I knew it would again change my vision for the day, but I kind of liked the idea of sitting at the foot of giant statues in the grass as I wrote. I didn't plan on spending much of the morning sitting in the garden; studying the plans for the enclosure Malcolm is building to protect the largest statue – a 34-foot high rendition of the Buddhist deity Vajrasattva, 'Indestructible Being'. I didn't plan that every time I got about 5 words of writing onto the page, Malcolm would chime in with another thought or idea about his design. I didn't plan for his suggestion that we take a lunch break at a local friend's property, where we would wander the garden of her sanctuary picking raspberries and wild cherries before swimming in her pond and drinking beer. I didn't plan that at this garden I would discover perhaps the closest replica of the type of garden Ash and Josh and I have been visioning for our new land (the type with enchanted paths of flowers and statues, fountains and willows, dragonflies, fruit trees, labyrinths and berries... so many berries). I didn't plan that Malcolm and his wife Vesna would join me at the end of the day to hike up to the top of the mountain and spend sunset sharing visions for when we all might meet up again.

All of this, if presented to me early in the day, compared to my clear and focused writing vision, would have appeared as unacceptable diversions from my very important path of writing... But somewhere between my first attempts to chisel down a few words before Malcolm's next building plan idea rose to the surface, and my second round of raspberry picking at the sanctuary, I decided to let go of my big plan and just relax into the day. If this is the way the river was flowing, maybe I just needed to go with it. Whatever valuable writing time was being used up here in this mountain valley, was being channeled into connecting with nature, connecting with close friends and living alongside the natural story of creation… And my theory was that the time would come back to me multiplied with new creative energy and raspberry-flavored inspiration when it was again time to write.

As the Universe would have it, about 15 minutes after I came to that realization, allowing myself to settle in to the spontaneous rhythm of the day, suddenly two things happened… Firstly, I realized that I no longer cared if I wrote a single word for the rest of the day, as long I was really there living fully. And with that, as if on cue, Malcolm put his tool belt on and quietly went to work up on the enclosure. Sure, he has continued to yell down each time a new bolt goes into place, but for the most part I've been down here in the garden ever since, quietly writing to my heart's content. And quite ironically, from this day and its funny winding path, has emerged this whole new piece for the book!

In Buddhism, the deity of Vajrasattva is said to represent 'complete purification of the obscurities to wisdom', opening the way for the qualities of enlightenment to be made manifest and rendered evident in our bodies and our lives. As I sit here in the grass at the foot of this giant effigy, I think I can see a slight spark of humor in his eye… it feels like he has gently taught me a lesson today about the obstacles in my own mind that sometimes keep me from experiencing the magic of a moment because I am so focused on the task at hand.

I'm reminded of a story I read in Paulo Coelho's book, *The Alchemist* (which I also discussed with Malcolm today!), where a young boy is given the task to tour around the halls of a great palace while carrying a spoon full of water, not spilling a drop. Some time later he returns, quite proud of himself that not a drop has spilled. The king asks him to describe the palace and artwork that he saw during his tour and the boy admits that he was so focused on carrying the spoon that he didn't actually see any of the artwork or details of the palace at all. To this (and I'm paraphrasing) the king replies that the secret to life is found in our ability to successfully carry the spoon while also taking in the beauty and wonders along the way.

And so it is, we must find the balance between living well and writing well. Between sticking to our plan of getting things done and allowing the so-called 'distractions' to perhaps lead us to even higher ground. The truth is that some days are for writing and some days are for living, and there are times when genuine focused effort and un-distractible commitment are required. But most days, if we are clear of our intention while being conscious of the rhythms of the moment, we usually get to do a bit of both, and each feeds and inspires the other. This is not to say that we should allow ourselves to be distracted from our committed mission of bringing through our great creative work (I have spent the past four hours now steadfastly typing), but in a very basic sense we can take heart with the knowledge that the better we live, the better also we will write. We may have to stay up late occasionally to finish what needs to be done, but if that is the case, at least our task will be alight with the fire of life.

Sometimes, when we are stuck or needing inspiration, the truth is we need to go pick raspberries for a while. And when our bellies are full of life's good fruit, we need to step from the path for a while and bring some of that magic through onto the page, the screen, the canvas or the clay… It is the responsibility of the artist to both experience life and to share the natural outward expression of what has been experienced, so that others may also taste the fruit, and be set out onto their own path of discovery.

It's now 10:57pm. I only just got home from the mountain, after scrambling to the very top for the sunset with Malcolm and Vesna, and feasting, literally feasting, our senses on 360 degrees of sunset magnificence. To the west, a crimson orange radiant ball lowering down through multiple layers of the Cascade Mountains. To our north, the rolling green forests of the Siskiyou Mountains. To our east, Pilot Rock, an ancient volcanic plug, which is almost an exact replica of my favorite Mt. Warning (Wollumbin) near Byron Bay in Australia. And to our south, Mt. Shasta. The guardian peak of all mountains in this region. Massive and truly magnificent… a wild swirl of clouds both circling and spraying up from her like mist on the back of an offshore wave. Driving down we stopped to gather wildflowers in at least seven colors and we discovered a spring bubbling out from the side of the mountain. It tasted like freezing cold honey so I took several giant gulps and filled up my bottle, knowing that diarrhea would be worth it if that was the price to pay (thankfully it wasn't). As we piled back into the car for the journey home, Malcolm concluded his description of the Buddhist deity Varjasattva, explaining that the primary offering and expression of purification from this deity comes in the form of our senses. That when the senses have been purified and illuminated, they actually become the five Buddhas, each reflecting a different aspect of enlightenment and pureness of being into our body and our being. As I reflect upon all of the little moments that made up our day… mountain breezes, wild fruit, swimming holes, human laughter, hawks cry, dancing dragonflies and wildflowers… each giving over to the next… most distracting me from what I thought I was supposed to be doing in order to lead me to some deeper food for my soul, I have an even fuller appreciation for this ever-present exchange between fires of life and the gift of creative expression. I can see the truth in the Varjasattva message for us, the writers of story. Not only do our purified senses have the capacity to enlighten our minds, our illuminated experiences have the wonderful ability to enlighten our entire creative path.

Entering the house, I'm aware that I'm still carrying the breakfast I left with this morning. I had fixed a fresh bowl of quinoa with almonds, blueberries and bee pollen for breakfast, but I was so keen to get up to the mountain and start writing, that I decided to take it with me. It's been with me each step of the way and here we are back at home together. I just took my first bite (11:03pm). I taste the sweetness of today's journey and find myself unfolding my computer as I do. I'll just write a little while I'm eating my breakfast, as I planned to do sixteen or so hours ago.

WRITING EXERCISE:
FOR THE BALANCE OF STORY AND LIFE

When the equation of living and creating is well balanced, we enter a sense of flow where 'everything nourishes everything.' On the creative path these two polarities can easily be confused and falsely justified. If we are social by nature we may quite easily justify procrastinating a night of needed writing in order to go out with friends, watch a film or take a walk. Under the guise of 'living our research' we can postpone writing for years. Likewise, if we are overly work-focused or more introverted by nature, we may find ourselves buried in our journal or diving right into the next draft of a project, when what we really need is to get out and take a big full breath of LIFE.

At this moment in your life and creative path, where do you fall in the balance between these two mutually required polarities?

LIFE EXPERIENCE ————————————————— *CREATIVE DELIVERY*

What can you do today, this week, right now to take a step toward bringing yourself into balance and full alignment with your highest creative expression? List 3 things you can do in the next seven days to enrich the exchange between the life you are living and the creative gifts that are ready to come through as a result.

Congratulations for completing Chapter 8 and the Climax of your *Writing the Story Within* journey! This is HUGE. I look forward to sharing the last two chapters truly as a gift to you as a writer, story steward and hero in life. Aho!

"...What happens is of little significance compared with the stories we tell ourselves about what happens. Events matter little, only stories of events affect us."
– Rabih Alameddine, The Hakawati

"Long before I wrote stories, I listened for stories. Listening for them is something more acute than listening to them. I suppose it's an early form of participation in what goes on. Listening children know stories are there.
When their elders sit and begin, children are just waiting and hoping for one to come out, like a mouse from its hole."
– Eudora Welty, One Writer's Beginnings

CHAPTER 9:

Your Closing Image

"Come to the edge, he said.
They said, we are afraid.
Come to the edge, he said.
They came,
He pushed them
And they flew."
– Apollinaire

Coming Full Circle
(Closing Your Story
and Beginning Your Path)

*"Even in literature and art, no man who bothers about originality will ever be
original: whereas if you simply try to tell the truth (without caring two pence
how often it has been told before) you will, nine times out of ten, become original
without ever having noticed it."*
- C. S. Lewis

Eight chapters and 30-some lessons ago, you answered the call of creative energy within you that was ready to be explored and expressed at new levels. You may have had a specific story or book idea in mind, or you may have just felt something deep within you stirring, waiting to be tapped into and experienced. For whatever reason, you said, "YES" to that part of yourself and began a new creative journey.

As is often true for the hero in story, what you initially thought brought you to the path may be different than what has emerged for you since. But whatever your *Writing the Story Within* journey has looked like (so far!), I want to acknowledge you for being here, where you are today! Whether you've stuck to the lesson plan and progressed steadily day-by-day or whether you've skipped around and now find yourself reading this chapter months or even years later, I trust that your own heroic self knows the high timing of your true creative path.

Anytime we answer a genuine inner calling and take steps to expand our true self and creative essence, we contribute to the GREAT STORY that's unfolding within each of us and our planet as a whole. We each have a vital piece to play in this great adventure tale, and the stories we live, create and share play a very important part.

As we explored in our Chapter 8 Climax lesson, the culmination of the Hero's Journey brings all that has been learned and experienced – inside and out – into a moment of fusion, where the hero has the opportunity (and often the necessity) to bring forth his/her true and highest self, while galvanizing and catalyzing the highest self of others. The hero moves from knowing the truth to being the truth on all levels. From the consciousness of 'to me' right up to the realization of life/God/true potential being lived and expressed 'as me'. The purpose of story is to transform, and our Climax moment is when that transformation is fully realized and expressed in the world.

While this moment usually comes near the end of the story, in truth it also marks a new beginning for our hero. It is a hallmark of all that has been, and an opening to the bright field of all that is to come. A beginning that may have been set into motion with the Opening Image or Call to Adventure hundreds of pages or minutes ago... and has taken us right to this very moment to be fully materialized.

As we lead, guide or follow our characters into the Closing Image of our story, we do so with a hint or glimpse of a whole new world opening before him/her. In *Avatar*, Jake Sully actually refers to this moment as his 'birthday', acknowledging that this moment marks a whole new phase of his existence. We are left with a Closing Image of the ceremonial ritual of transferring the life force of his human body into the body of his Avatar being, forever. One body dies and the other is born again into a new future among the Navi people. While we all received a glimpse of what this moment might look like in the very beginning (with Jake's Opening Image dream of flying over the jungles of Pandora), only right now as we arrive here to the end, do we truly see the circle closing and suddenly it all makes sense.

This is the nature of the Closing Image of our story. It is a poetic completion and quiet honoring of all that has been achieved and experienced. It often ties us back to the very beginning moment of our story, and in doing so, it shows us that while this journey has unraveled mysteriously one step at a time, there was a part of us that knew all along where we were going. There was a part of us that felt the deep whisper of this Closing Image moment in the distant echo of our initial entry into the story and the Call to Adventure that followed. And as we stand here in the moment of our completion, in our 'As Me' state of being, we can assume that this part of us that knew deep down what was coming, was also responsible for co-creating this journey in the first place. Whatever the origin of our journey may have looked like, it was most certainly catalyzed by that greater energy of life within, as a doorway to remember who we really are.

The following is a glimpse into a Closing Image of my own, which is a weaving of both my own story-writing and story-living paths, in the full circle moment that came to me in the closing hours of our recent journey to the US...

*

Time: 3:46 am
Location: Seat 56F, Air New Zealand flight 05. Flying over Nuku'alofa, South Pacific
We've been in the air for six hours. Three more to go before landing in Auckland, then onward another three to Melbourne where I'll reunite with Ash and Josh (after a final three hours in the car!). My travel day started 24 hours ago with a dawn barefoot walk

and IHOP (International House of Pancakes) breakfast with my brothers in Denver. Having burned the work-family-writing-packing candle at multiple ends right up to the moment of departure, I was pretty sleepy by the time I finished my plane tray of chicken-something, firm white bun with firmer butter and spongy lemon dessert (all of which hold an honored 'long flight only' place in my diet), so I watched half of a super hero movie and drifted off into nap-jerk-land until just a few minutes ago, when I bolted upright in my seat. My eyes focused on the flight status TV screen in front of me, and I found myself arriving at a fascinating full circle moment...

As I type this now, we are approaching the island of Nuku'alofa in the middle of the Pacific. Not an island I have visited or even consciously flown over in the past, but in glancing at the map, I notice that right in this very moment we happen to also be flying over the International Date Line. As soon I see that line on the map pictured directly underneath the little animated plane, I have a flash back to the first time I crossed this line just over 17 years ago. I had left my friends and family with a loose promise to return 1-2 years later. I remember hitting this exact spot on the journey and writing about it in my journal for about an hour.

I was baffled by the idea of skipping a whole day in time simply by crossing an imaginary line in the sea. As someone who has tried always to embrace the miracle potential in a single moment, I found myself wondering what magic moments might have been contained in that day that I was skipping simply by traveling west. As I tried to reconcile the time robbery equation the first time I faced it, I eventually arrived to a simple realization: If I truly believed that each moment held miracle potential, then all this time and day debate shouldn't really matter anyway. I could spend years chasing or running from time, or I could find a way to settle right into my shoes and simply be totally where I was. If I could bring 100% of my presence to the moment I was in, then what could and would be experienced in that moment would be far beyond the human confines of space and time anyway...

I hadn't left with the intention never to return. But in my moment-to-moment commitment to "squeeze the towel dry" my path had quite simply opened in ways well beyond what I had imagined. After seventeen years we came back to live in the US for the first time since I had left. Specifically in the past month, I have reconnected with many of the people I held closest to my heart before I left. Evening, soulful walks with my mom, café breakfasts and long heart-to-hearts with my dad, games of pool and fish tacos with my brothers. I have felt a sort of reclaiming of pieces of me that I never even realized were left behind those many years before. I have spent time in rivers and trees and mountain trails that hold deep cellular memories and flash backs of childhood. Laughter and road trip conversations. Snowdrifts, rock climbing and the creaking sound of early morning chairlifts. Inside jokes and movie quotes shared as a secret language with those I shared all of my rising years of youth with. I realize

*as I revisit these spaces that in my efforts to be present in the journey I have been on,
I have subtly blocked out many of the passages and doorways to my past. So in the
last month I have opened my heart to let them flood in. I have for the first time since I
left, fully allowed myself to stop, be still and really be back where I came from. Not in
a 'reliving the old days' way, but in a way that honors what has been, while allowing
each relationship and connection to rise fully into a new space that is relevant and
true for today. Getting caught up with all that we have each become.*

*Here in the wee hours of Monday morning with dark skies and deep blue ocean below,
I find myself snapping awake from slumber at the same moment in space and time
that I arrived to all those years ago on my first trip across the Pacific. Here in my
plane seat, listening to opera through plastic airplane headphones, I move quietly
across the International Dateline and arrive at a full circle moment of both returning
and of new beginning. I have spent much of the last month exploring what it means
to complete the sacred circle of a journey that began long ago, and here I find myself
arriving to an actual place of crossing a threshold from one day and time into another.
I did not realize it until now, but in a strange sort of way, this is the moment I have
been waiting for. As the tail of the plane crosses that imaginary line on the TV screen
before me, I breathe a moment of quiet completion, closing the circle of a journey that
began as young adventurer, opening to the presence of the hero in me. I give thanks to
the bold spark and spontaneous spirit that beckoned me out here in the first place...
and I give thanks for the golden embers that now draw me forward into the path
ahead. To challenge me to continue stretching my vision beyond the bounds of time
and space... To dream without limits and to give myself and all those I share this
journey with the opportunity to step with calm connectedness into the realization of
those dreams. While in one sense I have again said goodbye to the land of my birth
and a handful of those people I love the most in this life, this time I am doing so not
as a solo journeyman leaping blindly into space. This time I do so with deep peace
and excitement knowing that as I say goodbye to one part of my earth family, I am
returning to my tribe. Suddenly it seems acceptable to give up a day of time to be
here... perhaps it's just the admission price of the hero's journey of life.*

*As one journey ends, another begins again. I stand at the precipice with arms
outstretched, preparing to leap out and fly. Another breath and I open my eyes to see
that I already am.*

*

Today's lesson has two parts... one for your STORY and one for the writer you have
journeyed into BEING during the course of this book.

CLOSING YOUR STORY

We touched on the idea of the CLOSING IMAGE way back in Chapter 2 of our journey. At that time we each took a little time to envision where we wanted to end up. We started with our end in mind, with an image and a feeling. Having now taken time to drop in deeper in a variety of ways to your characters, to the themes, messages and key phases of your story, I invite you to take a few moments to reconnect with your story as a whole. To reflect on what you initially envisioned for your experience and to catch up to what you and your story have become along the way. To hear and see what new information and imagery your Muse may now have to share in terms of how this tale may end.

WRITING EXERCISE: YOUR CLOSING IMAGE

Take 5-10 minutes now to envision your way through your entire story from start to finish and beyond... and see what comes up for you. Knowing what you now know – and sensing what still may be in the process of being revealed – how might this story of yours come to a close in such a way that it brings us full circle to where we began, both lighting the path we have walked with new meaning and igniting a spark for what is yet to come?

As we asked ourselves in the very beginning, what is the fundamental feeling-outcome of this story? If you could leave your readers and viewers with one clear emotional truth, what would that be? Has your story journey delivered this feeling so far? How might you bring us right home to the very center as we step off the page and back into life? What is a fitting full circle moment for your hero to arrive to that will in some way capture the entire essence of the journey, without having to say anything at all?

Play with this with an open mind and see what wants to come through. Write freely and follow whatever image emerges. If you are not yet working on a specific story, or you have not yet arrived to the end, then perhaps this moment will give you a glimpse into the heartbeat of the story that is now ready to come through!

OPENING YOUR PATH

After you have taken some time to write and connect with the energy of your Closing Image, I invite you to take a few more moments to consider the same theme within your own path as a writer and creator. Through the pages of this book you have embarked upon and moved through a heroic journey of your own creative self. You've crossed thresholds and met tests and allies on the path… you have journeyed to your innermost cave, you have met with your Muse and you now return with the Elixir(s) of all the discoveries and new realizations about yourself and your craft that you have made along the way.

Just as with our hero in story, as we reach the Closing Image of our *Writing the Story Within* experience, this moment marks both an ending/completion/celebration and a new beginning, full of bold new possibilities.

As the hero of your own creative story in life, you came on this journey for a reason, and what happens from this moment forward will in a sense be the truest testament to that reason. Even if you are not yet consciously clear about where you will go from here, <u>who you are</u> will naturally infuse and inform each of your steps forward.

WRITING EXERCISE:
OPENING YOUR PATH

For you the writer and hero of your own path, I invite you to imagine you are standing at the precipice between the journey you have just walked and the path that lies ahead. Standing strong within the embodied gifts and discoveries of your adventure so far, fueled by the creative torch within… the journey ahead of you will be the perfect extension of what has come before, and will no doubt lead you into extraordinary new places.

In your mind's eye, take moment to observe and absorb the details, texture and vista of this path. Take a few steps forward and see what comes… What will the next phase of your own Hero's Journey bring you? What are you now being called to? Is it the spark of a new story ready to be lived and shared? Or is it the call of one now running deep, ready to be completed in full glory?

What Call to Adventure are you ready now, more than ever to answer? If you were writing the script of your life, the next chapter and phase of your own heroic experience, what new challenges, discoveries, elements and characters would you include? How will this story play out?

In the truest sense, our Closing Image is actually the Opening Image of a brand new journey.

The remaining lessons and exercises of this chapter are designed to help you anchor and channel many of the lessons from the *Writing the Story Within* experience directly into the mapping and creation of your story. They will challenge you to take what you have learned and put it into practice in a focused progression with one clear goal: **To bring that story inspiration through onto the page in deeply engaging, Universal form where it can be shared with the world.**

Enjoy these final pages as the first/next few bold steps in the mighty, worthy, noble endeavor of *Writing the Story Within* YOU.

> *"Because if we the storytellers don't do this,*
> *then the bad people will win."*
> – ***Christiane Amanpour***

The One Liner
(Saying it All in a Sentence)

"Much wisdom often goes with fewer words."
– Sophocles

Back in Chapter 2, we set a *heart*-based intention for our story, in order to get a sense for how we want people to walk away *feeling* as a result of experiencing our story. We asked ourselves what single gift or message we would love to have them come away with, and how we might boil that down to a feeling. In my experience, when I have a clear emotional sense for where my story path is leading (or any path for that matter), I naturally develop a sort of internal barometer that guides the many hundreds of simple and subtle steps and decisions along the way. No matter where the Muse may lead in terms of details, with my feeling-intention clearly anchored, I can write with great trust, knowing that the energy that transpires from my pen to the page and onward to the reader will align with the spirit of this intention. When we know how we want to feel at the end, and we let that feeling lead our actions now, the path almost always opens to a deeply fulfilling conclusion – often in ways that we never could have imagined.

*

I started exploring the inner technology of 'feeling-based intentions' in a tangible way many years ago in the surf. I had been surfing for several years and had found it to be one of the most deeply enjoyable but consistently humbling activities of my life. I loved the experience of being out in the water and the occasional victory of flying along a crystal green wave face when everything all came together, but more often than not I found myself leaving the water frustrated, having witnessed many great rides, but experienced very few. Then one day I realized that while I had managed to gather a certain amount of skills, I wasn't setting myself up for success on the inside…

In my anxiousness to 'get out there' I often arrived to the beach and threw myself into the water without consciously considering or intending what I actually wanted to experience or come away with. I was like a small ship heading out to sea without my bearings and without setting my compass for where I wanted to go. One day, I decided to begin a simple experiment. When I arrived to the beach ready to surf, rather than sprinting out into the water haphazardly, 'hoping' this session would be better than the last, I stopped at the water's edge and took some time to intend. As a loud part of my mind was barking at me to hurry up before I missed any more waves, I chose to take another breath and pause for a moment to surf on the inside instead. I watched a few waves come through and I imagined myself with all of my faculties, gliding effortlessly, dynamically along. I took another breath and imagined how I wanted to feel when this simple surfing session was finished. How did I want to feel as I stepped back out from the water and headed back to my car at the end of the session? I challenged myself to stretch inside until I arrived at a feeling that seemed totally unrealistic based on my previous experience (and the conditions of the day). But it felt like the highest feeling I could muster, so I went with it. It was a sort of blend between being speechlessly grateful and peacefully excited. That feeling I used to get on Christmas morning or skiing with my brothers in the trees on a deep snowy day. It was the feeling that I imagined I would have if I were to go out there and have a 'best wave of my life' experience out on the water. Some moment on a wave that was somehow different and beyond any other surfing moment I had ever had. It seemed a tall order indeed, but I realized that if I didn't at least give myself the gift of seeing the highest vision imaginable, the chances of experiencing the highest reality were slim to none. Plus, I didn't know how close I'd get to actually claiming this 'speechlessly grateful, peacefully excited' feeling in the water, so I figured I may as well indulge myself with the feeling for a moment on land! I took a few more breaths, sinking my toes into the sand, letting that good vibe settle, and when it felt like the right time, I stepped with a smile into the water. As soon as I started paddling out, the feeling started to shift into more of a tangible focus on the moment – the water, the currents, the other surfers – but there was a calm sureness to my movements that I had not noticed before. I felt good just being out there, I felt good duck-diving and paddling around others, I felt good looking at the way the mist curled off the back of each wave… I wasn't frantically trying to jockey myself into position to get my life's best ride, I was just out there following the good feeling that had started brewing on the beach. About two minutes later, right about the time I had completely forgotten about my whole intention setting process, a beautiful green wave rose up right before me and I found myself turning to meet it… catch it, and ride it with flow-filled precision, right back to the beach where I had started. I felt smooth and dynamic, fast and fluid… it was unlike any wave I had ever surfed before and it left me with one of those spontaneous smiles that little kids get when they are holding a funny secret. I blinked the salt from my eyes and stood there basking in a momentary feeling that registered a solid middle space between hugely grateful and spontaneously, peacefully excited. Wow. That was quick. It was perhaps the shortest surf session I had ever had and yet it delivered exactly what I had asked for. I bolted back down the path, bought muffins for Ash and Josh, and arrived home before they even knew I had left – except for the water in my eyebrows and the mysterious grin on my face.

*

The power of a clear, heart-based intention stretches well beyond the mist of an early morning surf session. In the past decade I have explored this simple process in virtually every arena of my life and have found it in most cases to quite literally to be the difference that makes the biggest difference in the enjoyment of the process as well as the fulfillment of the end result in pretty much everything I do (from business meetings to house hunting). This feeling-based intention setting process has also served as an incredibly potent creative tool on the writing path.

When racing toward a deadline or submission date, it can be very easy to leap onto the computer quite reactively and start punching keys, hoping for the best. But when I give myself and my writing the gift of stopping first to set a clear and undiluted intention, what emerges is always more deeply aligned, time-efficient and quite often well beyond what I may have initially imagined possible for the piece. This very section is an example of just such an experience. I sat down with the intention of completing this piece about the One Liner (which we will get to in just a moment!) and when I allowed myself to drop into the 'inner feeling' of the topic, it linked me back to the beginning of the book. With that, the surfing intention experiment rose into my mind as a way of sharing the tangible energy of this concept with you, the reader. Without setting my intention and taking time to feel how I wanted to feel at the end of the piece, I may not have ever made such a link, and the whole surfing description may have gone unwritten... The section may have been just fine without it, but maybe that little story will help make it more accessible to someone who may have otherwise missed out. Who knows? I trusted it like I trust the quiet power of a rising wave, and before I knew it I was writing myself into the center of what this section is really all about: **Anchoring the intention for our writing in such a way that our words pour forth in natural response, fulfilling the end-result feeling and realizing the greater vision – in ways that often go beyond our previous view of the possible.** This is why we stop at the water's edge before bringing surfboard to wave, pen to page. We set our internal compass and in this direction the Muse begins to sail.

Complementing the 'inner' focus of our intention, there are a few 'external' writing tools that really help us stay true to our vision. One of these is the One Liner.

THE ONE LINER
The One Liner serves a similar role to the heart-based intention in that it acts as a homeopathic dose of our overall story. A way of gathering a glimpse of the depth, magic and layers of our tale into one simple expression that alludes to it all, without giving too much away. The difference between the feeling-based intention of our story and the One Liner is that while the intention is something that we express on the inside when we think of our story, the One liner is something that we can look at, listen to and share with others. It's like a mission statement for the business of our story. And while this One Liner may eventually evolve into something called a 'log line' that may be used as a key piece

of marketing and promotion for the vision of our story (imagine the summary sentence that shows up on the poster or TV guide listing of virtually every film), initially, right here and now, it's just for us.

Basically, the One Liner is a one-sentence summary that captures the essence and thematic relevance of our story. A simple sentence that somehow gives us the ENERGY of the whole thing, and yet makes us want to read more... It is a great thing to know before we start the writing process, but often times it doesn't seem to show up or fully drop into place until once we have been on the journey and come full circle at the end. In the same way that it is sometimes easier to write the introduction to a story once we have written the end, it is sometimes easier to refine a clear One Liner, once we have taken time to really explore and express our story's themes on the page. So as we come full circle to our Closing Image, it seems a perfect time to reconnect with our intention and see what clarity may emerge as we consider how best to summarize our story into a single sentence.

The main thing to remember is that the One Liner is not set in stone. This is a changeable, mutable, malleable sentence and it may very well evolve and shift as your story drops into its polished form. So don't feel confined or trapped by it. Allow yourself instead to simply play with the idea of harvesting the absolute essence of your story into a single point of focus and see how the choice of different words resonates within your body as you use them to describe the story you have chosen to write. Discovering your One Liner can be a fun and rewarding exercise and the end result is powerful, when you have a sentence you can hold in your hand like a crystal ball and confidently say (at least to yourself), "This is what my story is about."

WRITING EXERCISE:
CRAFTING YOUR ONE LINER

To enjoy the process of discovering your One Liner, I suggest the following:

1. FEELING – Firstly take some time to connect (or reconnect) with your ANSWERS to the questions posed in the Chapter 2 section, Starting at the End: Your Heart-based Intention (page 41). Having been on the journey now for several days, weeks or more, take some time to revisit the simple question of how you would love your readers/ viewers to feel at the end of your story experience. Give yourself the gift of dropping into the answers to the questions in that section so that when you get to your ONE universal, emotional truth, you can really feel it. If you can genuinely ignite this feeling as you begin to write, you are already beginning to set yourself up for success on the story path.

2. CIRCUMSTANCE – Once you connect to the feeling of your story, the next step is to consider your story in a more tangible sense – the characters, the plot points, the journey itself, and to write a few summarizing sentences that capture the basics of 'what this story is about'. You might find it helpful to begin by quite simply writing, "This is a story about..." and then continuing with whatever naturally comes next. Initially stick with the tangibles, the specifics of what actually happens in the story (not so much the feeling of things but more about the external events). What is this story actually about?

3. MESSAGE – When you've anchored the feeling of your story and you've gathered a summarizing sense for what the story is about, the next step is to combine the energy of that emotional truth with the tangible essence of your story into a one-sentence summary of what this book/film/story is really about. ONE SENTENCE (two maximum to begin with, but try to whittle it down to one), with a fundamental aim that every word has a reason for being there and captures the underlying message or purpose of the story. If you think of your feeling intention as the sun, this sentence is like a ray of light that comes from that central place. Using a story like Kung Fu Panda as an example, while your hero's end result feeling (step 1) might be "peace and courage" and your tangible story summary (step 2) might be something like "A lazy panda bear orphan discovers his true destiny as a great martial arts warrior", you might end up with a final One Liner that says, "This is a story about the unlikely rise of a great martial arts hero, having the courage to step beyond what he thought was possible, and having the peace to accept himself just as he was." The creators of Kung Fu Panda might have seen it differently, but if I were writing the story, this sentence would have helped me stay on track. It sort of blends the two sentences together in an overall vision for the piece.

Depending on how you think and how you work, any one of the above three sentences can serve as an effective One Liner. Step 1 is the feeling, Step 2 is the circumstance and Step 3 is the ultimate message of your story. To me, step 3 is the most complete because it draws upon the circumstance and it delivers us to the feeling. Some One Liners may weigh more heavily toward the facts, yours might be something altogether different. There may be a time when you are asked to write a specific sentence in a certain way so that publishers or distributors can use it in their marketing of your master story, but for right now what matters most is how it sits, sounds and resonates for you, the storyteller.

When I was trying to come up with a good One Liner to describe this book, I went through a similar process. I connected first with my feeling-based outcome and came up with "inspired and empowered". My vision was for people to finish their experience of this book feeling a real sense of passion and accomplishment, like they had awoken qualities, aspects and brilliance within themselves that they perhaps did not even know existed. I wanted them to feel infused by their own unique voice and genuinely ignited to share and express it. I thought of the circumstance and I realized that I wanted this to be more than just a book... I wanted it to be an experience... a dynamic creative journey. In one sense I wanted to lead people into creative places within themselves they hadn't been before, but in another, bigger sense I wanted them to feel a sense of arrival, a coming home to a sense of creative connectedness within them that has been there waiting all along. And when we put those two aspects of my intention together, we ended up with the subtitle/ one liner, "*A Dynamic Creative Journey... Becoming the Writer You Came Here to Be.*" It fits and even feels quite good to say!

Bottom line is if you can say it in one sentence, then you have a simple, clear reminder at any stage of the writing process, to communicate with yourself and test the metal of every scene and story suggestion you receive. If you don't come up with your One Liner until after you have actually written the story, then it can be used like a laser during re-writes and editing to help you see where you have strayed from the path and how you may quickly and effectively come back. For the purposes of our journey here, the One Liner you come up with today will be greatly instrumental in helping you take the next step to writing a Treatment for your story (see the next two sections), to expanding that treatment into the story itself, and to eventually speaking about and pitching your story to others!

If you had one sentence right now to tell me what your story is really about, what would that sentence be?

The Nine BEATS
(Saying it All in 9 Moments)

OK... So you've had a chance to chew on your One Liner and you may now actually have three of them – one that captures the feeling, one that captures the circumstance and one that captures the message of your story. Our next step is to map this story out from your one-sentence summary into nine key Beats, tracking along with the 9 essential story moments and stages we have discussed as we've moved through each of the chapters of this *Writing the Story Within* journey. This is a *great* way to crystallize your understanding of the lessons so far and to really give yourself a tangible, measurable topographical map of your story. These nine beats are like the pylons of a bridge tracking through and holding up your story. You are not bound or restricted by these beats, and you can change these whenever you like and there will be many beats in between, but by tuning in and aligning yourself with these key archetypal milestones, you begin to feel your story ground into form and with this comes a great sense of freedom and empowerment to really maximize the energy of your story from start to finish.

In the average 120-minute feature film, each of the dividing lines on our story map (page 53) or each point on the spiral story map (page 208) generally signifies approximately 15 minutes of film time. These are not fixed times and can certainly vary and shift, but if you set your stop watch at the beginning of your next 10 films, you may be quite surprised to see how close to the mark these beats usually arrive. Much like a trail map of a great mountain adventure, we may find ourselves straying from the path from time to time, but jeez sometimes it's nice to have that map to refer back to when we get a little lost!

Here's how we're going to break it down...

Beginning with your One Liner summary sentence and a basic overview of what this story is really about… we can launch into a simple process of defining our nine key story beats as we have explored them in *Writing the Story Within*.

STAGE 1: Opening Image / Set-up – *Who is our character at the beginning of the story in his/her ordinary world? How does this story begin?*

STAGE 2: Catalyst / Call to Adventure – *What happens within the first few scenes of our story that shakes the tree and kick-starts our character on their journey? What is the hero of our story being 'called' to?*

STAGE 3: Stepping on the Path (Turning Point 1) – *Where does the initial Call to Adventure lead? What is the extraordinary world of this story and what is required of our hero to make* *the leap from his/her ordinary world?*

STAGE 4: Tests and Allies – *How do our characters cope with the extraordinary new world they find themselves in? What initial challenges must be faced, what new skills must be learned, what 'early wins' occur and who is there to help?*

STAGE 5: Point of True Commitment (Mid Point) – *What is our character's point of true commitment and what decision must be made in order for them to cross that line? How do the stakes rise from there and how does our hero respond?*

STAGE 6: Innermost Cave – *What is the ultimate emotional test for our hero in this story? What challenge or deep inner fear must be faced in order to claim the elixir of the journey?*

STAGE 7: Crossing Back (Turning Point 2) – *How does our character express what s/he learned or gathered in the Innermost Cave? What empowered decision does our key character make that allows/catapults them with great resolve toward the climax of our story?*

STAGE 8: Climax - *What happens at the apex of the story, when all the forces (inside and out) come together at the end? What inner conflict and external challenge is overcome and who shares in the power and triumph of this experience?*

STAGE 9: Closing Image – *How does this story end? What is the ultimate resolution of this journey and the message it leaves in our heart as we finish? How is this captured in the final image or moment of the story? How does it in some way tie back to our very first moment and Opening Image?*

Since we've spent a fair amount of time tracking the film story *Avatar*, I'll use it as an example here to summarize and clarify each beat...

This isn't a scientific formula and these beats may or may not line up exactly with how the film story creators mapped them out. This is just how I see and experience them as I watch the film. It's also not meant to be a big laborious process, so I'll see how quickly I can map it all out, purely based from memory. It's now 1:55am as I start this... let's see how long it takes!

AVATAR (A 9-BEAT GLANCE)

ONE LINE SUMMARY: This is a story about a disabled marine who discovers freedom, leadership and the interconnectivity of life through his relationship with a tribe of native beings on a futuristic planet being mined by US military.

1. OPENING IMAGE: Quadriplegic Marine, Jake Sully, wakes from a recurring 'flying dream' above the trees, to his reality in a spaceship on the planet of Pandora, where he has been asked to take the place of his twin brother in a research project merging human DNA with that of the native people.

2. CALL TO ADVENTURE: Merging with the 'Avatar' body intended for his dead brother, Jake is exposed to a new level of physical freedom and is recognized as an asset to the military department who is seeking to mine an expensive mineral from the native people's sacred land.

3. STEPPING ON THE PATH (Turning Point 1): On his first research trip into the jungles of Pandora, Jake is separated from his team and left to his own defenses (way over his head), until he is rescued by the female native warrior, Netyri and brought back to the tribe as a 'sign' from the tree spirits.

4. TESTS and ALLIES: Tentatively accepted into the tribe, Jake embarks on a journey to learn their sacred ways, and while he initially reports back strategic input to his military leaders, he slowly develops a deep appreciation for the way of the People and a love for his mentor Netyri.

5. MIDPOINT / POINT OF TRUE COMMITMENT: Forsaking his military mission, Jake postpones his return trip to Earth in order to be initiated into the tribe as one of the People (in hopes of negotiating a peaceful resolution with the military agenda) and consummates his love for Netyri.

6. INNERMOST CAVE: Following Jake's initiation into the tribe, his growing allegiance to the native people is discovered by his military superiors, leading to an escalation of conflict between the humans and the native people with Jake caught tragically in the middle.

7. CROSSING BACK (Turning Point 2): After being blamed for the destruction of the sacred 'Home Tree' and banished from the tribe, Jake risks all to capture 'Taruk', the great red sky dragon, regaining the trust of the People and galvanizing an army to defend against the military's advances on the sacred 'Tree of Souls'.

8. CLIMAX: Combining his military expertise with his new intuitive knowledge and alliance with the native people, Jake leads an indigenous army into battle with the human military, where the ultimate victory comes through the power of 'Eywa' (the Mother Nature spirit), sending beasts and animals from all directions to aid in the battle, in service of the 'balance of all things'.

9. CLOSING IMAGE: Having defeated the human military and claimed a new era of peace for Pandora, Jake claims his true role as a leader among the native people and gives up his human body to stay with them and truly 'fly' forever.

OK. It's 2:22. So it took me about 27 minutes. I could have spoken it to you in about 3 minutes, but I wanted to write it out and keep each step condensed in one sentence. It's a little late now, so this may not be exact, but it gives you an idea of how quickly you can map out the big beats of your entire story. I haven't gone into the real details here, but these main pillar moments will serve to guide us structurally, and the next steps will involve filling in the gaps with details and giving the whole thing feeling.

WRITING EXERCISE:
NINE BEATS, YOUR TURN!

Now it's time to put YOUR story through the same process and see what comes for you as you lay the basic framework of your story vision into the 3-Act Hero's Journey story form. Keep it loose and use this template as a way of clarifying the strong beats that you know of... and exposing those that may need more drilling into! Feel free to start with simple dot points and phrases, which you can hone into sentences later. Just have fun with it and delight in the fact that you can build the entire framework of your story right here and now.

OK. 27 minutes (or however long it takes you!)... GO!

SUMMARY SENTENCE

1 - OPENING IMAGE
2 - CALL TO ADVENTURE
3 - STEPPING ON THE PATH
4 - TESTS AND ALLIES
5 - POINT OF TRUE COMMITMENT / MIDPOINT
6 - INNERMOST CAVE
7 - CROSSING BACK
8 - CLIMAX
9 - CLOSING IMAGE

Once you've outlined these key story moments, you may wish to set them out into your own version of a story map or some other physical expression of how the beats connect to each other and what is in between.

If you could draw the highs and lows of this story, what would it LOOK like to you?

The Three Pager
(Fleshing the Beats into a Treatment)

Once you've expanded your one liner into a 9-Beat story map, the next step is to flesh those beats out into a more expanded summary outline, or what the film industry often calls a 'Treatment'. In my experience, this synopsis has a few key benefits. Some are for you, and some are for the people you might be sharing your story with (publishers, distributors, agents etc.).

In terms of marketing your story, the basic function of this summary (which may run between 1-25 pages, depending on who you ask) is to give people a chance to experience your story without taking the time to read the whole thing. It's basically like a great trailer for your movie, but in written form. It shares the main beats of the story and captures at least a glimpse into the feeling nature and the message of the story, with a fundamental purpose of leaving whoever is reading it with an insatiable yearning to read the whole thing. If you have caught someone's interest with the concept of your story (possibly with your One Liner!), the next thing they will likely ask to see is a Treatment/Synopsis of your story. If they love the One Liner and your summary, well then your script/manuscript is the next sparkling piece in line. There is an art to writing a marketable summary to sell your story, and there are some great books out there to help guide you with that. My desire in sharing this model here is more to help you sell your story to *you*.

The Treatment is your way of test driving your story to get a balcony view of the overall flow of its essential beats, scenes and turning points. When you are doing it for yourself, it can be in outline or dot-point form and can include as much or as little detail as you choose. What it allows you to do is to take your nine-beat summary and fill the gaps in between. To basically build a pathway from start to finish of all the major – and some of the minor – events in the story. What happens from start to finish on the outside, and how that influences the growth and transformation of your hero on the inside. This is not to stifle or limit what spontaneous magnificence may emerge in the process of writing out the entire piece, but to give you a dynamic framework to work from that will help inform each step while allowing your nervous system to relax, knowing that this magic house has a blueprint.

WRITING EXERCISE:
YOUR 3-PAGE TREATMENT

My invitation in this section is for you simply to take what you have created with your Nine-beat outline, and expand it out to include all the major events of your story with enough flesh to also give it feeling. Imagine the energy of a great trailer for the movie of your story, but in written form (With or without that classic American voiceover that comes with many film trailers. "One man... On a mission... To save the world..." J). Your synopsis will likely give us more information than a movie trailer would (because it will take us right to the end rather than leaving us hanging off the cliff), but you'll want to infuse your descriptions with the same type of pace and feeling that your overall story will carry.

Essentially, the nine-beat outline can be seen as the skeleton of your story, and now we're just going to add the vital organs and a few key pressure points! The flesh, blood, skin, hair and everything else is still yet to come, and these structural pieces, placed lightly into a short document will help guide the way. I suggest that once you have your Nine-beat structure in pretty good shape that you take a walk outside, get out of your head, then from a place of calm creative center, just give yourself a little chunk of time (maybe an hour) to write the summary of your story from your heart. Allow yourself to see that movie trailer for this epic tale of yours unfolding in your mind and just write what you see. Don't feel bound by the structural pillars, but rather allow them to free you into a genuine connection with the heart center of your story, and write from that place.

Write with passion and enthusiasm, as though you are writing for a slightly impatient child and your primary job is to keep him interested in what you have to say. With every sentence you are pulling us along, giving us just a little more, calling us to experience the adventure of your story. Don't force it. Let this treatment writing process unfold in a way that feels good, and trust where it takes you. Feel free to add little bits of dialogue if they emerge, to hone in on a few scenes that really capture your imagination and see where the characters want to go once you give them a little bit of room on the page. They may offer some fresh insight you hadn't even thought of in the process of mapping it all out.

Wherever you are on the story path, you've thought about (and lived!) your story for long enough to know where the heartbeat is. So just give yourself three pages (or less if that's all it takes) to simply bring us into that world. If you know why your story is important and you are clear about why you are here to tell it, this energy will naturally permeate every word you write and we will be there keen to follow!

If you had three pages to share the magic of your story in such a way to make us all want to read, hear and see more... what would you write?

CHAPTER 10:

Begin Again

"The only limit to your impact
is your imagination and commitment."
– Anthony Robbins

Produce Every Day
The Art of Showing up

In the realm of ideas everything depends on enthusiasm…
in the real world all rests on perseverance.
– Johann Wolfgang von Goethe

*

When I first arrived to the mountains of Victoria, Australia many years ago, while coaching skiing for the season at Mt. Buller, I was given a room in a big hotel that was used for employee housing. Most mountain staff members were sharing three to four (and sometimes more!) per room, but somehow my assistant coach 'Kenno' had snuck in early and worked out a way for us each to have our own room – sharing a bathroom between us. I was very impressed… until my first night when I discovered why the head of accommodation may have been willing to give us solo rooms at the far end of the hotel. One simple reason really… no heat. I'd spent the previous two months in Bali acclimatizing to rooms with no fans amidst sweltering equatorial heat, and now I had landed in the Australian Alps in the heart of winter with just a thin wall and cracked window separating me from the snowy world beyond. But, it was my own room and my own space and that alone was worth the price of sleeping in my ski gear. Within a few days I had made several new friends and one of them loaned me a small blow-heater (basically a large, square hairdryer) so that helped take the edge off. At least I was no longer seeing my breath most nights. During the next three months I entered one of the most simple and structured periods of my life. I was being fed three giant meals a day, I was coaching skiers and working out from dawn until dusk, and at night I was immersing myself in Australian mountain culture and falling steadily in love with Asheyana. There were some gaps between each of these primary pillars in my schedule each day and for the most part I used them to go for walks, write in my journal and draw on the walls of my room. The room was clearly on its last legs before a major remodel, so I decided to give it one last creative hurrah by penning a mural on the wall. I found that each day I would have a little bit of time for me, and quite early in the season I declared that with that time, I would produce something of genuine creative value each day. "Produce every day". That became my motto. It didn't matter whether it was a tree on the wall, a poem in the pages of my travel log or a self-timed photo on the mountain summit during sunset, before my head hit the pillow each night some small part of the Muse would have a chance to express itself through me. It felt good to produce every day and it seemed to flow over into other areas of my existence on the mountain. I noticed that with the consistent feeding of this creative flame, I naturally found myself immersed in creative experiences with others. Writing songs, playing music, skiing under the moon. This notion also flowed over into the ski-training arena. One day I showed up for training and it was pouring rain on the mountain. The team had already resigned themselves to a day of indoor soccer, but through my creative lens I could see potential benefits in heading out onto the mountain anyway. A creative challenge of sorts, to see how long we could last skiing in the rain. Some thought I was mad, others loved the idea, and despite the unuttered objections of most team parents (had they only been there at the time!), I grabbed my skis with a giant smile and headed out for what went down in history as one of our very best training sessions ever. Despite the sideways sleeting winds and sloppy, slushy conditions, once we were all soaked to the bone and freezing, nothing else seemed to matter. We had the mountain virtually to ourselves (except for the occasional ski patrol guy who would double-take at our good cheer) and at the end of the day we had "produced" some great training results and an inner spark of bonding that stayed with the team for months to come. All propelled from this inner engine of "Produce Every Day".

Several years later, I ran into a close friend Ant – we had met during that first season in the mountains. I hadn't seen Ant for years and I had forgotten all about my "Produce Every Day" mission. I certainly didn't remember ever mentioning anything about it to Ant during our time together… but apparently I had one night while playing darts. During our reunion evening, I met a few friends of his, one of whom approached with a giant smile as if he knew me and said with a knowing nod, "Produce Every Day." I smiled back but didn't really know what he was talking about, until he went to the bathroom and Ant explained that he had shared this idea with his friend following our season together years ago… who had embraced it and taken the concept to a whole new level. Infused by the idea of producing every day, Ant's friend had started a community art project that had taken off like wild fire. Basically, every day he, his roommates and whoever they could gather off the streets would come together at a certain time with canvases, paper, cardboard boxes and cupboard doors… and paint. Every day they painted something new and each day the group got a little bigger. After a couple of months they had literally hundreds of original paintings from artists of all walks of life and they ended up holding a massive, multi-medium, 3-day exhibition party that was sponsored by the local radio station! All from the simple commitment to Produce Every Day.

*

So as we move through the Closing Image of our Writing the Story Within journey, this is probably my greatest wish for you: that when you close the cover of this book you do so with an openhearted, expanded-minded, ignited-spirit commitment to producing every day. To every day in some way or another keep the energy of your creative river flowing. You may not write every day, you may not paint every day, but if you can commit to some form of creative expression every day, you will come to discover at the very least, the following four gifts:

1. The more consistently you commit to showing up and exploring/expressing your creative self, the more powerfully the energy of your Muse will rise to inform, inspire, guide and align you with meaningful, magnificent and fulfilling forms of creative expression. This is a 'practice' in the truest sense of the word and a new type of fitness for your mind, heart and body. From this practice you will build an internal creative strength and momentum that will expand greatly as it is channeled into specific projects. Your writing, painting, sculpting, music – and whatever else you put your hand to – will deepen, expand, refine and be more of a thrill for you (and others) to engage with.

2. As you do this on a regular basis (ideally every day), increasing your commitment and rhythmical connection to tangible creative endeavor, you will find that you become more intuitive and creatively aligned with who you are in LIFE. You will discover that all of these different mediums of artistic expression – while beautiful and worthy in their own right – are really just doorways to the ultimate creative masterpiece of you. You will begin to experience life as an artistic being and an expression of art and your way of seeing the world will enrich every activity and relationship you engage with.

3. Not only will your stories and other artistic creations ripple out to infuse and inspire the lives of others, as a byproduct of you simply committing yourself to your own creative path each day – going about the simple business of "Producing Every Day" – you will naturally and even unknowingly (as was the case with me in the mountains) open the pathway for many others to do the same. By creating and producing every day, you will increase the amount of positive creative flow in the world around you and others will begin to do the same in ways they never thought themselves capable.

4. Lastly (well, actually I could keep on listing benefits here for quite a long time, but I will probably stop after this one so you can get on with the business of producing), when you give yourself the gift of "Producing Every Day" you will find that you feel better about yourself and pretty much everything else in life. We are innately creative beings. When we stop or hinder the flow of that energy it has a way of circling back and spiraling inside of us, making us feel stuck, stagnant, scared and unconfident. But when we open the channels and let the water rush through for a while, carrying those ancient old logs and autumn leaves back out to sea, we find ourselves feeling clear, open and alive like a crystal spring. CREATING FEELS GOOD. It just does. Sing a song, write a poem, make a video and at the end you will notice (even if you are exhausted) that you have more life force flowing through you than you did when you began. As innately creative beings, our unique expression is one clear path to fulfilling our true purpose in this life. Even in the simplest ways, when we create, we raise our entire field of consciousness and that field flows outward into the world around us. So open the channels. Commit yourself to

Producing Every Day and watch as your health, vitality, energy, outlook, relationships, and other work in the world improves, expands and benefits as a result. Every time you pick up your pen, brush or instrument, you are bringing yourself to the fountain of life and filling your cup with the Elixir of the hero within you. And if that's not enough motivation to "Produce Every Day" well… maybe read it again!

One of the primary intentions of the whole *Writing the Story Within* experience (in written, spoken and workshop form) has always been to help people build an effective and inspired 'writing practice'. The lessons in this book, the workshops and mentorships are all designed to bring us to the page repeatedly, productively and open-heartedly until we recognize the act of writing as a natural expression of who we are. So that along with food, water, sleep and love, we give ourselves the vital gift of creativity each day.

If you have followed this book to this page then you have surely already taken huge steps to doing just that in your life. For this I truly commend you! In order to be here right now, you will have written a wonderful amount of stunning prose in the previous days, weeks or months. Looking back upon your journal and/or into the computer files of new stories started and perhaps even finished, you will likely see that you have already committed yourself in a significant way to your story path. Well done!

So what's your next step? Do you now have a story seed that needs watering? Do you have a screenplay concept you are ready to birth? Maybe you just want to take some time to congeal all that you have learned along the way and take the next few months to write the story of your life… the story of becoming the hero you are.

WRITING EXERCISE: PRODUCING EVERY DAY

Take some time to consider all that you are currently committed to each day. We are all committed to something, and from that commitment energy and experiences arise. What great things have come into your experience as a result of your current and past commitments?

Imagine if you were committed to Producing Every Day… something creative and inspired. What might that look like on a day-to-day basis?

When you think about the stories that you feel most inspired to write or create, what kind of commitment do you think it will take to bring them into full magnificent fruition? Are you ready?

Create and Deliver
(a.k.a. Putting Yourself Out There)

"So we went to Atari and said, 'Hey, we've got this amazing thing, even built with some of your parts, and what do you think about funding us? Or we'll give it to you. We just want to do it. Pay our salary, we'll come work for you.' And they said, 'No.' So then we went to Hewlett-Packard, and they said, 'Hey, we don't need you. You haven't got through college yet.'"
– Steve Jobs, Co-founder of Apple

One of the greatest joys in running the *Writing the Story Within* workshops and mentorship programs is having the opportunity to watch and listen to people share their writing out loud. Many who come to the workshops have never done this before and a lot of people don't even consider themselves to be writers, so the prospect of doing a simple creative writing exercise and then reading what they've written to a group they barely know… well, for many, is nothing short of terrifying. The joy I find in the experience isn't from terrifying innocent workshop participants, but in watching what happens in the room – and in the being of the reader – after they have shared and received positive feedback from others. No matter where the group has come from and no matter what 5-10 minute exercise I choose, I myself come away from each exchange with a feeling that we could pretty much take those raw writing pieces just as they are, bind them in a book and have them published… and people would buy and read and love that book.

OK, so the punctuation isn't always perfect and the grammar varies from person to person, but there's a raw aliveness in the work that many polished authors out there strive for. To this day I am not sure exactly where this comes from, but it never ceases to make me smile in wonder. It might have something to do with the open energy of the room. It might have something to do with the open energy of the assignments (no major agenda or pressure to 'nail it' or get it right). It might have something to do with the fact that most people often don't know they will be sharing their work when they first start writing… but what I have come to discover time and time again is that when you give someone a simple, open creative task and a few minutes to focus, what usually emerges is a small magic piece of their soul. They may begin writing about a paper napkin, autumn leaf or a staple gun, but through that little doorway, their creative voice will find a way to climb through and express. It may be just a simple paragraph, but by the time the reading is done, each person has not only shared a unique expression, they have also shared a unique view into themselves. We know them deeper just in hearing them read.

Going around the room, it is astounding to see how different each person's perspective, voice and world view is, and yet it is also powerful to see how united we are by the energy beneath the stories that we share. And how collectively we sort of fill in the gaps for each other. In other words, each person brings something unique and needed for the whole. Even when writing about the exact same thing, each person brings his or her slice of the pie, and by the time we have finished going around the circle there is wholeness present that was simply not there before. Had we finished the writing and skipped right into the next section without taking time to share, we would have missed out on something extraordinary. And while the initial precipice of 'putting it out there' can be pretty daunting to say the least, what each person comes to realize is that what they have to share is not only worthy and positively embraced... it is actually necessary to complete the creative energy of the group.

Through our schooling years many of us were taught 'how to write' with very specific rules that did not always leave a lot of room for the Muse to run free. As a result, many of us come into adulthood with a conditioned belief that we simply 'can't write right.' Add that to the cultural belief that it's incredibly difficult to get published, sell a screenplay or make a living from your writing, and most people will pretty much block themselves from considering the writing path before their Muse has a chance to whisper the magic it has in store.

Within the supportive arena of a workshop, making the leap from, "I can't write" to "I just wrote this and now I am reading it" is one of the most liberating experiences I have witnessed on the creative path. Sure there are times when tools and specific techniques can help to refine the expression of that path, but for many, the first big quantum step is just giving ourselves the permission to express, and to love what comes through just the way it arrives.

In the early years of my writing career, I spent time working on my own creative projects but never took the final step to put them out there (continually convincing myself they just needed a bit more work or polishing before they could be shared). Simultaneously, I accepted jobs working on projects for others where delivery was an absolute requirement, but the opportunity to freely create was limited. I didn't understand why my own stories, books and films weren't being fully embraced by the world... and then I realized it was simply because I wasn't putting them out there! My creative pot was full to the brim with energy and ideas, but without giving myself the opportunity to move that energy out into the world, it was starting to spiral around and burn me. And until I was willing to open the gates and start delivering what I really wanted to create I couldn't expect my situation to change.

At the time I had a magazine that I really enjoyed reading, and one day I had an idea for an article that I felt would really benefit the readers. I hadn't yet learned the proper way to send a 'query letter', but one Friday afternoon I just grabbed the number from the inside cover of the magazine and called. Because it was late in the day and the end of the week, it just so happened that the chief editor was the only one in the office so he answered the phone. We had a great chat, he liked my story idea and said, "Look, no guarantees until I see your writing, but if you can have it to me by the end of next week, I'll read it and see if it fits." I hung up the phone with a smile and dove right into the article. The next week I sent the article across and the editor loved it. I noticed for about a week afterward that I felt this sense of ease in my body that I had never felt while working as a hired writer even on much bigger projects. The following month I wrote another article and again, felt this incredible lift of energy in the simple process of sending it out. It was like I was gently pulling logs from my own creative river and each time I did, the water would run a little clearer. And by filling (or relieving) a gap within my own creative engine I was also fulfilling a need within the magazine. Before long I started receiving positive praise from readers, and that felt great but it was just frosting on the (gluten-free) cake that I was already enjoying in the simple act of creating and delivering my work.

A few months later I was approached by someone who had read one of my articles and wanted my help editing her book. I had never considered this as a path for my creative energy but at the time it was perfect. It allowed me to stay primarily focused on my own writing, while being paid to help another person with hers. And I noticed instantly that because my own river was already flowing, I naturally had more to give (with less attachment) to her project as well. The waters were running clear and the more I focused on creating and then in some way delivering what had been produced, the more energy I had for other projects and in truth, everything else in my life.

Years later I read a great blog post by Steve Pavlina, American author/speaker/entrepreneur, who shared his theory that the absolute key to staying prosperous during a financial recession was quite simply to keep your focus on 'creating and delivering value'. He talked about how whenever he and his wife need more money, rather than focusing on "Ok, how can we make more money this month?" they simply ask the question, "How can we create and deliver more value?" This really helped crystallize my experience of this balance between 'Producing Every Day' and 'Putting it Out There'.

By keeping our focus on creating value that people need and then delivering the value that we create, we naturally take the focus off of ourselves and put it onto the place or people that our creations will benefit. As we become a servant to the beneficial energy of our creations, we naturally open the gates for energy in all forms to flow. This very book you now hold in your hands is a product of my own commitment to keeping the energy of creativity flowing – not just in my own world, but in yours!

We could spend time worrying about how we are going to get our writing published, but in my experience, this usually just takes us away from our Muse and the very energy that will eventually open those doors of opportunity for us anyway. If we keep our focus on the simple act of answering the call and being true to our creations, with a commitment to delivering what has been created when we are done, we will usually find that the doorways of delivery and channels of distribution naturally rise to meet us on the path when the time is right. We might meet someone at a party, come across an old friend by email or be approached by someone we've never even met. It may require an act of spontaneous boldness like calling up the editor of a magazine late one Friday afternoon, but this does not need to be a daunting process. In fact, what I have come to discover is that the 'putting it out there' part can be filled with just as much magic as the 'Produce Every Day' part. We just have to be willing to take the first step... and then the next.

Up until a year ago, most of my major writing work had been in the film world, so I hadn't thought too much about how to publish books. I have a few friends who are well-published authors, but their relationships with their publishers always seemed to have a sense of mystique about them. In fact the whole publishing world seemed quite mysterious to me, and while I certainly dreamed of one day having a great publisher who was as excited about my creative projects as I am, I did not know where to even begin looking for such a person. In the mean time, with a commitment to finding some way to deliver what I had created, last spring I followed a simple impulse to advertise the *Writing the Story Within* online workshop/mentorship program in one of Australia's most widely read holistic magazines, *Living Now*. It was quite last-minute timing on my behalf, so the placement of the ad wasn't the best. The response was initially less than what I had hoped, and at first I wondered if the exercise was worth it. But then a couple of weeks later, Toni Carmine Salerno from Blue Angel Publishing sent me an email. He had seen the ad in *Living Now*, and wanted to know if I'd be interested in creating a book with the same title. Wow. Ash and I have always loved Toni's work and have often thought how great it would be to work with him on a project, but never quite knew how that would happen. But here he was, reaching out, inviting it to happen. Not with one of his projects, but with one of mine. We spoke on the phone and instantly felt a mutual excitement for the project and other opportunities to work together. Within a week, I had signed a contract for my first official book publishing deal – the *Writing the Story Within* book, CD and DVD. The mentorship enrolment was a little low that session, but it was perfect because it gave me a chance to dive right into the writing. Since then, through Toni's gracious spirit and creative encouragement I have felt safe to 'deliver' and share a few other creative seeds from my garden shelf, and as a result Blue Angel Publishing and I are currently working on several projects together. This is exactly the type of author/publisher relationship that I had always dreamed of finding, but never knew how or where. Here in a simple response to my willingness to 'put myself out there' in one way (with my workshop advertisement), the gift of this relationship quite literally found me.

Like our characters and heroes in story, we never really know what new relationship, creative adventure or doorway of opportunity may be waiting just around the corner of our simple impulses and desires today. The only way to find out what golden gifts the path may hold for us, is to continue taking steps. We do this well when we take our mind off of our self-concern of whether we are good enough or worthy, and get on with the business of creating and delivering value (in whatever way we know how!).

Wherever you are on your creative path and whatever your vision for future delivery of your creations may be, I encourage you above all to allow yourself to rest in one simple truth. The world wants and needs you to share your work as much as you want to share it. As much as you would love to have a great ongoing relationship with an editor, publisher, distributor or other, know well that these great humans also seek to have great relationships with visionary creative beings like you. Don't get caught up in the mystique of the publishing world, just pour your energy into your creative work and the rest will flow from there.

As competitive as the film and publishing worlds may appear to be, there has also never been a more accessible time to freely express and put yourself out there. With the absolute global proliferation of the Internet and social media, there are no limits to what can be created and delivered. You may set out to find the perfect publisher for your book or distributor for your film, or by taking simple steps to create and deliver your creative energy you may find that they come looking for you. In the process of taking one step after another you may even discover or create a whole new pathway of delivery that you never dreamed possible. "If you build it, they will come." If you create, with a commitment to deliver, the pathway of expression will find you!

TO LIVE, LOVE AND LET GO

For as long as we have been living here on earth we have been creating and sharing stories. With our stories we give meaning to our experience and with this meaning we create the context to perceive our reality. In this way we can see that the stories we live and share actually play a huge role in creating the world we live in. Pretty powerful stuff.

And story comes in many forms. It can be told, shown, sung, danced. You may write your story as a poem, a children's book, a film or a blog. You might even find that the story that you really came here to tell has already been written in the pages of your journal and all you have to do is cut and paste it into a place where others can experience it. Your role is simply to make yourself available to the creative energy that is ready to come through you onto the page… and to commit yourself to putting it out there when it does.

I am sitting here in the kitchen of a little farmhouse in New South Wales, Australia typing the last words of this book. It's Thursday night at 3:44am. I have to finish this tonight because it needs to be 'delivered'. The team at Blue Angel Publishing is patiently waiting, and tomorrow (actually, now it's today) my presence is needed to help move into our new home down by the beach in the town we have now claimed as our own. Throughout this book I have shared several small glimpses into the journey that has lead my family and me to this place on the path. And though I could never have planned for this moment to arrive just as it has (I hoped it would be done a few months ago!), I am quite suddenly realizing the perfection of the timing of completing this manuscript on the eve of our final arrival HOME.

Since my landing here several weeks ago, many pieces of our life have converged, merged, flowed-over and finally begun to fall powerfully into place. The house we will move into today is a symbol of where we now stand... A brand new chapter and Call to Adventure that is sure to send us out into the ocean of our own heroic selves in ways that we have never imagined or experienced before.

As I sat down at the table today, I took special notice of a wall hanging behind me, which has upon it a simple, anonymous poetic verse.

"In the end what matters most is
How well did you live
How well did you love
How well did you learn to let go."

I've read this verse several times, but today it seemed to jump out with a bit more punch. In fact it summarizes the very essence of our 'Putting it Out There' mission. Here's how I see it…

Our number one calling and responsibility is to *live* our story.
To immerse ourselves in the Hero's Journey of our life and to "squeeze the towel dry". If we are to create something of value to share with the world, a great place to start is to create and experience a beautiful life.

While the classic image of the writer is often one of solitude, isolated in a cabin somewhere, whittling away at some internal seed... In this journey I have invited you to consider the role of the writer in a different way... As a warrior with a pen and a hero on the path of life – engaged, connected, in tune, tapped in, turned on and aligned... Feeling the full scope of human emotions, feet wet and hands muddy. Rolling up our sleeves, then diving right into the river. Life makes the best stories of all. While the writing of your story will likely require disciplined focus, my invitation for us all is not to stop our life experience to write our story, but to keep a foot in both worlds... To write truthfully from a genuine place of being, doing and creating in the world. Our very first step (also in the quote above) is to LIVE.

Our second calling and responsibility is to *love*.
To embrace our unique experience and those we are having it with. To be present enough to the magic that is unfolding within and around us that we truly feel and experience that magic as it is happening – not just later when we look back. When we allow the energy of love to infuse our story we will naturally find ourselves compelled to capture and express it in some creative way. This is part of our second calling… It is a calling to love so much that the energy cannot be contained, but must be somehow brought forth and expressed.

To focus on the tiny light of a star long enough that it begins to speak to us. And when it does, our role is simply to honor its pulse and write what we see and hear.

Our third calling and responsibility, as the poem says, is to learn to *let go*.
By letting go I don't mean detaching and throwing our creations into the bin. I mean letting them go like you might imagine letting a previously caged eagle go from the top of a mountain.

If your story is worth living, it is also worth loving. If you love it, it's worth writing (or expressing in some other way). And if it's worth writing, in many cases, its worth sharing with the world. Your job isn't to control where it goes, but simply to bring it through and let it go. And as you do this with each story you feel drawn to share, you will find it gives birth to another… and another. Create and deliver. Put yourself and your stories out there. It's time for them to fly.

Yes, there will be stories and creations that you choose to keep close to home. Prayers and poems between you and the angels. You may not wish to publicly share everything that comes through onto the page, but when you complete them, give yourself and the creation the honor of releasing them at the very least through a quite reading to the stars, or to a lover or a friend. As Rumi says, "Sing Your Note."

Throughout the ages, story has been our way of communicating messages, honoring what has been and capturing the dreams of what may be. In this vital time on planet Earth, humanity needs new stories. Stories that share visions of what is possible and messages for a world we wish to create. Stories that lift us out of our tendency to spiral and focus on what is 'wrong', and to begin to see the light of new possibility revealing itself in even the most challenging circumstances and moments of life. If we can begin to see our life not just as a series of cycles and ages, chapters and phases, but as a great story that is unfolding… as a heroic journey revealing itself through us, as us, calling us on to higher aspects of our self each step of the way… We can begin to experience our true reason for being here as the Hero of our own life journey and a bringer of great stories and elixirs to the world.

If you have a story that you know would make a great film or book or song or poem… Live it. Love it. Bring it through and let it fly. Everything you need is within you now. Listen. Trust. Follow the whispered call of your heroic creative voice. Now is the time.

WRITING EXERCISE:
YOUR NEXT STEP

Standing here at the closing page of your Writing the Story Within journey… today is a new day. You have a new clear lens to see the world and all the magic in it. I have one final question to ask you. Something I have asked before and may certainly ask again. My invitation is that you will take a moment to quietly listen to the answer that comes from that deep wellspring within… And when it speaks that you will not hesitate, not doubt or question its call… but rather seize the very moments that follow to commit yourself anew to the path. To agree deep down to playing your part in this great creation story. To bring yourself to the page of life with an open mind and willing heart to step on the hero's path and follow where it leads.

I feel grateful well beyond these words to have had the chance to share this journey with you. I feel honored to participate, encourage and take part in this great creative wave, as people all around the world give birth to new stories and give rise to a new era of true creative freedom, expression and experience on our planet.

As you prepare to take your next bold step on the story path, I will ask you one more time a question I posed at the very beginning…

What stories wants to come through YOU?

Now is the time!

Remembering the Way of Miracles

"There are only two ways to live your life. One is as though nothing is a miracle.
The other is as though everything is a miracle."
*- **Albert Einstein***

Throughout this journey I have referenced several different stories and I have shared many glimpses and pieces of my own stories to demonstrate different points and key phases of story form. As a final gift, I'd like to share one last story from my experience that actually delivers a fairly comprehensive example, from start to finish, of the entire Hero's Journey story form that we have discussed and studied throughout this book.

When I wrote this story, I wasn't thinking about archetypal story or any of the lessons we have shared so far. I was simply recounting the progression of a powerful, transformative experience in my life. As I have hinted throughout this book, and as you will discover in the reading here, the way it happened and the way I found myself recounting it, quite naturally wound its way into the rhythms of all that we have been discussing so far. Not every episode of life contains every phase of the Hero's Journey we have discussed, but this one does a pretty good job. So climb inside and enjoy the read. You may wish to keep our Story map in mind as you read and see if you can identify the key beats, stages and moments of the hero's path along the way!

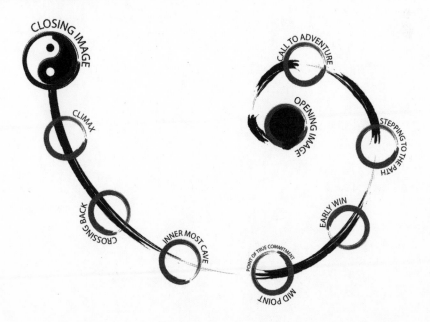

I have always been fascinated with the idea that miracles are meant to be a normal part of daily life and who we really are.

Recently, my family and I were plunged into an experience that called for the living validation of this theory. It is in some senses a very small story (about 14cm high), with stakes not as brooding as some of our current world issues, but this encounter has left us with a potent road map and reference point to the inner pathway of miracles, which has since rippled profoundly into all areas of our life. I share it here in hopes that it will trigger your own recognition of subtle patterns and miracle experiences in life, through the stories and creations you are living right now…

Missy went Missing

"Promise me you won't take her outside", were Asheyana's last words before she and our son Joshua left our home in the hills of Byron Bay for a weekend in Melbourne. As she said this, she cradled the feathery yellow bird in her hands – scratching it blissfully behind the ears – then placed her gently on my shoulder. Missy had come into our life the previous Christmas, and while I had never before considered myself as a 'bird owner', amidst the magic of getting to know this little being as she flew around our house and celebrated our arrival into each room, as she sprinted across my computer keyboard (adding words like "jk7?~" to my sentences) in times of great stress, as she stole Cornflakes from Josh's cereal bowl and gently cleaned herself in the mist of Asheyana's showers, we had all fallen deeply in love with her. And yet, part of me had remained conflicted about her captivity, wishing I could go outside with her, where she would be free to fly and return to us of her own will. My family's argument, which I also understood, was that she would never survive out in the wild… so why tempt fate?

About an hour after I said goodbye to Ash and Josh, and about five minutes before I settled into a weekend of very focused writing (with a major deadline waiting on the other end), I stepped outside to grab something off our verandah, somewhat unconscious of the fact that the little bird (who was as light as a feather), was still perched on my shoulder. We had been onto the covered verandah together before, and this would only be for a moment, but I could not have predicted what would happen…

As I stepped outside, Missy fluttered to the top of a hanging hula-hoop. As she landed on the plastic ring, it spun into motion, flipping her off balance into flight, off the verandah, into the open air! With calls of great distress, she circled over the house in a panic before crash landing into a high tree canopy. I raced into the yard, trying to call her down, but she just paced back and forth along the limb as if she didn't know how. Jumping onto the trampoline I tried to encourage her into flight from there… and for a moment I thought it might work. She gingerly opened her wings and stepped off the ledge, but something startled her mid-flight and she ended up flying straight over my head, into the rainforest of the National Park!!! A tiny yellow dot, panicking, screeching and vanishing in the distance.

With Asheyana's last words echoing painfully in my gut, I sprinted after Missy, up along the old fire track deep into the forest, calling and listening with every step. But she was nowhere. I may as well have dropped a goldfish fish into the ocean and swam after it. I was furious with myself for my casual disregard of Asheyana's deep wishes, horrified at the thought of having to tell her and Josh what had happened, and deeply disturbed knowing that our sweet little friend was flying lost in the jungle – into the territorial grounds of eagles, crows, magpies, snakes and more.

Two hours later, sweaty, scratched and already well behind my writing schedule, I vowed to myself and the Universe that I would do all in my power to bring Missy back. I did not know how, but I knew this must be done. I found myself voicing this intention clearly and repeatedly out loud – first to myself, then to the trees and the kookaburras. I went to the spring at the centre of the property and called out to the nature spirits and all who would listen. I asked for help. I stated my intention for her to return and my willingness to do whatever was needed to assist. The forest studied me in silence. I took a breath, thanked them for their help and bolted back to the house to see if Missy had arrived home yet.

I arrived instead to a call from Asheyana, checking to see how I (and little bird) was doing. I have often noticed that when we strongly state an intention to the Universe, among the first things to arise are symbols of what may be blocking our internal flow from receiving it. This is often misperceived as a setback, but in truth it is more like a weed rising in the garden after rainfall – it simply calls for gentle release, so we can get on with the mission of growing. In this case, my energy of clear intention to bring back Missy, was being squashed by my guilt and fear of telling my family what had happened – and I knew it. As much as I had hoped to have this situation solved before I spoke with Ash, here we were on the phone, and I knew the only way forward was honesty. I told her what happened, and after swearing, crying and hating me for a few minutes, thankfully she turned, and in a voice of startling clarity, said, "Bring her back, Chip. We have to bring her back."

We both fell very quiet on the phone. Then from that silence, an idea began to rise. Knowing that we are all energetically connected and that animals often communicate with pictures, we decided the best thing to do was to turn the intention of Missy's returning into a picture. Something we could revisit in our mind over and over and something that would build a genuine positive feeling in our bodies. With no sign of a yellow bird anywhere, it seemed a tough time to initiate a visualization experiment, but we knew the energy had to start somewhere.

I asked myself what could be the very highest outcome of this experience. Initially I couldn't get past the devastating vision of having to tell Josh what had happened, but slowly I moved through other more 'realistic' scenarios until I eventually came to an image… an image that felt in this moment to be nearly impossible, but one that to me represented the highest possible outcome.

The image was of Missy flying right into my chest and me catching her. I imagined the feeling of overwhelming relief and gratitude we would feel for this to happen, and for a moment I allowed myself to feel it. Somewhere in the field of all possibilities, there must be a probable reality of Missy coming home; so we both decided to hold that vision above all others, and to do our best not to doubt the universe's infinite capacity to line up with our intentions. This vision would be our message. We would share it with a few key friends and we would return to it over and over, letting ourselves feel the feelings of the image.

From there it would be up to me to listen and follow whatever impulses may arise to help bring us closer to its realization.

We hung up the phone and, as the sun went down on this first day, quiet inklings began to rise in me of steps I could take to build the energy of Missy's return. The first was to record my voice whistling and calling out to her (something she always responded to). So I positioned our stereo speakers at the window and much to our neighbors' curiosity, I began pumping this recording into the forest. As darkness fell, I knew she was out there shivering on a limb somewhere. Maybe she could hear me.

The next morning I rose with an increased sense of focus. If she was still alive, she would still be somewhere in the region – so I turned up the stereo volume and left it on repeat as I made up a sign to distribute and headed into town. On the way, I repeatedly stopped at the sound of whistles in the trees – often engaging in lengthy call and response exchanges before realizing I was talking to the wrong bird. "Prepare to buy a puppy", was the best vote of confidence I got from a friend I passed in town as I handed him my flyer, but I would not let this deter me. She was coming home.

Each time I hung up a flyer, I paused to look at her photo, imagining Missy flying into my chest and how incredibly grateful I would be. Shortly after hanging up the last flyer, something subtle happened that I would not normally attach significance to, but on this day it meant the world… There in the very small town of Mullumbimby, in the space of three minutes, two different people (a kid on a bike, then an old man in a car) went out of their way to approach me and ask for directions. Never before nor since has this happened. So I took it as a sign – I must be putting out the energy of navigation in some way or another.

A short drive – and many whistle stops – later, I arrived home and discovered another piece of the puzzle… As I sat on the verandah trying to get a fragment of my writing project done, I became aware of an immense amount of bird activity above the yard. In the space of an hour, I saw two wedge-tail eagles, a hawk, several crow families, kookaburras, a pack of rainbow lorikeets and a huge flock of doves – so many more than usual. They were hovering, circling and mingling in almost eerie ways around the house, as though they had been called there and wondered what for. It seemed whatever we were doing was having a magnetic effect of sorts… but perhaps it needed to be more clear focused. For as the sun went down on the second day, still no sign of Missy.

That evening we returned to our meditative images and I told Asheyana the next time I called her it would be with tears in my eyes from Missy's return. We both wanted to believe this and felt encouraged by the signs, but with a cool winter night on the way and a rain forecast the following afternoon, we knew our window of time was narrowing.

Morning of day 3, I rose to a phone call from my aforementioned friend. He had good news and bad. The good news was that he remembered hearing a story of a bird returning to its owner after flying off for several days. The bad news was that on closer inspection of my flyer, he noticed that I had written the WRONG contact phone number!

This was not the first opportunity I had to spiral into self-judgment, but somehow I knew this would not help. I decided instead to try embracing the wisdom of Aikido and 'accept the hit as a gift'. There must be a gift in this somewhere… I zoomed back into town, and carefully began renumbering every one of the flyers I hung up the day before. Halfway through, I felt my energy begin to rise and I realized that this activity was like a mantra to the message. It was giving me the chance to once again look at full color images of Missy at home, and to really connect with the vision of her return.

I knew I had put out a pulse that was being received in some way by the animal world, and despite the passing hours and the growing rationale against it, I continued to 'feel the vision' of Missy's return to my chest. This focus was of course intermingled with waves of doubt and fear of the worst possible scenarios, but I noticed that whenever a fearful image would rise, I would let it move through with a breath, then I would simply return to my vision. If she freely chose to live out her days as a wild yellow dart in the woods, then I would try to accept this, but if she wanted to return, my job was to help…

If she was having a hard time finding home, perhaps I could do more to bring home to her. So I lit a fire in the stove as a smoke signal, maxed out the stereo volume and basically folded our house inside out. I brought her cage, food and much of my wardrobe out into the yard, hanging them up in the trees. I ate cereal, played music and typed on my computer. I spent the day doing all the things she was most familiar with, but doing them outside. The yard looked hilarious but for some reason it felt like the right thing to do.

Hours passed, fires dimmed and storm clouds began to build. Just before sunset, I gathered an armful of firewood on my way into the house, and as a token gesture, let out one final whistle, as I had done hundreds of times in the past few days. Turning toward the house in surrender, I suddenly heard in the distance… a familiar response. I whistled again. This time the response came louder. I had always been mystified how birds like penguins know the unique call of their young in a colony of thousands, but in this moment I knew this was for me. I dropped the wood and bolted into the trees, whistling and listening with each step. As I came to a narrow clearing, my eyes rose to the top of an 80-foot gum tree, where a tiny yellow form paced back and forth looking down. I whistled once more, and in a moment of surreal magnificence, she took flight with wings of new confidence and dive-bombed through the clearing… right into my CHEST! Just like the image we had dared to hold. I grabbed her with both hands and scrambled up to the house. With tears of disbelief pouring down my face (man, I didn't realize how much I loved this bird!) I called Asheyana and heard the conversation unfold that we had rehearsed and imagined.

"She's back! I have her! She's OK!"

That night as I watched Missy eat her weight in seed and gratefully settle back in to her human home, I recounted the tale with Asheyana, unraveling many incredible lessons Missy had taught us. Lessons about clearly stating our highest intention and building energy around the FEELING of that vision – even when it seems out of reach. Lessons about listening to our highest wisdom, taking simple practical steps when called to and being willing to flow with what comes. Lessons about letting doubts and fears arise and release as we continually return to our higher focus. I realized that no matter how far-fetched our dreams and ideas may seem, if we can envision them and build energy around them in our bodies, then there is nothing we cannot create. In truth, this is perhaps one of our greatest callings – to continually stretch ourselves to see greater possibilities beyond our 'apparent' reality; to know that our world is an ever-evolving reflection of the visions we hold clearest and share most deeply with those around us. Whether we are calling a tiny bird back from the forest or calling healing to our body… whether we are seeking resolution to a challenging personal situation or peace in a land of conflict… whether we are calling for a new home or new vitality in the elements of our living planet… the pathway is the same. It starts right here with the visions we hold and the energy we build around them. While it is often crisis and challenge that bring us into the focus of our infinite creative capacities, it doesn't have to be that way. In truth these moments of greatest challenge may simply be helping us remember how incredibly creative and powerful we are all the time – when we open our view of what is possible and come together, for the higher good of all.

*

"Miracles are a retelling in small letters of the very same story which is written across the whole world in letters too large for some of us to see."
- C.S. Lewis

Now it's your turn. Bring *your* miracles onto the page.

And I look forward to meeting you on the path of story!

With Peace and Gratitude,
Chip

Recommended Reading

I am actually quite a slow reader – like one page a night (on a good week!). Strangely I often find I gain much simply by having a book sit on my bedside table for several months next to my head as I sleep. Along with a certain percentage of thought transference that I like to think happens naturally with it just sitting there, my wife Ash usually picks the book up, reads it quite quickly and shares with me the most special parts. I love that. This of course often sparks my curiosity, causing me to begin reading the book in earnest – which is great too.

For those who want to explore more about the inner framework of story, the following are a few books that have had a positively powerful influence on my writing journey.

The Hero with a Thousand Faces by Joseph Campbell

Story by Robert McKee

Save the Cat!: The Last Book on Screenwriting You'll Ever Need by Blake Snyde

The Artist's Way: A Spiritual Path to Higher Creativity by Julia Cameron

The Writer's Journey: Mythic Structure for Writers by Christopher Vogler

Myth and the Movies: Discovering the Myth Structure of 50 Unforgettable Films by Stuart Voytilla

Inner Drives: How to Write and Create Characters using the Eight Classic Centers of Motivation by Pamela Jaye Smith

Writing the Character-Centered Screenplay by Andrew Morton

Writing down the Bones: Freeing the Writer Within by Natalie Goldberg

About the Author

An internationally published author, screenwriter and creative guide, Chip Richard's writing career spans the mediums of feature film, fiction, poetry and journalism. With an honors degree in English from Dartmouth College, Chip made his mainstream screenwriting debut as the writer of the critically acclaimed feature film, *One Perfect Day*, and spent three years as head writer for Lightstream Pictures in the USA, facilitating an international team of writers, animators and storyboard artists. Chip is a regular contributor to *Living Now* magazine in Australia, and works in a creative consulting capacity with authors and projects ranging from novels and children's books to documentary film.

Merging a foundation of formal training with decades of professional experience and soulful adventure, Chip carries a deep faith in the magic of life, a passion for human potential and a zest for igniting the creative gifts of others. His love of story and reverence for our living planet has propelled him to create the *Writing the Story Within* experience (book, CD, DVD and mentorship program) as a pathway for individuals of all walks to bring their creative visions through onto the page... and out to the world for the good of all.

To learn more about the *Writing the Story Within* mentorship experience and Chip's other work in the world, please visit: **www.chiprichards.com**.

Also Available in this Series

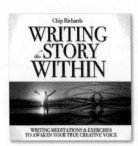

Writing the Story Within - Audio CD
Writing Meditations & Exercises to Awaken Your True Creative Voice

The *Writing the Story Within* audio CD brings together a collection of simple yet profoundly effective lessons, meditations and exercises designed to empower writers of all levels to access that deeper voice within and express their creative visions freely on the page. As a stand-alone experience or dynamic complement to the *Writing the Story Within* book and DVD, the *Writing the Story Within* CD is a rich, creative journey in and of itself. Through a progressive series of lessons and interactive writing meditations, you will gain essential tools for developing your creative project and experience yourself stepping through resistance and powerfully onto the page. You will emerge feeling connected, aligned, and creatively inspired to take the next steps in your writing journey.

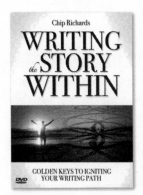

Writing the Story Within - DVD
Golden Keys to Igniting Your Writing Path

The *Writing the Story Within* DVD is a two-part video experience designed to clarify your creative vision and light a torch of new possibility on your writing path. The first part of the program dives into the archetypal story form of the Hero's Journey, leading viewers on a personal exploration through their own life experience to discover an ancient language and framework for writing and sharing stories of all types with the world. The second section shares a collection of essential 'Golden Keys' to building and sustaining an authentic, heart-connected and universally engaging writing practice. Practical tools and approaches for new and experienced writers to deepen and expand their writing to a whole new level. Set amongst the beautiful story rhythms of the natural world, the *Writing the Story Within* DVD is like a personal mentorship session that will leave you feeling alive with the energy of your true creative potential, and aligned with clear pathways to boldly venture into the heart of your own writing journey.

"Your story is about to jump forward in ways you cannot even imagine, and someday you'll look back and realize that it started when you began reading this book."
- James Twyman
Bestselling author of *The Moses Code* & *Emissary of Light*

"*Writing the Story Within* is a wonderfully enjoyable, dynamic book by a man of talent and huge heart. It's a consciously creative and practical manual that I highly recommend to anyone looking for a way to harness and hone the wisdom of their life's experience and share it with others."
– Brandon Bays
Author of *The Journey*

"If there's any book that's going to inspire you to start writing, *Writing the Story Within* is it! Packed with plenty of practical exercises to help you get words on the page and really engage your readers, it also offers a wealth of writing advice which covers all aspects of crafting a great story. I highly recommend this book to all budding writers!"
– Inna Segal
Bestselling author of *The Secret Language of Your Body* and
The Secret Language of Colour Cards

"Chip is one of the most creative and collaborative people I have worked with. With his florid writing style, unique life experiences, and keen insight into the human spirit, Chip has a knack for getting to the heart of character and key story moments while keeping the overarching theme flowing steadily on course."
– Paul Giacoppo
Writer, Cartoon Network, Marvel Animation Studios, DC/Warner Bros.
Digital Character Supervisor, Industrial Light & Magic, Lucasfilm

---

"Chip Richards is one of the best writers I've had the pleasure of working with over 21 years of editing and publishing Australia's favorite holistic magazine.
He is a master storyteller and paints amazing word pictures. His sometimes quirky turns of phrase are a delight, demonstrating his skill in playing with the language. His philosophies and morals are robust and mature and so he not only writes well, but his messages are strong, clear and an exceptional voice for the planet and humankind."
– Elizabeth Jewell Stephens
Editor & CEO, Living Now Magazine

"I'm loving seeing an archetypal journey presented through my own experiences. I wake up every morning looking forward to the next lesson, and I go to bed every night, excited about the inspiration I get from dreams and the relaxed ponderings before sleep. Thank you Chip, I kind of like being my own hero!"
– Bronwyn Smith

"I found these lessons to be an awesome tool to engage in a deeply insightful enquiry into myself, where I am at and who I am. Each lesson provides an opportunity for me to exercise a different writing muscle in myself, and despite some resistance (and some creaky sore muscles that have not been used in a while!), I experience huge growth in myself and in my writing ability each time, and every piece I write has relevance to my inner story as well as the fictional story I am writing. This work is deepening my connection with my inner creative spark, the result of which is a fire of creative work that is building each day."
– Penelope Law

"Before I started this journey, I was getting lost in the detail and overwhelm of writing my first novel. This course is helping me stand back, and allow the magic from within to simply unfold, without effort. I am loving how each exercise just seems to be exactly what I need in the moment and is giving me real tools to write within the loose structure of the hero's journey, as well as giving invaluable insight into how to bring the central character to life by understanding their deepest desires and purpose. I highly recommend Chip, and *Writing the Story Within* to anyone who is thinking about writing, or wants to deepen in their ability to write from the heart... Thanks Chip, you rock!"
– Carolyn Dickenson

"*Writing the Story Within* is a wonderful merging of creativity and spirituality! Chip's teaching and writing draws me in and helps me integrate so much information on all levels. It's a holistic experience and speaks to the heart as well as the head. Every day is another little adventure and investment in my own creative journey!"
– Anne-Marije Bussink

"*Writing the Story Within* has recharged my love of free writing with a structure and depth that reflects and gives me new levels of understanding in the pivotal moments of my own life journey."
– Louise Moriarty

Notes

Notes

Notes

Notes

Notes

Notes

Notes

Notes

Notes

Notes

Notes

Notes

For more information on this or other
Blue Angel Publishing titles,
visit our website at:

www.blueangelonline.com